'Once in a generation a book comes along that sends a shockwave through the literary world, dramatically rewriting our understanding of Shakespeare. This masterpiece of scholarly detective-work allows us to see how the Bard we know was shaped by very human impulses: admiration, envy, the hunger for success, the spirit of cooperation, or simply the inability to get a phrase from a rival's play out of his head. To read this game-changing book is to see Shakespeare and his milieu with new eyes. A stunning contribution to the field that I cannot recommend highly enough!'

Chris Laoutaris, author of *Shakespeare's Book: The Intertwined Lives behind the First Folio*

'A weighty study, rich with insight, that helps us see Shakespeare not as a sacred solitary genius but as a powerfully responsive writer among other writers. Darren Freebury-Jones draws hitherto unrelated plays into striking new relationship with one another. You won't look at early modern drama in the same way again.'

Will Tosh, Head of Research, Shakespeare's Globe

'*Shakespeare's borrowed feathers* tackles the most polarising questions of early modern drama with authority, dexterity, and style. This intimate portrait of Shakespeare's creative community gives the most familiar plays, players, and playwrights new life.'

M. L. Rio, author of *If We Were Villains*

'Solitary genius? Thieving magpie? We live in copyright times, obsessed with Best. Freebury-Jones explores Shakespeare's world, where playwrights collaborated with, borrowed from, and were influenced by one another. How exciting for actors nowadays to be reminded that "The play's the thing". Not authorship or provenance but Story-Power.'

Bruce Alexander, actor

Shakespeare's borrowed feathers

Manchester University Press

Shakespeare's borrowed feathers

How early modern playwrights shaped the world's greatest writer

Darren Freebury-Jones

Manchester University Press

Published by Manchester University Press
Oxford Road, Manchester, M13 9PL
www.manchesteruniversitypress.co.uk

British Library Cataloguing-in-Publication Data
A catalogue record for this book is available from the British Library

ISBN 978 1 5261 7732 2 hardback

First published 2024

Typeset
by Cheshire Typesetting Ltd, Cuddington, Cheshire
Printed in Great Britain
by Bell & Bain Ltd, Glasgow

Contents

Introduction: Plucking a crow

In late September or early October of 1592 a pamphlet appeared in London bookstalls that sent ripples through the Elizabethan literary community and would impact Shakespeare criticism for centuries to come. The tract was titled *Greene's Groatsworth of Wit, Bought with a Million of Repentance* (1592). The entry in the Stationers' Register, which constituted a form of copyright during the period, features the curiously ominous phrase, 'uppon the perill of Henrye Chettle', who bore responsibility for making a clean copy of a manuscript attributed to the recently deceased playwright and prolific writer of prose works and poetry Robert Greene. Henry Chettle, another dramatist and pamphleteer, claimed to have reproduced Greene's work as closely as he could. But he felt compelled to delete particularly offensive material. One passage that wasn't deleted, however, has ruffled the feathers of generations of Shakespeare critics:

> there is an upstart Crow, beautified with our feathers, that with his Tygers heart wrapt in a Players hyde, supposes he is as well able to bombast out a blanke verse as the best of you: and being an absolute *Johannes fac totum*, is in his owne conceit the only Shake-scene in a countrey.

What can we make of this passage? Is this a case of a jealous author punching down at the new kid on the block? Are these the words of a man in the twilight of his life and career railing against the injustices of commercial drama? An enduring image of Robert Greene is a 1598 woodcut engraving of him 'suited in death's

1

livery', beavering away at his writing desk and resembling an ear of corn or a pensive banana. As is the case with many diatribes of the period, the passage is cryptic and has been interpreted in diverse ways.

This is the earliest reference to Shakespeare as an actor-dramatist in London. It's framed as a warning from Greene, initially in the guise of the personage Roberto, to fellow university-educated writers, the sharp-penned Thomas Nashe, the erudite George Peele, and the devil-may-care dramatist Christopher Marlowe, about a certain 'Shake-scene'. A grammar schoolboy from the country, a mere player. One of 'those Puppets (I meane) that spake from our mouths, those Anticks garnisht in our colours', who considers himself to be a *Johannes Factotum*, a Jack of all trades who's had the audacity to turn his hand to writing plays.

This is a book about Shakespeare's borrowed feathers and the community of playwrights working in early modern London. It's an exploration of Shakespeare's engagement with the plays of these contemporary dramatists, including matters of authorship, varying modes of collaboration, such as co-authorship and revision, as well as the ways in which Shakespeare was influenced by, imitated, or adapted plays by fellow playwrights. In this respect, although it's a non-dramatic work, *Greene's Groatsworth of Wit* provides not just a starting point but the structural fulcrum for this book. London was a narrow, intensely competitive world, where writers lurked, like Shakespeare's mischievous sprite, Puck, in a gossipy bowl. We can imagine the whispered voices growing louder as devilish drunkenness gives way to wrath in taverns, the clamour of eager tongues as writers pass each other in the theatres, or meet at the central aisle of St Paul's Cathedral, in the publishing and bookselling centre of London. The discussions that arose between Elizabethan writers in the wake of the pamphlet's publication, and the theories it has spawned among generations of Shakespeare scholars, are inextricably linked to the pillars of this study: authorship, collaboration, adaptation, and imitation. Shakespeare is often regarded as an influencer, and he was certainly influential among his contemporaries, but his plays are also filled with voices blended together, seemingly confounding distinction at times, his texts bearing the ghostly traces of his friends, his rivals, his predecessors.

The authorship of *Greene's Groatsworth of Wit* was a matter of vigorous discussion in Elizabethan England. Whose hand was responsible for the offending passage? Accusatory fingers were pointed at Chettle, who claimed in his pamphlet *Kind-Heart's Dream: Containing Five Apparitions with Their Invectives Against Abuses Reigning* (1592) that Greene's papers had merely come into his possession; the content was all Greene's. Chettle noted that one or two playmakers were offended and, given that they couldn't be avenged on the dead, they were taking their frustrations out on him, a living author. To what degree did Chettle collaborate with the dead man? Was he simply an editor who had followed his copy but not put a word in himself, as he claimed? Another playwright and pamphleteer who was accused of having a hand in *Greene's Groatsworth of Wit* was Thomas Nashe, who protested in his *Pierce Penniless His Supplication to the Devil* (1592) that the lying tract didn't contain the least word or syllable from his pen, nor was he involved in the printing of it.

During the 1960s a scholar named Warren B. Austin claimed that the pamphlet wasn't written by Greene: it was a forgery by Chettle. Austin took a pioneering approach: he applied a computer-aided technique to distinguish Greene and Chettle's writing styles.[1] His study has led some scholars to conclude that Greene wasn't responsible for the notorious passage. The attribution to Chettle, however, has been countered by Richard Westley, who found that the calculations pointing towards Chettle's, rather than Greene's, authorship were limited to small handpicked samples and subjective criteria that inevitably favoured the former author.[2] This might serve as a cautionary tale to readers dazzled by purely statistical approaches to matters of authorship.

Approaches towards determining authorship continue to be debated in attribution studies, a field characterised by the kind of hostility we find in the *Greene's Groatsworth of Wit* passage, an imbalance of *laus et vituperatio*, or praise and opposition, more befitting plays composed during the so-called 'Poets' War' than modern scholarship.[3] In this book we will undertake a journey through the many layers and theories surrounding what Shakespeare wrote, whom he wrote with, and who influenced him. Grasping some of the methods that lay behind certain new attribution theories will broaden our understanding of the extent to which Shakespeare engaged with playwrights such as Christopher Marlowe, Thomas Kyd, George Peele, and Thomas Middleton, fully revealing just how valuable a field of study this really is. Navigating the blurry lines between authorship and influence remains the biggest obstacle in attribution studies, particularly in the case of shared language. It isn't insurmountable, though: when it comes to authors repeating their favourite phrases or images, the surrounding text tends to be the same in terms of vocabulary, poetic rhythm, and other features of style. In the case of verbal borrowings, the surrounding text is often quite different, and these phrases are repeated in later plays.

Since the nineteenth century attribution scholars have conducted textual sleuthing to discriminate writers' styles. They've scrutinised verse habits, diction, vocabulary, and parallels of thought, language, and dramaturgy between authors' recognised works and plays suspected to be by the same hands. These are the fundamental principles of authorial dramatic style, and there's safety in applying as many different methods as possible. But several new attribution methods derive from fields like information theory and genetic studies. The suitability of these approaches for analysis of early modern plays is open to question. After all, plays are complex literary and performative artefacts. They were sometimes produced by multiple co-authors or revisers. They occasionally derived from actors, maybe even scribes attending performances who pricked their piratical ears up and scribbled down the dialogue, the equivalent of filming a movie at the cinema on your phone. It seems fair to say that fierce debates concerning the authorship of the *Henry VI* trilogy or the anonymous domestic tragedy *Arden of Faversham* (1590) are unlikely to be resolved any time soon.[4] What approaches best help us to distinguish early modern dramatists' styles? In seeking to answer that question this book provides a picture that increases our knowledge of Shakespeare's working relationships with contemporary playwrights, the friendships and rivalries that helped to form his thoughts, his writing processes.

Discussions and debates about authorship aren't limited to the provenance of *Greene's Groatsworth of Wit* itself: the pamphlet has implications for Shakespeare's authorship of the *Henry VI* plays. In the late eighteenth century the editor Edmond Malone reached the conclusion that Shakespeare wasn't responsible for the chronicle history plays titled *The Contention between York and Lancaster* (1594) and *The True Tragedy of Richard Duke of York* (1595). He proposed that the surviving quarto (a small book produced by folding a sheet of paper into four leaves) and octavo (an even smaller book in which the sheet was folded eight times to produce sixteen pages) editions were composed by Greene and Peele as joint authors, or that Greene was the author of one play and Peele the other. According to Malone, Shakespeare drew from these texts in order to produce the plays known as *Henry VI Part Two* (1591) and *Henry VI Part Three* (1591) in the 1623 First Folio (the posthumously published collected works in a larger format), arousing Greene's umbrage in *Greene's Groatsworth of Wit* and eliciting the targeted paraphrase of York's line, 'O tiger's heart wrapped in a woman's hide' (1.4.138), from *Henry VI Part Three*.[5] Another theory is that *The Contention between York and Lancaster* and *The True Tragedy of Richard Duke of York* were put together by actors aiming to reconstruct Shakespeare's plays from memory. They are mangled abridgements of Shakespeare's plays. Or maybe the quarto and octavo editions represent earlier versions of Shakespeare's plays, which were later revised by Shakespeare? We'll wade into debates on the authorial provenance of the *Henry VI* plays later in this book: with the pendulum continuing to swing between affirmation and rejection of authorship theories, this book provides a major intervention in our understanding of Shakespeare's dramatic development.

Malone's theory paints Shakespeare as a plagiarist. But the *Greene's Groatsworth of Wit* passage chimes with Greene's combativeness with actors in general. Maybe Shakespeare was able to 'beautify' himself in other playwrights' feathers because he'd delivered their words on stage and had gained first-hand experience of what worked for audiences in terms of language, verse cadence and registers, and dramatic devices? The passage has also been interpreted as targeting Shakespeare 'as a writer of bombastic blank verse, but also as someone who employs bombast better than his contemporaries'. The 'feathers' are 'stylistic flourishes, of his contemporaries', but it's 'how he made use of them' that 'makes Shakespeare's early plays not simply appropriative and imitative but distinctly Shakespearean'.[6] Chapter 1 shows that Shakespeare's rhetorical training and his background as an actor were fundamental to the development of his dramatic style. The trained habit of *imitatio* was intrinsic to the composition of Shakespeare's plays.

How might we go about plucking a crow and determining the origins of each of his feathers? Literary debts can be measured in a variety of ways, be it through allusions, studies of similarities in dramatic narrative and structure, characterisation, and explorations of the ways in which dramatists appear to have parodied each other. This book relies on each of these approaches and, in some respects, shares the same aim as Stanley Wells, whose study *Shakespeare & Co.*[7] seeks to bring Shakespeare's contemporaries to life by elaborating on his relationship with each of them, thereby casting light on Shakespeare himself. Bart van Es's book *Shakespeare in Company* argues that Shakespeare wrote in terms of a company of actors, performers, and other theatrical staff, developing his individual style precisely because he knew how to work with others, such as the comic actors Robert Armin and William Kempe.[8] This book considers other playwrights in a similar way by showing how Shakespeare made use of theatrical resources, both from his own company and from others. A major point of difference from previous investigations is that this book provides the most systematic account of Shakespeare's debts to his contemporaries ever provided by using modern databases and drawing from more recent theories about authorship and the order in which plays were written.

The computerised methods now at our fingertips illuminate these old plays in ways their authors cannot have begun to imagine. Pervez Rizvi has developed a database of 527 plays dated between 1552 and 1657, called *Collocations and N-grams*, an invaluable aid for identifying links between early modern plays.[9] This resource is a revelation. It has been endorsed by the leading scholars in the field of early modern authorship studies and has already led to exciting new discoveries.[10] It seems fair to say that the database has raised the discipline to a new level. In the past researchers relied on manual searches of databases such as *Literature Online* or *Early English Books Online*, and, while it's likely that other resources will become available in future years, the fact that results in *Collocations and N-grams* are automated means that its findings are of lasting value. Users can suddenly discover every continuous word sequence (or 'n-gram') shared between plays, such as the phrase 'from the purpose of', which Shakespeare repeats in *Julius Caesar* (1599) and *Hamlet* (1600). Users can also discover so-called 'collocations', matching phrases broken up by intervening words, such as Shakespeare's association of 'hounds', 'greyhounds', 'mongrel', and 'spaniel', which are separated by the words 'grim' and 'or' in *King Lear* (1605) and 'and' in *Macbeth* (1606). We can read such phrases according to dramatic context, recognise the ways in which verbal parallels can be interlinked by situation and characterisation. *Collocations and N-grams* also contains numerical data demonstrating which plays of the period share large numbers of phrases according to such factors as common authorship, chronology, genre, and influence. The numbers give us unparalleled insights into the words of these writers.

Shakespeare, like every other commercial dramatist of the period, borrowed phrases from plays by his contemporaries. However, earlier scholars making cases for similarities between dramas had to rely on their reading memories, with no way of knowing whether a locution was truly distinctive in the surviving canon of dramatic works. We can now check just how many times a phrase is repeated in plays of the period and establish whether similarities exceed expectations. The rarer a word combination is in *Collocations and N-grams*, the higher its value for determining links between plays. This book provides an accurate account of the influence of fellow playwrights' language on Shakespeare's dramas. We'll look at the summary spreadsheets for plays written by each of Shakespeare's major contemporaries; these plays are ranked according to the numbers for unique phrases they share. The major finding when it comes to statistical analysis of phrases shared between early modern dramas is that authorship trumps other factors, such as genre, influence, or chronology.[11] Take for example the spreadsheet for *Macbeth*, which ranks every other play of the period in comparison to Shakespeare's dark tragedy according to the number of phrases found in no other pair of dramas:

MATCHING PLAY
 1. *Julius Caesar*
 2. *Alphonsus, Emperor of Germany*
 3. *The Woman Hater*
 4. *The Great Duke of Florence*
 5. *Coriolanus*
 6. *King Lear*
 7. *Hamlet*
 8. *The Turk*
 9. *Philaster*
10. *The Two Angry Women of Abingdon*

If we weren't sure who wrote *Macbeth*, we'd need only look at the titles *Julius Caesar*, *Coriolanus* (1608), *King Lear*, and *Hamlet* near the top of the spreadsheet to finger its author. Common authorship or deliberate imitation become the likeliest explanations when plays share large numbers of distinctive word combinations that can't be dismissed as commonplace expressions in the theatrical vernacular of the period; the former should be complemented by analysis of verse style, vocabulary, and overall dramaturgy. Deliberate imitation can be seen in one of 195 unique (meaning they're not found elsewhere in the 527 plays in *Collocations and N-grams*) combinations of consecutive words shared between Thomas Dekker's play *The Wonder of a Kingdom* (1622) and John Day's *The Parliament of Bees* (1626): 'all that treasure dry who hoards up wealth is base who spends it brave earth breeds gold so I tread but on my slave'. The chances of the playwright John Day repeating this whopping combination of words by accident is infinitesimal. In fact, it's long been recognised that Day borrowed whole passages of text from Dekker. Modern methods confirm existing theories: the sheer number and nature of such extensive shared phrases can't be coincidental. But as this book shows, *Collocations and N-grams* often challenges existing theories in startlingly compelling ways.

In the first chapter we'll see how Shakespeare's grammar-school education and his background as an actor helped him to engage with the works of fellow dramatists through imitation, adaptation, and parody. Several playwrights of the period were also actors and would develop an intimate familiarity with plays in which they'd performed. The necessity for actor-dramatists to possess extensive verbal memories meant they could draw from a variety of plays when composing their own works. This chapter situates Shakespeare in the original theatrical culture in which he worked. It was a deeply collaborative period in which playwrights would have worked closely with theatre managers, actors, and fellow dramatists. We will discover the ways in which dramatists collaborated with audiences and with each other, taking account of shifting theatrical milieus, advances in stage technology, and changes of playing spaces during Shakespeare's career.

Later chapters deal with Shakespeare's relationships with his Elizabethan predecessors, such as John Lyly, who established several precedents for Shakespeare's plays, and whose earlier Romances Shakespeare seems to have consulted when composing plays for the indoor Blackfriars Theatre, where Lyly's plays had previously been performed by the Children of Paul's company. In *Shakespeare & Co.*, Stanley Wells devotes less than three pages to Thomas Kyd, but around thirty pages to Christopher Marlowe. The third and fourth chapters of this book reveal that Shakespeare's relationship with Kyd has been grossly underestimated. Kyd's influence on Shakespeare appears to have been just as profound as Marlowe's. These chapters also deal with the thorny issue of distinguishing Shakespeare's early style from Kyd and Marlowe's, the two playwrights he most closely emulated at the beginning of his career and with whom it's been proposed he collaborated.

Chapter 5 casts a spotlight on Robert Greene's underappreciated impact on Elizabethan stage conventions, and the benign influences Greene had on Shakespeare's dramaturgy, whereas their relationship has often been framed in malignant terms. In the following chapter we'll discover the degree to which George Peele's plays influenced Shakespeare's early dramas, particularly in the genres of tragedy and chronicle history, before turning our attention towards Shakespeare and Peele's collaboration on *Titus Andronicus* (1592). Collaboration could take many forms and it's a matter of debate whether Shakespeare and Peele worked simultaneously on this play, or whether Shakespeare revised an older, possibly unfinished, work by Peele.

The seventh and following chapters show the ways in which other dramatists, such as Thomas Dekker, John Marston, and Ben Jonson, and the emerging genres in which they wrote, intersected with Shakespeare's dramatic trajectory later in his career. The book then turns to Shakespeare's engagement with the plays of Thomas Middleton and those associated with John Fletcher and Francis Beaumont. By testing theories that Middleton revised several Shakespeare plays, and by delving into the textual layers of Shakespeare and Fletcher collaborations, we can increase our understanding of the working methods shared between these playwrights.

The book concludes by looking at the ways in which the compilers of the First Folio helped to create the image of Shakespeare as *sui generis*, a solitary genius, and how that has impacted the ways Shakespeare is written or spoken about today. We can expand our knowledge of other 'Shake-scenes' of the period through proper acknowledgement of Shakespeare's debts to, indeed his reliance on, these playwrights, taking more methodical approaches than have been used in the past. This is a never-before-seen look at the men behind plays of the period and the genetic and generic makeup of Shakespeare's works. We are about to encounter major revelations. It was Shakespeare's late plays, not his early ones, that most recall Lyly. Kyd had more of a direct and persistent influence on Shakespeare than Marlowe did. We've been getting the title *The Taming of the Shrew* wrong all these years. A scene of madness that it's long been thought Shakespeare added to his bloodthirsty tragedy *Titus Andronicus* was probably there all along. Full recognition of early modern drama as a communal enterprise casts new light on Shakespeare's career and has the potential to transform our understanding of not only Shakespeare's output but early modern drama as a whole.

1

A player's hide

We don't have enrolment records for Shakespeare's grammar-school education, as is also the case with other literary figures of the period like Robert Greene. But it seems more than likely that between the ages of approximately seven and fourteen Shakespeare would have attended King's New School, which was just a short walk from his home in Henley Street, Stratford-upon-Avon, and was also the site of the Guildhall. King's New School, established in 1553 by the royal charter of King Edward VI, was free for boys in the borough and tradition holds that John Shakespeare 'bred' his son 'for some time at a Free-School'. During the summer months Shakespeare would have attended the school between six o'clock in the morning and five in the evening, and between seven in the morning and four o'clock in the evening during the winter months when the sun was less inclined to show its head. Shakespeare's education would have been robust enough to equip him with the knowledge and skillset he required to write poetry and plays.

Schoolboys of the period would have encountered Latin anthologies such as the Dutch humanist Desiderius Erasmus's *Cato* and Leonard Cullman's *Sententiae Pueriles*, as well as Aesop's *Fables* via a Latin translation.[1] Shakespeare would have been expected to speak Latin with his school fellows in the playground, and even with his family at home. In the classroom he'd also hunch over the works of classical writers such as Terence, Horace, Ovid, and Virgil, in their original Latin. The fibrous influence of such writers can be detected in Shakespeare's works, particularly those written early in his career, such as the narrative poems *Venus and Adonis* (1593) and *The Rape of Lucrece* (1594). These are two of his most explicitly Ovidian works, the former deriving from Book 10 of *Metamorphoses*, and the latter drawing from Ovid's *Fasti*. Ovid also served as a source for several of Shakespeare's plays. The tale of Pyramus and Thisbe is contained in Book 4 of *Metamorphoses* and provided Shakespeare with material for *Romeo and Juliet* (1595) and the play-within-a-play in *A Midsummer Night's Dream* (1595). The sensational violence of the *Henry VI* plays and *Titus Andronicus* owes much to Ovid's, as well as the Roman philosopher and tragedian Seneca's (on whom more in later chapters), influence.

Shakespeare's early works are 'often spectacularly imitative and as a result his personal voice is much less distinct',[2] and yet these early plays are 'as consistently imitative as his contemporaries'.[3] Shakespeare isn't renowned for coming up with his own plotlines, but it's worth stressing that he was writing during a period when emphasis was placed not on telling new stories but on retelling existing stories in innovative ways. This was reflected in the standard school curriculum instituted by Erasmus and John Colet, for which *imitatio*, *parodia*, and *translatio* served as bedrocks. Against this background of an education that prized imitation and advised students to read as many different types of author in order to fill up their storehouse, it's hardly surprising that Shakespeare might attempt to 'bombast out a blanke verse as the best' of other playwrights when he appeared on the London scene. The pedagogical emphasis on bettering imitated sources would have been drilled into him at school.

One method that students would have undergone was known as 'double translation', for which they'd be required to translate a passage of Latin into English prose. The original would then be taken away and students would need to replicate the original as closely as possible.[4] The Erasmian emphasis on memorisation and improvisation would have also prepared Shakespeare for a career as an actor, and it's worth noting that schoolboys would have acted out scenes from the works of Terence and Plautus. Moreover Shakespeare could have attended performances by travelling players at the Guildhall, perhaps joining his father, who, as an alderman from 1564 onwards and High Bailiff from 1568, might preview such plays to make sure they weren't subversive, and then grant the players a licence to perform in public.

Shakespeare's thorough immersion in classical rhetoric, the language of persuasion, as learned at school in the writings of Cicero, Quintilian, Erasmus, and later Henry Peacham's treatise, *The Garden of Eloquence* (1577), would have been of particular use to a budding actor-dramatist. Erasmus was committed to teaching schoolboys to argue *in utramque partem*, voicing two sides of a question in the art of formal controversy. Shakespeare's works often display an antithetical thought process: he frequently weighs up competing arguments. This is reflected in Shakespeare's language, in which one image tends to give birth to another, often diametrically opposed, image with remarkable speed, giving us the sense that Shakespeare's mind is running faster than his pen and supporting Ben Jonson's claim in *Timber, or Discoveries* (1630) that Shakespeare 'had an excellent fancy, brave notions, and gentle expressions, wherein he flowed with that facility that sometime it was necessary he should be stopped'. It's also worth bearing in mind Erasmus's *Copia: Foundations of the Abundant Style*, first published in 1512, with its emphasis on verbal abundance, plenitude, variety, resourcefulness of discourse, and the desire to write, to release and bring to life all nuances of language, thought, ideas, associations, and figurative richness. The impact of *copia* on Shakespeare and the seductions of overwriting might help to account for Jonson's complaint and the occasional excessiveness of his verbal, poetic, and circumstantial complexity and detail.

In consulting Renaissance rhetoric tracts Shakespeare would have encountered such devices as *anaphora*, a figure of repetition in which words and ideas are repeated at the beginning of successive clauses, as in this example from *Henry VI Part One* (1592): 'Between two hawks, which flies the higher pitch, / Between two dogs, which hath the deeper mouth, / Between two blades, which bears the better temper' (2.4.11–13). Shakespeare would have also developed knowledge of *polyptoton*, the repetition of words stemming from the same root, and *antithesis*, such devices playing important roles in Richard's skilled manipulation of Lady Anne

14

Neville in *Richard III* (1592), as he bends and twists language to achieve his aims: 'That laid their guilt upon my guiltless shoulders' (1.2.98). Shakespeare would have been taught how to employ *epistrophe*, a particularly tricky device to sustain in which several lines or clauses end with the same word, as in Titus's despairingly melliflu-ous speech in *Titus Andronicus*: 'If they did hear me, / They would not mark me; if they did mark, / They would not pity me' (3.1.33–5).

Figures of repetition would no doubt benefit Elizabethan players when it came to learning lines, including long, declamatory speeches. Having embarked on a career as an actor in London, Shakespeare experienced training in rhetoric and memorisation not too dissimi-lar to his school lessons. This would inform his dramatic writing when composing roles for himself and other members of his playing company. Although writers could choose from over two hundred of these figures of speech, there was a high degree of individual expres-sion open to them, and Elizabethan authors can be distinguished through the rates and ways they employ rhetorical devices. While the university-educated dramatist George Peele seldom grasps their full dramatic potential, Shakespeare showcases the efficiency of the rhetorical training he received at grammar school.[5] There are key dif-ferences between Shakespeare's and Christopher Marlowe's rhetoric: Shakespeare's instances of '*congeries*' (the device known as *accumu-latio*, which creates a heaping effect) in the *Henry VI* plays expand 'the semantic connection with the idea with which it is meant to connect'. Marlowe's usage is comparatively 'flat: words do not add to the meaning of an idea, they repeat the same point'. Shakespeare's appropriation of bombastic language serves to create 'a heap of com-plementing ideas in the *Henry VI* plays' that contrasts with the 'col-lection of cold gems' on show in Marlowe's *The Jew of Malta* (1589).[6] Paying close attention to the different ways Shakespeare and his early modern contemporaries employed rhetoric in their plays can cast fresh light on authorial styles. Such approaches have important implications for plays of uncertain authorship.

Unlike dramatists like Marlowe and Greene, there's no record of Shakespeare attending university. This is hardly an anomaly in the context of the community of playwrights working in early modern London: several other dramatists aren't known to have attended university, such as Thomas Kyd, Nathan Field, and Jonson. The last author in that list prided himself on his learning in particular. The author of *The Second Part of the Return to Parnassus* (1601), performed at St John's College, Cambridge, declares, in the voice of the comic clown, William Kempe, that 'few' university-educated dramatists 'pen plays well' and that 'our fellow Shakespeare puts them all down'. Shakespeare's grammar-school education likely approximated a modern Classics degree. We can compare Shakespeare to Greene, who was entered as a sizar (undergraduate) at St John's College in 1575, receiving a BA in 1580, transferring to Clare Hall in Cambridge for his 1583 MA, and later receiving an MA from Oxford University. Despite supposedly receiving a superior education, university dramatists like Greene commit startling learning errors in their plays, including the jumbling of references to classical mythology.[7] Early modern university education served a primarily vocational purpose that wouldn't necessarily have equipped students with greater skills and knowledge when it came to writing plays and poetry.

It's worth considering too the kind of verse that Shakespeare would have encountered when delivering speeches written by supposedly better-educated dramatists, or at least hearing those speeches in performance, either during rehearsal, in the tiring (dressing) areas when listening out for his cues, or maybe as an audience member. The thudding end-stopped lines found in the plays of many Elizabethan contemporaries contrast with Shakespeare's use of caesura, or pauses within verse lines, enjambment, in which one line strides into the next, and so-called 'feminine' endings, lines concluding in unstressed eleventh syllables, the most famous example being the final syllable -*ion* in Hamlet's line 'To be, or not to be; that is the question' (3.1.58). In a classic study the scholar Philip Timberlake examined the rates of 'feminine' endings in English blank (unrhyming) verse drama up to 1595.[8] He gave percentages for these endings in scenes as well as averages for plays. His findings revealed that Shakespeare employed 'feminine' endings more frequently than many of his Elizabethan contemporaries, who tended to stick to the ten-syllable line, such as Greene (whose sole-authored plays range from averages of 0.1–1.1 per cent 'feminine' endings), Peele (1.5–5.4), and Marlowe (0.4–3.7). These findings suggest that Shakespeare recognised the need for linguistic flexibility from the very beginning of his career, averaging 15.3 per cent in *The Comedy of Errors* (1593) and 16.8 per cent in *Richard III*. There are striking differences between Shakespeare's early style, perhaps attributable in part to an actorly ear, and the styles of university playwrights. Later in this book we'll discover that Thomas Kyd, Shakespeare's fellow non-university-educated dramatist, was a surprising innovator.

Shakespeare's profession as an actor meant he could draw from the verbal dimension of plays he had seen or acted in as well as their verse cadences: he could adapt the contexts in which his contemporaries placed utterances with considerable facility. Shakespeare evidently had a powerful associative memory which helped him conjure pertinent images or plot points. This prodigious memory is traceable in part to his grammar-school education but, more importantly, also to his background as a player. He'd have worked under conditions in which several plays were performed six days a week, during a period that placed more emphasis on aural understanding than is the case today. Early modern players needed to retain lines from numerous roles in plays both old and new. Shakespeare appears to have acted throughout his dramatic writing career: a cast list printed in the 1616 Jonson Folio informs us that Shakespeare was one of the principal comedians in *Every Man in His Humour* (1598) and he's also listed among the principal tragedians in *Sejanus* (1603). Described as 'Our Roscius', the English equivalent of that honourable Roman actor, in an early seventeenth-century book annotation,[9] Shakespeare might very well have taken many of the monarchical roles in his plays; the poet John Davies of Hereford tells us he often played kingly parts. Finally Shakespeare is listed as one of the principal actors in his own plays, in the First Folio, although we can't confirm any specific role he took. Traditional accounts have him playing the ghost of Hamlet's father and the old man, Adam, in *As You Like It* (1599), roles that serve important structural purposes and would help Shakespeare keep an eye on proceedings during performance. He's even supposed to have filled in for Lady Macbeth when the actor playing that role died, another of the wild and occasionally whirling theories attached to the 'cursed' Scottish play.

During his career as an actor and playwright, Shakespeare would encounter significant changes in genres and stylistic registers. When he first appeared on the scene, likely in the late 1580s to early 1590s, playing spaces were abuzz with tragedies, chronicle history plays, and comedies, genres in which he would write within his first few years as a dramatist. Additional genres or sub-genres of the Elizabethan period included the so-called 'Turk play', the morality play, biblical dramas, and, in the case of *Arden of Faversham*, the domestic tragedy, which was developed during the Jacobean period in such plays as *A Woman Killed with Kindness* (1603), *A Yorkshire Tragedy* (1605), and *The Witch of Edmonton* (1621). In competing to create new plays within existing genres and experimenting by conflating genres, dramatists ransacked literary materials for inspiration, including the Bible, Italian works (from novellas to Roman tragedies and comedies), and chronicle materials often found in expensive tomes, such as Raphael Holinshed's *Chronicles of England, Scotland, and Ireland* (1577; 1587). Playwrights would draw from distant events to inform their dramatic narratives, characters, and themes. But the seeds of their own time also contributed to their blooming imaginations.

Dramatists would find plenty of material for their works, particularly those dabbling in tragic matters, wherever they looked. Crossing London Bridge, the eyes of traitorous heads, preserved in tar and impaled on spikes, would gaze down at them. Death was everywhere, tearing through families, tearing through Shakespeare's home town, tearing through London and often forcing theatre closures. Strange screams of death in the city would be accompanied by the roars of entertained crowds watching a cry of hounds attacking a bear tied to a stake. The creature could do nothing but fight the course. Sometimes a bull was sacrificed instead of a bear. On rare occasions a chimpanzee was strapped to a horse's saddle and audiences found it highly entertaining watching this poor monkey clinging on for dear life. There were plenty of theatres of cruelty to attend. If Londoners didn't fancy blood sports such as bearbaiting or cockfighting, they could pay just a penny to witness the heftier cost of treason: hangings, beheadings. Beyond the veil of death, that customary houseguest during Shakespeare's time, there was always the unknown, the instruments of darkness, the shadows lingering over newborn babes, the chattering of voices in the winds that drove the boats arriving at docks. 'So you like violence, cruelty, bloodshed? You are interested in a world elsewhere? You are superstitious?' we can imagine the playmakers ask. 'Come to our tragedies. There will be ghosts and witches and demons. You can travel the globe. The stage will be littered with corpses. All this we can truly deliver!'

Genres would continue to shift as Shakespeare's career progressed, as shown by the popularity of city comedies, the comedy of humours (which focuses on character traits or so-called humours), and Romance plays, with mixed-mode writing prevailing in the tragicomedies in particular. In tandem with the gallimaufry of genres, dramatic diction and linguistic registers underwent considerable changes, from an emphasis in earlier plays on Poulter's measure, which alternated between lines of twelve and fourteen syllables, to plays written in largely end-stopped iambic verse (alternating five unstressed syllables and five stressed syllables). The heavy ornateness and rhetorical patterning of many Elizabethan plays gradually shifted to more economical language sometimes resembling real speech, although we'll see later that some pre-Shakespearian plays succeeded in fusing lyrical verse with colloquial, naturalistic dialogue. Striking insights into prosodic progression are afforded by the 'feminine' ending test: younger Jacobean writers would overshadow the high rates in Shakespeare's early plays, to the extent that ten-syllable lines became the exception rather than the norm.

In the course of this book we will discover the remarkable extent to which Shakespeare drew from the language of contemporaries writing in numerous genres and in various stylistic registers, employing his powerful aural memory when it came to plays that hadn't yet reached print. A useful test case can be found in another actor-dramatist of the period: Ben Jonson. In *Satiromastix* (1601) Thomas

Dekker mocks Jonson, in the guise of the character Horace, for play-ing Hieronimo in Kyd's *The Spanish Tragedy* (1587) with a group of travelling players:

> I ha seene thy shoulders lapt in a Plaiers old cast Cloake, like a Slie knave as thou art: and when thou ranst mad for the death of Horatio: thou borrowedst a gowne of Roscius the Stager (that honest Nicodemus) and sentst it home lowsie (1.2.354–6).[10]

This is the only evidence we have that Jonson played the protagonist in Kyd's popular tragedy. Jonson's acting career is, perhaps delib-erately on Jonson's part, not well-documented. But he is recorded as a 'player' who both 'acted and wrote'.[11] *The Spanish Tragedy* was a play that Jonson repeatedly mocked, drawing from its lan-guage to depict the play as outmoded.[12] Jonson's relationship with Kyd's drama gives us a great opportunity to test out the *Collocations and N-grams* database. Turning to the summary spreadsheet for *The Spanish Tragedy*, which ranks that play against all others in the database according to numbers for unique phrases, we discover that Jonson's *Poetaster* (1601) is listed sixth. These plays share sixteen phrases found in no other play. The results are fascinating: in paro-dying *The Spanish Tragedy*, Jonson filches large stretches of text from Kyd, the longest combination running to twenty consecutive words ('I am thy foe and fear shall force what friendship cannot win thy death shall bury what thy life conceals'). But Jonson also assim-ilates Kyd's phrasing into passages that aren't obviously parodic, like when the braggart captain, Tucca, says that poets **'are a sort of poor**, starved rascals' (1.2.169),[13] which uniquely echoes a speech delivered by a servant in *The Spanish Tragedy* and serves as a cue for the actor playing Hieronimo: 'Here **are a sort of poor** petition-ers' (4.7.46).[14] Another echo, found elsewhere only in John Studley's translation of Seneca's *Agamemnon* (1566), occurs when the alle-gorical figure of Envy speaks of 'Spy-like suggestions, **privy whis-perings**' (Induction.25), which recalls Kyd's line: 'For fear the **privy whispering** of the wind' (3.4.80). Did Jonson's engagement with *The Spanish Tragedy* as an actor, reader, or even a spectator, help him not only to echo Kyd's play for parodic purposes, but also to recycle Kyd's language below the level of conscious thought?

In *Satiromastix*, Horace claims to have played 'Zulziman' in 'Paris Garden' (4.1.122–3). This could be a reference to the play-within-a-play in *The Spanish Tragedy*, or maybe Kyd's full-length treatment of that playlet: *Soliman and Perseda* (1588).[15] Judging by the play's comparatively scant performance and printing history, *Soliman and Perseda* wasn't as popular as *The Spanish Tragedy*. But there are indications that Jonson was familiar with the language of the play, possibly from having acted in it. In *Poetaster* he echoes the allegorical personage Love's line, **'From whence I sprung'** (1.Prologue.30), in Ovid's speech: 'unlike the line **from whence I sprung**' (1.1.38). Seemingly trivial verbal echoes like 'But stay let me see' (found in 3.4.241 of *Poetaster* and 5.4.116 of *Soliman and Perseda*) and 'first by chance' (5.2.46 of *Poetaster* and 2.Prologue.14 of *Soliman and Perseda*) can be found in no other play of the period. The evidence suggests that Jonson had an extraordinary retentive memory of serviceable phrases in the theatrical vernacular of the time. Verbal echoes in the plays of dramatists who were also actors, such as Robert Wilson, Anthony Munday, Thomas Heywood, Jonson, and Shakespeare aren't always concentrated in possible cue lines or any specific characters' speeches. This makes it difficult to tell which roles they might have taken in plays from which they borrowed. To complicate matters further: it was a practical necessity that early modern actors would need to double roles and 'Performing in a play brings to the actor a general familiarity with the text as a whole' because 'he needs to give half an ear to what is being spoken on stage if he is not to miss his entrance cues'.[16]

Jonson most likely acted with the company Pembroke's Men, for whom Shakespeare seems to have begun his career as an actor-dramatist in London, under the patronage of Henry Herbert, Second Earl of Pembroke. The company is listed on title pages for several early plays associated with Shakespeare: *Henry VI Part Three*, *The Taming of the Shrew* (1592), and *Titus Andronicus*. At the beginning of Shakespeare's career Pembroke's Men faced commercial rivals in companies such as the Queen's Men, formed in 1583 at Elizabeth I's command,[17] and the Lord Admiral's Men, patronised by Charles Howard, who became Lord High Admiral in 1585. There was also

Lord Strange's Men, associated with the Stanley family, especially Ferdinando Stanley. In 1590 that company allied with the Admiral's Men, and they eventually formed the company known as Derby's Men when Ferdinando Stanley attained his father's title.[18] The Queen's Men boasted some of the star actors of the Elizabethan period, including Robert Wilson and James Burbage, whom they subsumed from the company Leicester's Men, as well as John Adams and the famous clown Richard Tarlton, attained from Sussex's Men. Their repertoire consisted of works by major Elizabethan dramatists, such as Greene, Peele, and perhaps, from around 1583–85, Kyd. The Admiral's Men's leading actor was Edward Alleyn, who contributed his sonorous voice and lengthy stride to the company in 1589, and their repertory also consisted of plays by dramatists such as Kyd, Marlowe, and George Chapman. Strange's Men acquired Alleyn in early 1591 and their repertory included the dramas of Thomas Lodge, Thomas Nashe, Kyd, and Marlowe. Elizabethan plays often recurred in other companies' repertoires and the 'circulation of dramatists between companies may have involved underhand dealings at times' in 'contexts that involve collaboration, competition, and deception'.[19] A particularly sneaky example can be found in the case of Greene, who wrote *Orlando Furioso* (1591) for the Queen's Men but spied an opportunity to sell that play again to the Admiral's Men when the Queen's Men went on tour.

Given that the company performed at court in 1592–93, Pembroke's Men likely existed several years before that and attracted major playwrights of the era, including Shakespeare, Marlowe, and possibly Kyd. Pembroke's Men suffered financially disappointing tours in the early to mid-1590s and their fate seems to have been sealed by Jonson and Nashe's play *The Isle of Dogs* (1597), which offended the Privy Council. Nashe attempted to shift blame on to Jonson and the actors, Gabriel Spencer and Robert Shaa, claiming that he authored 'but the induction and first act of it, the other foure acts without my consent, or the least guesse of my drift or scope, by the players were supplied'. Shakespeare seems to have left the company several years before this debacle. He might have spent a short period working for Derby's Men around 1593,[20] before joining Lord Chamberlain's

Men, who, together with the second Admiral's Men, would dominate the London playing scene in the 1590s. Alongside Shakespeare
the Chamberlain's Men included such big-name actors as Richard
Burbage, Henry Condell, John Heminges, and William Kempe, and
they produced plays by Jonson and Dekker. Shakespeare evidently
had his fellow actors in mind when composing his plays: famously,
the 1599 second quarto of *Romeo and Juliet* features a stage direction calling for Kempe's entrance, while directions in *Henry VI Part
Three* name the actors Gabriel Spencer, Humphrey Jeffes, and John
Sincler, the last also appearing in *The Taming of the Shrew* and
the 1600 quarto of *Henry IV Part Two* (1597). Shakespeare would
be aware of the strengths and weaknesses of his company of players:
he would know that Burbage was a powerful performer who could
elicit pathos from audiences but that he didn't have the strong-
est singing voice; we seldom find roles Burbage is believed to have
played breaking into song. Shakespeare would be aware of Kempe's
physical abilities; after all, Kempe famously Morris-danced his way
from London to Norwich in 1600. But the dramatist would also be
conscious of Kempe's penchant for an extempore performance style,
placing the warning in Hamlet's mouth: 'And let those that play
your clowns speak no more than is set down for them' (3.2.38–9).
Shakespeare sought opportunities to maximise comic potential in
Sincler's physical appearance: emaciated and ague-skinned. Actor
and role were often inextricable in Shakespeare's mind's eye.

In 1603 King James, monarch of Scotland since 1567, became
King of England as well as patron of the Chamberlain's Men, leading to the genesis of the King's Men. Their actors also included
the likes of the fiercely satirical clown Robert Armin; Alexander
Cooke, who was often attached to prominent female roles; and John
Lowin, a player with a talent for imbibing long speeches and home-
speaking in comic roles. The company's repertoire featured works
by Francis Beaumont and John Fletcher. They continued to perform
long after Shakespeare's death in 1616 and King James's death in
1625, even after the theatre closures of 1642. Upon James's accession
the Admiral's Men became Prince Henry's Men, named after the
monarch's eldest son. Queen Anne's Men were named after James's

wife and amalgamated members from Oxford's Men, which had been patronised by the Earls of Oxford, and Worcester's Men, who had been given a licence to perform in London by the Privy Council in 1602. That company's repertoire included plays by Dekker, Henry Chettle, and Thomas Heywood. Lady Elizabeth's Men were formed by James's daughter, receiving their royal patent in 1611 and performing plays by dramatists such as Jonson and Thomas Middleton. Alongside adult acting companies there were troupes of child actors such as the Children of the Chapel, who performed works by the likes of Jonson, Beaumont and Fletcher, Chapman, Middleton, John Day, and John Marston, while the Children of Paul's had performed plays by John Lyly at court and their repertoire included works by Chapman, Marston, Middleton, and Dekker in later years. The Children of the King's Revels, formed by the poet Michael Drayton and Thomas Lodge's nephew, Thomas Woodford, were active during 1607–9, performing plays by such writers as Lording Barry, John Day, and Gervase Markham. The revival of children's companies at the beginning of the seventeenth century must have had a colossal impact on London theatre. In this thriving period of drama playwrights like Shakespeare would need to keep a keen eye on plays produced by rival companies in order to service what was essentially a commercial operation designed to generate income.

It was also a deeply collaborative period and Shakespeare would've worked closely with theatre managers as well as other players throughout his career. With the possibility of several different plays being performed per week, theatre managers needed to make sure their companies were supplied with fresh material. It might take as little as six weeks to write some of the plays we consider classics today, with an additional three weeks of rehearsal to bring a play from page to stage according to some estimates.[21] Theatre managers would commission an author to write a plot, which would be read to the company before work on the play proper began. Other dramatists could base a play on these scenarios, such as Chapman, who was commissioned by theatre impresario Philip Henslowe to write a play based on a plot by Jonson in 1598. Practically every commercial dramatist of the period appears to have co-authored plays, and nearly two-thirds of the 282 plays mentioned in Henslowe's diary, which details his theatrical operations, were produced by more than one writer.[22] Co-authors sometimes divided their labour according to acts, judging by Nashe's testimony for *The Isle of Dogs*, or one author might take over for an entrance or an exit. However, co-authors could contribute speeches in so-called 'French scenes', passages of text in which no character enters or exits. Thomas Dekker contributed 'a speech in the last scene of the last Act of the boy who had killed his mother' in the lost collaboration with William Rowley, John Ford, and John Webster, *Keep the Widow Waking* (1624). Most often divisions of labour were determined by character, theme, and plot elements. In the case of Greene and Lodge's *A Looking-Glass for London and England* (1589) the dramatists were largely responsible for separate plotlines: Greene took care of much of the plot involving Rasni and the comic business with the clown, Adam, while Lodge contributed the scenes involving the Usurer as well as Jonah. When a play was finished, dramatists were expected to transcribe the drafts into 'perfect' or 'fair copies', or at least commission professional scribes themselves. For co-authored plays one of the dramatists might take responsibility for compiling sections, perhaps touching up their co-authors' scenes and passages to make the play as homogeneous as possible, as seems to be the case with Philip Massinger, who could rarely resist tinkering with Fletcher's passages in plays such as *The Little French Lawyer* (1620).

Revision, another form of collaboration between dramatists, was commonplace during the period. This might include posthumous collaboration, a reviser collaborating with the dead, as in the 320 lines added to the 1602 edition of Kyd's *The Spanish Tragedy*. Sometimes a dramatist might be called on to finish a work that one of his colleagues had failed to complete: Fletcher's *The Noble Gentleman* (1626) appears to have been finished by another hand after Fletcher died in 1625. Was Shakespeare employed to tinker with and patch up older plays? Evidence suggests that, like Jonson, Middleton, Webster, and James Shirley, he was indeed occasionally commissioned to revise the plays of other dramatists. Shakespeare would likely contribute, in some way, to texts in which he didn't have a direct hand. He would take part in discussions between authors and actors during the planning stages. Changes to play scripts could occur during rehearsals or in performance: actors might suggest or make changes to scripts, although playing companies usually relied on the dramatist to alter his own play.

The actors' scripts contained each of their lines as well as their cues, which consisted of the last few words of preceding speeches (not the whole play). Players like Shakespeare would therefore need to be alert during performance, relying heavily on their aural understanding. Shakespeare might aid himself and his fellow actors by writing memorable cues, particularly in the case of rhyming couplets, which would be easier to hear and remember for players waiting in the tiring areas. The 'fair copied' play would also be transcribed into a prompt book, to be used during performance by the prompter, or book holder, who made sure actors entered the stage when required and that music and props were on cue.

Through performing in the plays of other writers as well as in his own, Shakespeare would be deeply conscious when composing his dramatic works of the requirements of his fellow players. He would also be cognisant of the necessity to collaborate with audiences. He'd need to bear in mind the very dimensions of a stage, the strengths and limitations of various playing spaces in London, from inns to theatres to courts and palaces, as well as the spaces his company would encounter on tour. Inn yards serving as playing spaces when Shakespeare came to London included Bell Savage on Ludgate Hill; the Bull in Bishopsgate Street; and the Bell Inn and Cross Keys on Gracechurch Street. Purpose-built playhouses included the Theatre on Curtain Road and the Curtain Theatre in Shoreditch. The Museum of London Archaeology (MOLA) has discovered that the stage at the Curtain was around '14 metres long, running across the width of the playhouse. Its immense proportions meant that it allowed for linear movement and was ideal for hosting certain types of plays – specifically those that included sensational dynamic fight scenes'.[23] One of several reasons for the popularity of the history play genre seems to have been the opportunities these plays provided for entertaining action sequences. Shakespeare took advantage of this in several of his earliest dramatic efforts, such as *Henry VI Part Three*, a play exploding with bloody battles. It's been estimated that from the opening of the first public theatre in London in 1576 until Shakespeare's death in 1616, over one-third of all surviving plays include battle scenes.[24] South of the Thames, situated in Surrey, was Newington Butts, while the Rose playhouse was located on Bankside. Plays associated with Shakespeare were performed at each of these venues, but it was for the Globe playhouse in Southwark, reconstructed from the timber of the Theatre in 1599, that he wrote most of his plays. For a penny, which could fetch you a loaf of bread at the time, Elizabethan audience members at the Globe could join the 'groundlings' (or 'stinkards', a term highly suggestive of the mixture of smells encountered at the Globe playhouse, including ale, shellfish, and urine) in the yard, or pit. For two pennies, audience members could sit in the gallery, paying a third penny for the luxury of a cushion. Wealthier citizens could pay around a shilling for seats in the boxes, where it was more about being seen by other audience members than necessarily having the best seats for watching the play. Prices appear to have increased during the seventeenth century, with admission being charged at around sixpence.

Audiences at the Globe would consist of the gentry, foreign ambassadors, butchers, tailors, leather workers, trainee lawyers, apprentices, shopkeepers, and thieves, as well as citizens' wives and sex workers. The whole sweep of the city of London.[25] Shakespeare was writing for eclectic audiences from all sorts of socioeconomic backgrounds. He'd need to make sure the characters, themes, and subject matter of his dramas were topical and applicable. Catering to an audience of up to three thousand, Shakespeare would be aware that there would be an awful lot going on in the theatre before a play even began: in the pit thieves might be picking pockets, sex workers might be peddling their wares, fights might break out. Shakespeare grabs audiences by their purse strings through stimulating opening scenes: an *in medias res* dispute between Iago and Roderigo in *Othello* (1604), the appearance of three witches in *Macbeth*, or a shipwreck at the beginning of *The Tempest* (1611). In the Prologue to *Sapho and Phao* (1584) John Lyly wishes audiences would content themselves with 'soft smiling, not loud laughing' (Prologue.9) during comedies.[26] But interactions between players and audiences at the Globe might have been rowdily dialogic at times. In 1965 David Warner received a response from an audience member when, playing the role of Hamlet in Stratford-upon-Avon, he asked: 'Am I a coward?' (2.2.573). Did Richard Burbage experience a similar relationship with early modern spectators?

Players collaborated with audiences to work on their 'imaginary forces' (Prologue.18), as the Chorus puts it in *Henry V* (1599). With performances taking place during the afternoon, Shakespeare employs auditory techniques and sensory descriptions to convey setting and mood: he establishes that it's dark through the opening question of *Hamlet*: 'Who's there?' (1.1.1). He transports audiences from London to the heat of Verona with statements like 'The day is hot' (3.1.2) in *Romeo and Juliet*. He helps his audience suspend their disbelief when it comes to apprentices taking the roles of heroines, employing hyperbolic language to turn the young boy playing Desdemona in *Othello*, clad in a wig and dress, into 'a maid / That paragons description and wild fame' (2.1.62–3). Shakespeare aids his actors, especially the less experienced young boys in the company, by incorporating stage directions in his dramatic language, as in Romeo's pointy line, 'See how she leans her cheek upon her hand' (2.1.65). Shakespeare is also deeply conscious of just how long a costume change might take. On the stage blood would have blood. And there were plenty of kinds: it could take the form of dyed vinegar, vermilion paint, or be drawn from calves or sheep (older animals were generally avoided as theirs was less drippy). Blood was often contained in a pig's bladder and concealed within a player's clothing for murderous scenes, and Shakespeare even shows an awareness of just how long it takes to clear away stage blood, as the Macbeths are required to do following King Duncan's murder. Shakespeare's plays are clearly products of a man of the theatre who had first-hand experience of rehearsal processes and performing on stage. His dramas often reference the Globe stage itself, as in Hamlet's line, 'this majestical roof fretted with golden fire' (2.2.302–3), which alludes to the stage cover known as the 'heavens'. Shakespeare takes full advantage of stage columns or pillars, which not only served an architectural purpose but also offered opportunities for conceal-ment, overhearing, and multi-patterned staging, as in the gulling of figures such as Malvolio, Paroles, and Othello. Shakespeare has the dimensions of the 'thrust', or 'apron', stage in mind when using the technique of 'teichoscopy', the synchronous discussion of events, as in the moment Pandarus describes the soldiers to Cressida in 1.2 of *Troilus and Cressida* (1602), or when the Widow, Mariana, and Diana discuss a passing troop with Helena in 3.5 of *All's Well that Ends Well* (1605). He makes maximum use of the cellarage and trap door, particularly for supernatural figures, such as the 'old mole', Hamlet's ghostly father, who 'Canst work i'th' earth so fast' (1.5.164), as well as special effects for storm scenes, such as lightning bolts created by pyrotechnics, or thunder, which could be simulated by rolling a cannon-ball across the rafters or via beating drums.

From 1608 onwards Shakespeare's company performed during the winter months at the indoor Blackfriars Theatre where the company could take advantage of artificial lighting. Candlefire would need to be relumed between acts. Admission for this theatre was likely higher than at the Globe so Shakespeare was catering for more upper-class citizens accustomed to spectacle, as witnessed in masques of the period, and courtly dialogue. These considerations can be found in late Shakespeare plays like *The Tempest*, with its amorous aris-tocratic figures engaging in witty repartee, Miranda and Ferdinand, and Shakespeare's capitalisation on innovations in stage machin-ery, such as the 'quaint device' (3.3.52.2 SD) that makes a banquet table disappear in that play. Shakespeare's late style, which has been described in terms of 'a pervasive self-consciousness, an artist's play-ful delight in calling attention to his own virtuosity', continues to emphasise 'aural patterns' or auditory techniques,[27] as we'll see in the chapter on Ben Jonson. For Shakespeare drama was a primarily aural experience. He frequently writes of hearing, rather than seeing, a play. In *The Taming of the Shrew* the Lord says to the travelling players: 'There is a lord will hear you play tonight' (Induction.91) and 'yet his honour never heard a play' (Induction.94). A servant tells the drunkard Christopher Sly: 'they thought it good you hear a play'

(Induction.130). In *A Midsummer Night's Dream*, Theseus states: 'I will hear that play' (5.1.82). In *Hamlet*, the title character says that 'We'll hear a play tomorrow' (2.2.538–9).

Shakespeare's aural understanding was key to the development of his drama. That understanding derives in large part from the fact that, as well as being a poet and playwright, he was also a player. His actor's memory provided a crucial conduit, affording Shakespeare significant insights into the dramaturgical techniques of plays composed by fellow writers. He was used to hearing and delivering their words on stage and adapting them to varying contexts for his own plays with considerable dexterity.

2

John Lyly

It would take a decade until Shakespeare was born into the great stage of life. Business contracts were being drawn up to ensure England wouldn't become a satellite of Spain. Uprisings caused by concerns over Mary I's marriage to Philip II were swiftly quashed. Kent is where Thomas Wyatt, son of the sonneteer who shared his name, was born. The younger Wyatt would have a rebellion named after him. He bade farewell to his head, his limbs, his bowels, and his genitals at Tower Hill in 1554, a typically low end for high treason. Meanwhile, back in Kent, a diocesan official named Peter and his wife, Jane Burgh of Burgh Hall, North Yorkshire, met their eldest son, John Lyly (1554–1606), for the first time.[1] John was in distinguished familial company. His grandfather, William, was author of the most widely used Latin grammar textbook in England, while his uncle, George, was a cartographer responsible for an important map of the British Isles, as well as a humanist scholar. John Lyly was educated at Magdalen College, Oxford, where he received his MA in 1575. He took another MA at Cambridge in 1579. Having moved to London, Lyly followed in his family's writerly footsteps and achieved literary fame with the publication of two prose Romances: *Euphues: The Anatomy of Wit* (1578) and *Euphues and His England* (1580). The hugely influential style of English prose in these works would later become known as 'Euphuism', a term deriving from the name of Lyly's protagonist.[2] Lylian stylistic tropes include a self-conscious approach to language with corresponding structures in a series of clauses, as well as references to mythology and nature.

Having revolutionised English prose, Lyly embarked on a dramatic writing career. His canon of plays consists of *Campaspe* (1583); *Sapho and Phao*; *Galatea* (1584); *Endymion* (1588); *The Woman in the Moon* (1588); *Midas* (1589); *Mother Bombie* (1589); and *Love's Metamorphosis* (1590). Unlike Lyly's other plays, *The Woman in the Moon* is written in blank verse rather than prose. Often labelled 'comedies', Lyly's dramas actually push against rigid generic distinctions, his *Campaspe* described as both a 'comedy' and a 'tragical comedy' in its printed text. Lyly's earliest plays were performed at the first Blackfriars Theatre, which he leased by 1583, the year in which he married the heiress Beatrice Browne, and most of his dramatic works were performed by the Children of Paul's. Unlike practically every other playwright of the period Lyly doesn't seem to have co-authored any plays or written with the more 'common stages' in mind. His plays were often performed privately for Elizabeth I, whose last four parliaments he sat on as an MP between 1589 and 1601. Lyly was keen to become Master of the Revels, a position that would mean he'd oversee royal festivities and take responsibility for stage censorship, but, to his grave disappointment, his petitions to the Queen were in vain. Lyly spent the final years of his life at his wife's home in Yorkshire before dying of unknown causes in 1606.

Lyly's influence on Shakespeare's dramas can be seen in the mannerisms and craftsmanship of comedies such *A Midsummer Night's Dream* and *Love's Labour's Lost* (1596), while Sir John Falstaff appears to parody Euphuism in *Henry IV Part One* (1597) when he impersonates Prince Hal's father:

> Peace, good pint-pot; peace, good tickle-brain. –
> Harry, I do not only marvel where thou spendest thy
> time, but also how thou art accompanied. For though
> the camomile, the more it is trodden on, the faster it
> grows, yet youth, the more it is wasted, the sooner it
> wears. (2.5.401–6)

Falstaff's comic bombast and florid analogies could be interpreted as Shakespeare's rejection of Lyly's model. But such parodies could instead be of Elizabethan courtiers who imitated the dramatist.[3] Lyly's style can in turn be seen as parodic, particularly through the character of Sir Tophas in *Endymion*, a braggart, or *miles gloriosus*, who anticipates Falstaff. The lineaments of Falstaff's characterisation are found in Sir Tophas's inflated language:

> There cometh no soft syllable within my lips; custome hath
> made my wordes bloudy, and my hart barbarous: that pelting word
> love, how watrish it is in my mouth, it carrieth no sound; hate,
> horror, death, are speaches that nourish my spirits. I like hony, but
> I care not for the bees: I delight in musicke, but I love not to play
> on the bagpipes: I can vouchsafe to heare the voice of women, but
> to touch their bodies I disdaine it, as a thing childish, and fit for
> such men as can disgest nothing but milke. (2.2.124–31)

Lyly's style has also been described as 'notably supple and varied', with the language of *Endymion* shifting from 'measured and formal dialogue' to 'staccato rhythms' and 'colloquial and punning' comic scenes.[4] The plot of Sir Tophas and servants in the courtier Endymion's household runs alongside the plot of a spell cast by Tellus as revenge for Endymion's falling in love with Cynthia. *Endymion* reveals Lyly's reluctance to pigeonhole his plays into specific genres: slicing away at distinction with the broad strokes of his powerful pen, Lyly has his Prologue say that it is 'neither Comedie, nor Tragedie, nor storie, nor anie thing' (Prologue.9–10). Lyly's dramas therefore anticipate Shakespeare's later works, which often defy generic classification.

Several elements of Shakespeare's comedies can be traced to Lyly, from cross-dressing heroines to the use of song to battles of wit. In *The Two Gentlemen of Verona* (1594), *As You Like It*, and *Twelfth Night* (1601) Shakespeare exploits opportunities to experiment with the androgynous attractiveness of boy actors playing female roles, who in turn disguise themselves as boys. This harks back to the exploration of cross-dressing heroines in Lyly's *Galatea*. In that play the two heroines, disguised in male clothing, Galatea and Phillida, become attracted to each other, without realising they're both female. The comic business between Rosalind, disguised as the boy Ganymede, and Phoebe in *As You Like It* closely resembles Lyly's explorations of female agency and homosocial relationships. That said, Rosalind's speech at the end of Shakespeare's play emphasises the true gender of the boy playing her. At the conclusion of Lyly's play Venus transforms one of the women into a boy so that they can marry, but Lyly chooses not to specify who is transformed. Unlike many comedies of the period, *Galatea* refuses to emphasise a restoration of normative gender roles at its conclusion. The ending of *Twelfth Night*, in which Viola remains dressed as a boy when she partners up with Duke Orsino, is probably as close as Shakespeare got to approximating Lyly's transgressive approach to comic resolutions.

In *A Midsummer Night's Dream*, Shakespeare echoes Lyly's *Sapho and Phao* and *The Woman in the Moon* by depicting his drama as a dream. Just as Puck tells audiences that the events of the play are 'no more yielding but a dream' (Epilogue.6), the Prologue at the Court for *Sapho and Phao* entreats the Queen to 'imagine yourself to be in a deep dream' (Prologue.10). The Prologue for *The Woman in the Moon* describes the play's events as 'but the shadow of our author's dream' (Prologue.12), which anticipates Puck's line 'If we shadows have offended' (Epilogue.1). There's a distinction to be made, though: Puck is very much a part of the play, a member of the cast, whereas the Prologues' messages to the Queen can be said to operate outside of Lyly's dramatic worlds.[5] In *Sapho and Phao*, Venus commands Cupid to make Sapho fall in love with the ferryman Phao. At the end of the play Sapho adopts Cupid, who usurps the goddess of Love. Shakespeare again differs from Lyly in his reluctance to include deific figures, such as Cupid, in the *dramatis personae* of his plays: approximately 13 per cent of Shakespeare's plays feature an onstage deity and they usually take on an illusory or performed role. On the other hand, six of Lyly's eight plays depict deities as onstage characters.[6] Shakespeare nevertheless seems to have drawn from Lyly in order to interrogate the boundaries between the world of the play and the reality of the audience.

The Tophas–Epiton–Bagoa trio in *Endymion* resembles Armado–Moth–Jaquenetta in the lower plot of Shakespeare's comedy *Love's Labour's Lost*. Parallelism between noble characters and lower-class characters is important for the dramatic thrust of both plays, while Don Armado, another affected braggart in the mould of Sir Tophas, speaks in an excessive, Euphuistic manner. Most importantly *Love's Labour's Lost* shares Lyly's inclination to interrogate comic resolutions, to conclude his plays with lovers parted from each other.[7] The men must wait a year and a day for their lovers to mourn the death of the Princess of France's father. Modern digital techniques inform traditional literary-critical approaches towards Lyly's influence on Shakespeare in remarkable ways. A technique called 'Discriminant analysis' has been applied to common three-word phrases. The method correctly identified the author of 84 per cent of early modern plays and got thirty-four out of thirty-seven tested plays by Shakespeare correct. This technique is clearly powerful and also succeeded in correctly assigning all of Lyly's plays to him. But one spectacular failure occurred: the method claimed there was a 92 per cent chance that John Lyly wrote *Love's Labour's Lost*! The assignment of *Love's Labour's Lost* to 'Lyly's Euphuistic world' can be considered 'a stroke of statistical brilliance in its own right'.[8] The cold, hard numbers reflect the nuanced dramaturgical relationship between Shakespeare's play and Lyly.

That method relied on the frequency of commonplace phrases. What about the findings for unique phrases in *Collocations and N-grams*? What do they tell us about the relationships between Lyly and Shakespeare's plays? We're given an altogether different picture. The highest-ranked Lyly play for *Love's Labour's Lost* is *The Woman in the Moon* at a lowly sixty-fifth. Despite their similarities Lyly plays don't feature highly in the spreadsheet comparing *A Midsummer Night's Dream* to all other plays of the period either: *The Woman in the Moon* is again the top Lyly play, at sixty-two, followed by *Campaspe* at sixty-five. Shakespeare wasn't overly familiar with Lyly's dramatic language near the beginning of his career, even if he was familiar with Lyly's prose Romances. His later plays such as *As You Like It* and *Twelfth Night* appear to have been more influenced by Lyly's dramaturgy than his earliest efforts. The highest-ranked Shakespeare play of this period in any of the Lyly spreadsheets is *The Comedy of Errors*, ranked thirteenth for pairs of plays involving *Mother Bombie*, with Lyly's play ranked eleventh in the spreadsheet for Shakespeare's play.

The language of Lyly plays performed by children at court would, however, seep into the works of dramatists writing for adult companies performing at public playhouses, and vice versa. George Peele's *The Arraignment of Paris* (1584) was performed by the Children of the Chapel. The title page of the 1594 quarto text of *Dido, Queen of Carthage* (1588) attributes the play to Christopher Marlowe and Thomas Nashe and claims that it was also played by that company of boy actors. Peele's play consistently features highly in Lyly play rankings. *Sapho and Phao* shares more unique phrases with *Dido, Queen of Carthage* than does any other play. Thomas Kyd's commercial dramas display Euphuistic mannerisms: in his verbal tennis matches, Lyly likes to contradict statements with sentences beginning 'Ay, but', his *Campaspe, Endymion, Galatea,* and *Midas* each featuring five instances or more of that colloquialism. This stylistic habit can be found on six occasions in Kyd's *The Spanish Tragedy* and eight times in *Soliman and Perseda*. Other plays that have long been attributed to Kyd, such as *King Leir* (1589) and *Arden of Faversham*, also have high counts for 'Ay, but': it can be found on seven occasions in *King Leir* and nine times in *Arden of Faversham*. Kyd is the only known dramatist, other than Lyly, to use this colloquialism with some consistency. On the other hand, apart from in *Henry VI Part Three* (eight instances), Shakespeare seldom uses it (he averages one instance per play in his canon), and his usage in that earlier play was possibly influenced by Kyd rather than Lyly. Plays that have been given to Kyd feature highly in the spreadsheet for unique phrases shared with *Endymion*: *King Leir* is ranked twelfth, *Fair Em* (1590) twenty-fifth, and *Arden of Faversham* thirty-third.[9] In a contrast as stark as Cleopatra on the muddy banks of the Nile, the highest-ranked early Shakespeare play is *The Taming of the Shrew*, at fifty-six, again suggesting that Shakespeare wasn't overly familiar with the verbal texture of Lyly's plays near the start of his career. We'll discover more about Kyd's canon and his influence on Shakespeare's dramas later in this book. For now we can see that although an author's influence can be mediated by the plays of other authors, Lyly's courtly dramatic language, not just the language of his prose works, influenced playwrights writing for commercial playing spaces.

The top Shakespeare play in the spreadsheet for *Endymion* is *Cymbeline* (1610), at thirteenth. The top four plays in this spreadsheet are all by Lyly who, like every other author of the period, was evidently prone to repeating himself. Turning to the spreadsheet for *Cymbeline*, we discover that Lyly's *Endymion* is ranked seventh. It's the only non-Shakespeare play in the top seven that was written before Shakespeare's Romance. As in the spreadsheet for *Endymion*, this statistical fact reveals the power of authorial self-repetition in these rankings. It also reveals, for the first time, that Shakespeare must have consulted Lyly's play directly when composing *Cymbeline*. Shakespeare's knowledge of the play was likely reading-based; after all, *Endymion* had been available in quarto form since 1591. This discovery strongly suggests that Shakespeare was harking back to Lyly when writing for the Blackfriars Theatre. As we saw earlier, Lyly's comedies had been performed in the first playhouse at the old Blackfriars monastery space. Were some of Lyly's plays performed at the second Blackfriars, where Shakespeare's plays would be put on? It's possible: the Children of the Chapel, who appear to have revived Lyly's *Love's Metamorphosis*, played there from around 1597.

Like Lyly before him Shakespeare shakes a fist at generic boundaries in *Cymbeline*, a play that fuses comic and tragic matter and, at the risk of sounding like Polonius, features historical, pastoral, and Romance elements. The play feels like a greatest hits package, the *Now That's What I Call Shakespeare!* of the canon. *Cymbeline* also features a cross-dressing heroine in Imogen, who disguises herself as the servant, Fidele. The play's courtly tone and ornate style are sometimes reminiscent of Lyly's dramas. Shakespeare brings a god on to the stage for this generically elusive play, a rare occasion in his dramatic corpus but very frequent in Lyly's canon. Hymen appears in *As You Like It*; Diana features in *Pericles* (1607); Apollo in *The Winter's Tale* (1611); and Ceres, Juno, and Iris in *The Tempest*. Jupiter's appearance in *Cymbeline* occurs during a scene that combines Lyly's liking for theophany, the presentation of onstage deities, with his emphasis on dreams: Jupiter visits the sleeping protagonist Posthumus and leaves a tablet with a prophecy inscribed on it on Posthumus's chest. The oracular dream is marked by a visually impressive cue, the *deus ex machina* exploiting the theatre's technical apparatus: '*Jupiter descends in thunder and lightning, sitting upon an eagle. He throws a thunderbolt*' (5.5.186.1–2 SD). The appearance of this mythological figure must have given audiences at the public theatres a visually delicious taste of the grand court entertainments experienced by upper-class citizens.[10] *The Woman in the Moon* presents a distinctive cosmogonic myth to Protestant audiences, in which the goddess of Nature breathes life into the first woman. Jupiter had previously made an appearance in Lyly's play, where he reveals his influence to Pandora: 'I may not blame thee, for my beames are cause / Of all this insolence and proud disdaine' (2.1.77–8). Similarly, the god of sky and thunder in Shakespeare's play reveals his transcendent sway: 'Our Jovial star reigned at his birth, and in / Our temple was he married' (5.5.199–200).

The phrase 'stately cedar' is unique in *Collocations and N-grams* to *Endymion* and the Soothsayer's interpretation of the tablet in *Cymbeline*: 'when from a **stately cedar** shall be lopped branches' (5.6.438–9). Another rare match with *Endymion*, the phrase, 'the beams of the sun', can be found in the same scene of *Cymbeline* and is again delivered by the Soothsayer:

> the Roman eagle,
> From south to west on wing soaring aloft,
> Lessened herself, and in **the beams o'th' sun**
> So vanished. (5.6.471–4)

Strikingly, both phrases cluster in a single speech in Lyly's play, delivered by Endymion:

> No Tellus; thou knowest that the **stately Cedar**, whose
> toppe reacheth unto the clowdes, never boweth his head to the
> shrubs that growe in the valley; nor Ivie that climbeth up by the
> Elme, can ever get hold of **the beames of the Sun**. (2.1.93–6)

It's interesting that the parallel speeches in *Cymbeline* concern the Soothsayer's interpretation of Jupiter's prophecy: Shakespeare appears to have had Lyly's deific figures as well as his dramatic language in mind. Jupiter's appearance isn't unique to these plays (he also features in the works of Ben Jonson and Thomas Heywood). But it's notable that in its generic slipperiness, the use of onstage deities, the emphasis on dreams, and the phrasal links with *Endymion*, *Cymbeline* recalls Lyly's dramas more so than any of Shakespeare's other Jacobean plays. Shakespeare had of course written plays for indoor performance throughout his career, plays to be performed at court or on tour. But he'd have been especially conscious of the Blackfriars Theatre and its audiences when composing this play. Did this stimulate further interest in Lyly's dramas performed at that site? Did Shakespeare want to learn more about how Lyly had entertained audiences there? Here Shakespeare emerges as a playwright who was deeply aware of his dramatic predecessors, his theatrical venues, his audiences.

In his eulogy on Shakespeare, published in the First Folio, Ben Jonson writes of 'how far thou didst our Lyly outshine' (l. 29). Rather than taking Jonson's line as a snipe at Lyly, it's testament to how enduringly Lyly's light shone, the comparison occurring decades after his plays were first performed. Shakespeare adorned himself in Lyly's feathers, particularly when it came to explorations of homosocial relationships and disguised heroines. He seems to have learned a great deal from Lylian dramaturgy, the older playwright's genre-bending brilliance, throughout his career. And as time limited all the learnings Shakespeare could receive, he turned to Lyly once again for inspiration in his late Romance *Cymbeline*.

3

Christopher Marlowe

Like Lyly, Christopher Marlowe (1564–93) hailed from Kent.[1] He was the son of a shoemaker, John Marlowe, and his wife, Katherine. In 1578 he enrolled at King's School, Canterbury, and two years later he attended Corpus Christi College, Cambridge, on a scholarship. He received a BA degree in 1584 and an MA in 1587, despite some reservations from the university due to Marlowe's frequent absences. The Privy Council defended these absences on the grounds that Marlowe was engaged in activities that benefited the country: did Marlowe work as an 'intelligencer' for the government under the spymaster Sir Francis Walsingham, the Elizabethan equivalent of M in the James Bond movies? It's likely that Marlowe moved to London before receiving his MA, announcing himself on the theatrical stage in the 'high astounding terms' (Prologue.5) of *Tamburlaine the Great, Part One* (1587).[2] He also wrote poetry, including a translation of Ovid's elegiac couplets, while *The Passionate Shepherd to His Love*, which Shakespeare paraphrased in *The Merry Wives of Windsor* (1597), was published posthumously in 1599.

Marlowe was accused of writing a heretical poem calling for the murder of Protestant refugees, which was posted on the walls of the Dutch church in Broad Street on 5 May 1593.[3] Marlowe's roommate in London for approximately two years, fellow playwright Thomas Kyd, was dragged into ensuing tragedy when the Council's officers discovered 'vile hereticall Conceiptes denying the deity of Jhesus Criste our Saviour' during a search of their lodgings, which Kyd affirmed 'he had from Marlowe'. At the time Marlowe was staying at the courtier Thomas Walsingham's house in Scadbury, Kent.[4] While Marlowe was enjoying this gorgeous manor, a huge brick and timber building, surrounded by ancient oak trees, as well as ash, sycamore, alder, and sweet chestnuts, Kyd was arrested and tortured in Bridewell prison. Kyd's protagonist in *The Spanish Tragedy* frequently calls for 'Justice, O justice' (4.6.27), and the injustice Kyd faced was exceptionally bitter, especially as the 'fragments of a disputation' found in his possession belonged to a harmless tract from 1549 by the historian John Proctor. Yet Marlowe was accused of atheism by several contemporaries, including Kyd, Robert Greene, and the double agent Richard Baines, who had stayed with Marlowe 1591–92 in the Dutch town of Flushing in the Netherlands, where they became embroiled in counterfeiting coins. The similarities in charges of atheism levelled at Marlowe can be interpreted as 'practically establishing the truth of Christopher Marlowe's alleged reckless and scornful heterodoxy'.[5]

Awaiting a decision on his case concerning the inflammatory poem known as the 'Dutch Church Libel', Marlowe spent 30 May 1593 in a public house in Deptford owned by the widow Eleanor Bull. He was accompanied by three men: Ingram Frizer, Nicholas Skeres, and Robert Poley. All three had been employed by either Thomas Walsingham or the late Francis. Marlowe was stabbed to death by Frizer during a quarrel over a bill.[6] Was this the outcome of malicious words having violent ends? Or was this an assassination covered up by professional liars and confidence tricksters? The clergyman and theologian Thomas Beard claimed that he was 'stabd in the head with a dagger' and, like his brilliant Machiavellian villain, Barabas, 'dyed swearing'.

We can imagine Marlowe's parents searching in vain for his unmarked grave in Deptford. Their hair streaked with white, faces lined like maps detailing their history, an enduring love that had known tragedy and comedy in equal measure. Memories propping them up. Remembrances of their little boy surrounded by his sisters, Margaret, Anne, Jane, and Dorothy, in their house on the corner of St George's Street and St George's Lane. Laughing, joking, bickering. Those voices suddenly sounding clear in the couple's ears. Little Christopher's smiles materialising in the dull stone of St Nicholas's Church and the gravestones surrounding them. His laughter joining in with the choral breeze and the ditties of ancient trees. Might that laugh have eased John's weary heart during troublesome times involving debt? Had Marlowe's eyes sparkled with such keen interest in John's tales that routines like attending church and examining leather become fun? His parents had found themselves lost in a labyrinth of death, their boy, a springing rose snipped before his time.

Marlowe lives on, however, through a phenomenal, if tragically stunted, dramatic canon of seven plays: *Tamburlaine the Great, Part One, Tamburlaine the Great, Part Two* (1587), and *Doctor Faustus* (1588), performed by Lord Admiral's Men; *Dido, Queen of Carthage*, performed by the Children of the Chapel and later featuring in the repertory of the Admiral's Men; *The Jew of Malta*, which migrated between Lord Strange's Men, Sussex's Men, and the Admiral's Men; *Edward II* (1592), performed by Pembroke's Men; and *The Massacre at Paris* (1593), performed by Strange's Men and later the Admiral's Men. Did Shakespeare start his dramatic writing career with Pembroke's Men? If so, all of his plays would have competed with Marlowe's with the sole exception of *Edward II*. Marlowe's plays are associated primarily with the Admiral's Men and the great actor Edward Alleyn. As we have seen, Alleyn moved over to Strange's Men in early 1591 and Marlowe seems to have also 'attached himself to Strange's Men, and in this way crossed the outer threshold of Ferdinando Stanley's personal retinue'.[7]

The majority of Marlowe's plays can be considered collaborative in some way. The *Tamburlaine* plays appear to have been abridged by Richard Jones, who printed them in 1590 and added a finger-wagging note:

> I have (purposely) omitted and left out some fond and frivolous Jestures, digressing (and in my poore opinion) far unmeet for the matter, which I thought, might seeme more tedious unto the wise, than any way els to be regarded, though (happly) they have bene of some vaine conceited fondlings greatly gaped at, what times they were shewed upon the stage in their graced deformities.

The tragic portions of the 1604 quarto of *Doctor Faustus* tend to be attributed by and large to Marlowe, with an unknown collaborator assigned the comic scenes. Thomas Nashe and Henry Porter have both been plausibly suggested as Marlowe's co-author.[8] In 1602 Philip Henslowe paid Samuel Rowley and William Bird 'for ther adicyones in docter fostes', which seem to have been integrated into the 1616 edition of the play. The 1594 quarto title-page ascription of *Dido, Queen of Carthage* to Marlowe and Nashe, however, isn't supported by rigorous testing. Independent studies have failed to unearth any evidence of Nashe's hand in the play's verbal fabric.[9] Could Nashe have provided the author plot? Did he contribute in an editorial capacity? Nashe understood how integral the author's plot was to fashioning a play, praising Robert Greene as his 'crafts master' at 'plotting Plaies'. Thomas Heywood contributed Prologues and Epilogues to *The Jew of Malta* for a 1633 revival, and possibly added more to that play, while Thomas Dekker might also have had a revising presence.[10] The undated octavo of *The Massacre at Paris* is a textual mess. It is manifestly corrupt, likely pieced together from hazy memories. Marlowe's dramatic voice might seem distinctive, but it's also undeniably polyvocal.

Shakespeare's borrowings from or allusions to Marlowe's dramas are extensive: no fewer than eight Shakespeare texts actually quote Marlowe's works, which emphasises 'the firmness with which Marlowe's influence rooted itself in Shakespeare and developed, for it continued to thrive for 18 years after Marlowe's death, roughly from 1593–1611, the remainder of Shakespeare's career'.[11] The most famous echo is surely the Player's speech in *Hamlet* (2.2.471–500), which recalls Aeneas's tale in *Dido, Queen of Carthage*, beginning 'Whereat he lifted up his bed-rid limbs' (2.1.250). Shakespeare recreates the '"feel" of a Marlovian speech' and 'half-affectionately' exaggerates its stylistic features, pushing his deliberately archaic verse 'over the verge of absurdity'.[12] Shakespeare's debt to Marlowe's play is echoed in Hamlet's own display of his verbal recall. Hamlet remembers a thirteen-line speech he 'chiefly loved, 'twas Aeneas' tale to Dido' (2.2.448–9), which he delivers with 'good accent and good discretion' (2.2.469–70) even though he's only heard the 'speech once, but it was never acted, or, if it was, not above once' (2.2.437–8). Hamlet nevertheless wrestles with beginnings: '"The rugged **Pyrrhus**, like th'Hyrcanian beast"– / 'tis not so. It **begins**' (2.2.453–4); 'where he speaks of **Priam's** slaughter. If it live in your memory, **begin**' (2.2.450–1). *Collocations and N-grams* reveals that Shakespeare's association of the word choice 'begin' with these mythological figures echoes Marlowe's play: 'He ripped old **Priam**; at whose latter gasp / Jove's marble statue **gan** to bend the brow, / As loathing **Pyrrhus**' (2.1.256–8). Hamlet, overawed by the Player's delivery of the speech, with 'all his **visage** wanned, / Tears in his **eyes**' (2.2.556–7), conjures 'Hector's ghost, / With ashy **visage**, bluish sulphur **eyes**' (2.1.201–2). Wisps of Marlowe's ghostly presence are traceable in Shakespeare's most famous ghost story. Marlowe also casts a pall over the enchanted island in Shakespeare's *The Tempest*: 'When Prospero says "I'll drown my book", he is clearly echoing Faustus' last unfulfilled promise, "I'll burn my books"', which suggests, in the words of scholar Jonathan Bate, that 'Shakespeare' was 'still haunted by Marlowe' in the twilight of his career.[13] Marlowe's ghost actually enters *Love's Labour's Lost* in the shape of the 'messenger of death' (13.3) Mercadé, who steps out of *The Massacre at Paris* to puncture the romantic comedy with news of a dead King and father.[14]

Marlowe appears to have learned a great deal from Shakespeare's historical tetralogy, while Shakespeare in turn drew from his chronicle history *Edward II* to produce *Richard II* (1595), a play similar in both plot and language, particularly Richard's rhetoric, which often rings Marlovian. And yet the most striking references to Marlowe's works occur, curiously enough, in a pastoral comedy: *As You Like It*. While Shakespeare sometimes quotes Marlowe for parodic purposes, such as through Pistol's bombastic rants in *Henry V* evoking the *Tamburlaine* plays, the callbacks to Marlowe in *As You Like It* seem poignant. Phoebe quotes line 176 from the First Sestiad of Marlowe's poem *Hero and Leander*, published in 1598: 'Dead shepherd, now I find thy saw of might: / "Who ever loved that loved not at first sight?"' (3.5.82–3). Touchstone alludes to Marlowe's death: 'When a man's verses cannot be understood, nor a man's good wit seconded with the forward child, understanding, it strikes a man more dead than a great reckoning in a little room' (3.3.11–12). These lines echo the Jewish moneylender Barabas's opening speech in *The Jew of Malta*: 'Infinite riches in a little room' (1.1.37).

Shakespeare engaged more fully with *The Jew of Malta* in *The Merchant of Venice* (1596), alternatively known as 'The Jewe of Venyce' according to the Stationers' Register entry of 1598. Comparisons between the plays must have been drawn by contemporary audiences. Shakespeare built on Barabas's relationship with his daughter, Abigail, when he depicted the Shylock–Jessica relationship. Marlowe's play draws a savagely satirical portrait of Christians, Jews, and Turks alike, whereas Shakespeare takes Marlowe's variety of stereotypes and paints a more balanced and, admittedly, more conservative, picture.[15]

Shakespeare's most direct borrowing from *The Jew of Malta* must be Aaron's speech in *Titus Andronicus*, which is closely modelled on Barabas's conversation with his villainous sidekick Ithamore:

As for myself, I walk abroad o' nights,
And kill sick people groaning under walls:
Sometimes I go about and poison wells;
And now and then, to cherish Christian thieves,
I am content to lose some of my crowns,
That I may, walking in my gallery,
See 'em go pinioned along by my door.
Being young, I studied physic, and began
To practise first upon the Italian;
There I enriched the priests with burials,
And always kept the sexton's arms in ure
With digging graves and ringing dead men's knells:
And after that was I an engineer,
And in the wars 'twixt France and Germany,
Under pretence of helping Charles the Fifth,
Slew friend and enemy with my stratagems.
Then after that was I a usurer,
And with extorting, cozening, forfeiting,
And tricks belonging unto brokery,
I filled the jails with bankrupts in a year,
And with young orphans planted hospitals,
And every moon made some or other mad,

And now and then one hang himself for grief,
Pinning upon his breast a long great scroll
How I with interest tormented him.
But mark how I am blest for plaguing them,
I have as much coin as will buy the town. (2.3.179–205)

Shakespeare remembered Barabas when writing this obstinate speech for his delicious villain:

Ay, that I had not done a thousand more.
Even now I curse the day – and yet, I think,
Few come within the compass of my curse –
Wherein I did not some notorious ill,
As kill a man, or else devise his death;
Ravish a maid, or plot the way to do it;
Accuse some innocent and forswear myself;
Set deadly enmity between two friends;
Make poor men's cattle break their necks;
Set fire on barns and hay-stacks in the night,
And bid the owners quench them with their tears.
Oft have I digged up dead men from their graves
And set them upright at their dear friends' doors,
Even when their sorrows almost were forgot;
And on their skins, as on the bark of trees,
Have with my knife carved in Roman letters,
'Let not your sorrow die though I am dead.'
But I have done a thousand dreadful things
As willingly as one would kill a fly,
And nothing grieves me heartily indeed
But that I cannot do ten thousand more. (5.1.124–44)

Barabas lists his evil deeds in self-contained units of information frequently beginning 'And', whereas Shakespeare flips a coin in his similar use of the device *polysyndeton* by linking alternatives in lines such as 'As kill a man, or else devise his death; / Ravish a maid, or plot the way to do it' (5.1.128–9). This emphasises the malevolent possibilities of Aaron's scheming mind, aggrandising Marlowe's already grand schemer. Although these speeches correspond structurally as catalogues of evil deeds, they share few verbal links, almost as if Shakespeare deliberately avoided paraphrasing his textual and oratorical stimulus. However, the phraseology of Marlowe's play as a whole was clearly at the forefront of Shakespeare's mind when he wrote this speech. Thanks to *Collocations and N-grams*, we now know that the string of three words, 'curse the day', is unique in drama of the period to *The Jew of Malta*: elsewhere in Marlowe's play Barabas says, 'So that not he, but I, may **curse the day**' (1.2.194). The phrase 'deadly enmity' also occurs in Marlowe's play and can be found on just four occasions in the database, with *The Jew of Malta* providing the only example predating *Titus Andronicus*: 'To be at **deadly enmity** with Turks' (2.2.33). Shakespeare also seems to have recalled a line in Marlowe's *Dido, Queen of Carthage*: 'Wound **on the barks of** odoriferous **trees**' (3.1.116). Marlowe's is the only play written before *Titus Andronicus* in which the phrase 'on the bark of', linked with the word choice 'trees', appears. Alongside linguistic elements borrowed from Marlowe we also get snapshots of Shakespeare's irrepressible self-repetition: the phrase 'had not done a' has its closest parallel in his *Henry IV Part Two*: 'As thou **hast not done a** great while' (2.2.20–1). Shakespeare recycles the image 'within the compass of my curse' in the moment when Margaret berates the court in *Richard III*: 'Nor thou **within the compass of my curse**' (1.3.282). Surprisingly, the phrase 'kill a fly' can be found in just one other Elizabethan play, *As You Like It*: 'By this hand, it will not **kill a fly**' (4.1.104). The influence of Marlowe's language on early Shakespeare is patent: despite their unequal canon sizes, there's a much larger proportion of rare phrases in *Collocations and N-grams* shared between this speech and Marlowe's dramatic canon than Shakespeare's.

That Marlowe's dramas exerted a considerable influence on Shakespeare is beyond dispute. That influence tends to be discussed in, rather appropriately, hyperbolic terms, although some pseudo-biblical claims might give us pause: according to one scholar, Marlowe 'first, and he alone, guided Shakespeare into the right way of work', and 'Before him there was neither genuine blank verse, nor genuine tragedy in our language. After his arrival, the way was prepared; the paths were made straight, for Shakespeare.'[16] Here Marlowe is John the Baptist, paving the way for Shakespeare's Jesus Christ. The poet T. S. Eliot rightly pointed out, however, that 'Kyd has as good a title to the first honour as Marlowe' and 'Shakespeare was not taught or guided by one of his predecessors or contemporaries alone'.[17] Yet the muscularity of Marlowe's bombastic blank verse, with its ornateness, exuberance, and densely packed hyperboles, seems to have pricked the ears of other dramatists. His 'distinctive voice', particularly in the majorly successful *Tamburlaine* plays, with their 'archaic imperatives, the outlandish and resplendent images, the recourse to cosmic forces' and 'classical and biblical parallels', appears to have been 'transplanted wholesale from Marlowe's plays' into those of other Elizabethan playwrights working to entertain audiences and satisfy theatre managers.[18] That voice echoes palpably in passages written by the likes of Greene, Nashe, Thomas Lodge, and indeed Shakespeare.[19] There are moments of breathtaking beauty in these plays, as in the protagonist's only soliloquy in *Tamburlaine the Great, Part One*:

> If all the pens that ever poets held
> Had fed the feeling of their masters' thoughts
> And every sweetness that inspired their hearts,
> Their minds and muses on admirèd themes;
> If all the heavenly quintessence they still
> From their immortal flowers of poesy,
> Wherein as in a mirror we perceive
> The highest reaches of a human wit;
> If these had made one poem's period
> And all combined in beauty's worthiness,
> Yet should there hover in their restless heads
> One thought, one grace, one wonder, at the least.
> Which into words no virtue can digest. (5.2.161–73)

These lines astound in a different way to Tamburlaine's ranty imperatives and self-aggrandising verbal flexing. Here Marlowe muses on the inability to fully encapsulate meaning. He wishes to tear down walls, to gnash away at constraints, to digest the indigestible, express the inexpressible. He aspires to the 'highest reaches of a human wit', to translate 'one thought, one grace, one wonder'. Tamburlaine's power in battle gives way to a stunning glimpse into Marlowe's quest to overpower poetry. Marlowe refused to be confined by poetic media and the wide universal theatre of life. Was his tragic end a foregone conclusion? How could other writers of the period not try and emulate such celestial poetry?

The pervasiveness of Marlowe's dramatic language in the works of other writers has proved tricky for statistical studies.[20] But the numbers for phrases shared between Marlowe and Shakespeare plays in *Collocations and N-grams* spring surprises. The database consists of spreadsheets for each of its 527 plays, ranked in comparison to all other plays according to the numbers for unique phrases, which are divided by the combined word counts for each pairing. Shakespeare's works don't feature highly in the spreadsheets for the *Tamburlaine* plays: the highest-ranked Shakespeare play is *Henry IV Part One* at position forty for *Tamburlaine the Great, Part Two*, with the plays' fixations on the noise of battle possibly spurring similar language. Shakespeare plays aren't mounted particularly high in the list for *Doctor Faustus* either, with *King John* (1596) at position thirty-seven, while *Richard III* is placed in thirty-fifth position in *The Massacre at Paris* spreadsheet. The top Shakespeare play in the list for *Dido, Queen of Carthage* is *Troilus and Cressida* at sixteen, but this can be explained by the fact that the events in both plays intersect with the Trojan War. On the other hand Marlowe's habit of repeating his favourite phrases plays a powerful role in the spreadsheets for his plays: *The Massacre at Paris* is the top-ranked play for *Edward II*, and the two *Tamburlaine* plays are in the top ten for the *Doctor Faustus* spreadsheet. It's a fact that strikes hard and fast, like a dagger to an unsuspecting forehead: Marlowe's dramatic language was far more prominent in the plays of dramatists other than Shakespeare. But there can be no doubt that Shakespeare drew from the linguistic texture of *The Jew of Malta* when he used the play as a model for Shylock's revenge in *The Merchant of Venice*: Shakespeare's play is in the very top place in that list. Shakespeare recalls the dehumanising language that the Christians use to describe Barabas, 'when they **call me dog**' (2.3.24), for Shylock's speeches, 'You **called me dog**' (1.3.126) and 'Thou **called'st me dog**' (3.3.6). Shakespeare takes this passage from Marlowe's play and turns it into a refrain for *The Merchant of Venice*, in which the word 'dog' is linked to the Jewish character on eight occasions, whereas in *The Jew of Malta* it's directed primarily at Barabas's enemies. It's possible that Shakespeare recalled the language of the play through his aural memory, having attended it during some of its many performances. The earliest surviving edition of *The Jew of Malta* is dated 1633.

The numbers for *Edward II* reflect the dramaturgical links between that play and *Richard II*, ranked twelfth in the spreadsheet for Marlowe's play. Matching phrases include Lancaster's line in Marlowe's play, 'None be so **hardy as to touch the** king' (2.3.27), which Shakespeare varies in the Lord Marshal's speech: 'On pain of death, no person be so bold / Or daring-**hardy as to touch the** lists' (1.3.42–3). Special attention should be paid to the compound form employed by Shakespeare: 'daring-hardy'. From the very beginning of his career Shakespeare had a higher rate of use for compound forms than many of his contemporaries, including Marlowe, who largely avoided them in his plays.[21] Even when phrases are unique to two plays, differences in style can be perceived through close reading.

Looking at some of the phrases shared between *Edward II* and *Richard III*, which is ranked nineteenth in the spreadsheet for Marlowe's play, we can again see the ways in which Shakespeare appropriated Marlowe's dramatic language early in his career. The phrase 'the murderer dead' is unique to these plays. In *Edward II*, Young Mortimer asks Matrevis: 'Is't done, Matrevis, and **the murderer dead**?' (5.6.1). The word combination forms part of a straightforward question in Marlowe's play. Shakespeare recycles it in 1.2 when Lady Anne Neville curses Richard:

> O God, which this blood mad'st, revenge his death.
> O earth, which this blood drink'st, revenge his death.
> Either heav'n with lightning strike **the murd'rer dead**,
> Or earth, gape open wide and eat him quick. (1.2.62–5)

The words are the same, but the poetic context in which they're placed is noticeably dissimilar. Unlike the Marlowe example Lady Anne's speech is rhetorically charged, the balanced arrangement of her lines (the device known as *isocolon*) signalled by the exclamatory 'O' employed in the vocative. Shakespeare takes Marlowe's interrogative and switches grammatical mood, transforming the line into a deadly imperative. We can contrast Marlowe's use of *isocolon*, or *parison*, when Faustus surrenders his soul:

To give me whatsoever I shall ask,
To tell me whatsoever I demand,
To slay mine enemies, and aid my friends. (1.3.96–8)

The tripping effect of Faustus's speech corresponds to a character who often employs Sophist logic. Shakespeare employs the same scheme to intensify Anne's deeply emotive speech. Another phrase shared between *Edward II* and the scene in which Richard engages in a verbal bout with Lady Anne occurs when Young Mortimer intervenes between Edward and Gaveston: '**The life of thee** shall salve this foul disgrace' (2.2.83). Lady Anne curses Richard: 'More miserable by **the life of thee** / Than thou hast made me by my dear lord's death' (4.1.75–6). The exchanges in Marlowe's play take the form of rapid, single-line dialogue, a firework display of words that crackle away in Young Mortimer's violent offer to stab the King's lover, Gaveston. Shakespeare's violence is concentrated in Anne's bitter insults.

Shakespeare once again remembers Young Mortimer when the assassins hired to murder Clarence dither: "Swounds, 'tis even now at my elbow, persuading me **not to kill the** Duke' (1.4.142–3). Here Shakespeare remembers the warrant for Edward's death in Marlowe's history play: 'Fear **not to kill the** King, 'tis good he die' (5.4.9). Marlowe writes the letter in blank verse, whereas Shakespeare employs the same language for a prose speech befitting the lowly station of the First Murderer. Shakespeare also seems to have had Edward's murderer in mind, the terrifying Lightborn, who tells the monarch: '**Far is it from my heart** to do you harm' (5.5.46). Marlowe's mounting thoughts creep into Richard's ironic protest that he has no desire to be King: '**Far be it from my heart**, the thought thereof' (1.3.150). Shakespeare's recollections of Marlowe's speeches appear to have been stimulated by dramatic context and characterisation. Shakespeare often repeats the language of *Edward II* to fulfil his own dramatic functions, to enflesh his characters, as manifested in Richard's ironical statements. He also remembers scenes of physical violence in Marlowe's play but borrows from his predecessor's language to serve purposes of oratorical violence, as in the assault on Richard's ears undertaken by Lady Anne. In short Shakespeare's integration of Marlowe's dramatic language doesn't amount to slav-ish imitation. Did Shakespeare recognise the power of his own verbal recall to stimulate audience members' memories of similar dramatic situations explored by Marlowe? He certainly recognised opportuni-ties to do something fresh with those phraseological origins. The wording might be the same, but the surrounding text is markedly different, particularly in terms of the varying media and the impas-sioned invocations that draw from a larger store of rhetorical devices employed by Shakespeare. For all their similarities, Marlowe and early Shakespeare's dramatic styles are demonstrably different.

In the autumn of 2016 a sensational announcement brimmed in headline fonts across various news outlets. The story went that Shakespeare wasn't just influenced by Marlowe, but actually collabo-rated on some of his earliest plays with him. The attribution of parts of all three *Henry VI* plays to Marlowe was enshrined in the *New Oxford Shakespeare*, an edition that made startling claims about the extent of Shakespeare's collaborations with other writers. The idea of Marlowe and Shakespeare working closely together is hard to resist. These global claims thrill the imagination. Shakespeare has fully entered the realm of big data. But how reliable are the digital meth-ods used to credit Marlowe and Shakespeare jointly on the title pages of these plays? In the past attribution scholars have been successful in identifying the hands of other writers in Shakespeare collabo-rations through highlighting measurable differences in verse style, phraseology, and vocabulary between acts, scenes, or passages of plays. Such differences can be discerned through good old-fashioned reading. The results might be put into tables, but readers can at least check those results by opening up the plays themselves. Several new methods lying behind recent authorship theories claim to detect lin-guistic patterns that not only evade readers but lie beneath the level of an early modern author's consciousness, such as 'function' words. Words like 'thou', 'you', 'and', 'of', and 'the' serve grammatical func-tions. Unlike 'lexical', or 'content-bearing' words, function words have low semantic content and are said to operate below an author's consciousness.

So-called 'stylometric' methods rely on the frequencies of words ripped from a text, bagged up like groceries for computation, and stripped bare of meaning. Readers are seldom equipped to query let alone contest the explanations provided for tables or graphs. Many of the methods lying behind recent claims of Marlowe's hand in early Shakespeare plays aren't corroborated by alternative approaches, be they statistical or non-numerical. Scholars who are versed in digital methods have highlighted issues that might make us pause awhile when it comes to claiming Marlowe's co-authorship, rather than his influence on Shakespeare at the beginning of his career. In a book about Shakespeare and his engagement with other authors, it'll be useful to give an account of some of these complex mathematical methods that claim to tell authors apart. This will also give us an opportunity to delve deeper into similarities and differences between Shakespeare and Marlowe's styles, or 'feathers'.

The *New Oxford Shakespeare* team contend that the presence of both Shakespeare and Marlowe in the *Henry VI* plays is established by a variety of tests.[22] The trilogy works brilliantly on stage, an epic of *Game of Thrones* proportions (minus the dragons and the disappointing finale), and yet these plays aren't performed nearly often enough today. The decision to attribute parts of all three dramas to Marlowe in the *New Oxford Shakespeare* edition is based partly on a 2009 study involving function- and lexical-word tests.[23] The methods are known as Zeta and Principal Component Analysis. The Zeta method works out what an author's 'marker words' are by comparing the word use in a set of plays attributed to them to the word use in a set of plays by other authors. Zeta measures the frequency of those 'marker words' in a play of uncertain authorship, while Principal Component Analysis, or PCA, is a reduction method that helps researchers summarise information. The frequencies of words are subjected to statistical processing and the findings are presented in graphs designed to distinguish one author's segments (each segment consisting of two thousand words) from another. According to this approach, text portions that fall far away from the centre of a graph, these portions being represented by a dazzling display of circles, diamonds, and squares, indicate differences of authorship, while those that score close to the centre suggest common authorship. However, numbers, like words, can be interpreted differently. It's been shown that the positions of some segments that supposedly support a theory of Marlowe's authorship have Zeta scores for the non-Marlowe types which are just as high as scenes not assigned to Marlowe. This approach to interpreting data has been deemed too crude to be reliable.[24] This goes not just for Zeta but also for the use of PCA, given that in both methods an imaginary line is drawn across a graph with the two territories supposedly belonging to different authors, as if they were Pyramus and Thisbe. One scholar who has reproduced these methods observes that they're 'less potent' than 'practitioners of computational-stylistics studies claim', can 'hardly prove that Marlowe was Shakespeare's collaborator on the *Henry VI* plays', and that the 'test results provide no magic solution to the centuries-long issue of the authorship' of these plays.[25]

Other issues include the variant spellings of early modern plays, bearing in mind that Shakespeare spelt his own name in six different ways! In the Zeta study the word '"Countries"', we are told, is in the top 50 of 500 Marlowe marker words, but Marlowe uses it only twice across his entire corpus of six plays', and '*1 Henry VI* doesn't contain the plural "countries"; Joan la Pucelle is using the possessive "country's"'.[26] Here we see the importance of interpreting dramatists' word choices by leafing through the plays ourselves. It's possible that the Zeta method actually measures disparities in author canon sizes (Shakespeare's canon, of course, is much larger than Marlowe's) rather than stylistic differences, and that issues of genre sensitivity undermine results, with history plays, for example, sharing more similarities than tragic and comic plays. It might be argued that, despite such critiques, these methods have high success rates on plays of known authorship, as impressive as 98 per cent in some cases.[27] But when the method has been replicated by other research teams, no evidence has been found that the separation of text portions reveals anything about authorship. The questionable interpretations of graphs in the 2009 study have led some experts to conclude that all its results should be disregarded.[28]

What about author methods that, if so inclined, we could check for ourselves by reading the plays and counting their features by hand? *Henry VI Part Two* and *Henry VI Part Three* average high percentages for 'feminine' endings of 10.4 and 10.7 respectively.[29] These results present a major obstacle to assigning large parts of the *Henry VI* trilogy to Marlowe, who 'only once reaches 8.0 per cent' in 'single long scenes',[30] meaning scenes that contain over one hundred verse lines. In total the scenes that aren't by Shakespeare (1.1–2; 2.3; 4.2–10; and 5.2) in *Henry VI Part Two* according to the Zeta method average 10.7 per cent 'feminine' endings, which is far too high for Marlowe, but characteristic of Shakespeare's practice. Marlowe averages 3.7 per cent 'feminine' endings in *Edward II*, his highest percentage for a sole-authored play. Some of the scenes in the fourth act of *Henry VI Part Two*, where Marlowe's hand can supposedly be traced, have the highest percentages for 'feminine' endings in the entire play. The play's third act, in which Shakespeare's contribution is mainly concentrated according to the 2009 study, averages a strict percentage of 12.0 'feminine' endings. Act 4.3–9, in which 'the likeness of Marlowe in style and vocabulary' is 'strong' according to Zeta,[31] average 21.3 per cent eleven-syllable lines, flying well beyond Marlowe's reach. If Marlowe had a hand in *Henry VI Part Two* and *Henry VI Part Three*, he must have more than sextupled his use of 'feminine' endings, revolutionising his verse style. Curiously, he then reverted to the verse habits of his previous plays in the later dramas *Edward II* and *The Massacre at Paris*, the later play averaging 1.4 per cent.

If we look at the highest percentages Marlowe reaches for single scenes in his plays, we discover the following rates for 'feminine' endings: 12.5 per cent in *Doctor Faustus*; 9.6 in *The Jew of Malta*; 11.1 in *Edward II*; and 12.5 in *The Massacre at Paris*.[32] These are high percentages, so what exactly is the problem with the figures for the *Henry VI* plays? These percentages aren't for 'long scenes' but for small samples of text: eight lines in *Doctor Faustus*; thirty-one lines in *The Jew of Malta*; eighteen lines in the *Edward II* scene; and eight lines in *The Massacre at Paris*. These scenes combined make up a grand total of sixty-five lines, whereas the scenes attributed to Marlowe in *Henry VI Part Two* total a whopping 1194 lines that reach a figure for 'feminine' endings vastly higher than anything Marlowe ever achieved for a similar sample of his dramatic work: nearly 11 per cent. The closest Marlowe gets to his peak of 8.0 per cent 'feminine' endings for a scene of over one hundred verse lines occurs in *The Jew of Malta*, 5.9, followed by 4.5 per cent in *Doctor Faustus*. These three scenes represent by far the highest figures Marlowe reaches in sufficient sample sizes across his entire dramatic canon. As one scholar has put it: the 'verse' in Shakespeare plays 'may be Marlowesque without being Marlowe's'.[33] In fact we can see that Shakespeare's verse style was significantly different from those of university-educated dramatists such as Marlowe.

There are other telling markers of Shakespeare's authorship in these scenes that could help to distinguish his early style from Marlowe's: 'while recent computational statistics have argued that' scenes in *Henry VI Part Two* match 'the profile of Christopher Marlowe, the insistence' of Shakespeare's 'wordplay is not a good fit for Marlowe's style'.[34] Whereas Shakespeare's plays display a penchant for wordplay based on proper names, Marlowe's works simply don't feature the kind of wordplay appearing in the *Henry VI* plays.

The Cade rebellion in *Henry VI Part Two* has been given to Marlowe. These portions, written largely in prose, apparently 'stray beyond the bounds of Shakespearean style in a way quite unlike other early plays we know to be Shakespeare's'.[35] But Marlowe used little prose in his sole-authored plays and the language and craftsmanship of these scenes are typical of Shakespeare. The dramaturgic devices employed to keep Jack Cade in his place are strikingly close to Shakespeare's depictions of mobs in *Julius Caesar*, *Sir Thomas More* (1601), and *Coriolanus*.[36] In particular the pricking of Cade's inflated speeches with comic, prose asides is a favourite device of Shakespeare's. Cade is an imposter, a royal lookalike who pretends he is a Mortimer, leading to some dodgy puns about him being a bricklayer (as in 'mortar'). One member of the *New Oxford Shakespeare* team, using a method known as 'microattribution', on which more later, has attempted to account for the fact that these portions share affinities with Shakespeare that are alien to Marlowe's dramas by suggesting that Shakespeare wrote the prose and Marlowe the verse speeches in 4.2.[37] Is it really likely that when Shakespeare reached the scenes introducing Cade and his fellow rebels, roles designed specifically for the clowns in his company, he chose to write the prose speeches and then handed the verse lines over to Marlowe?[38] Many of the scenes that stylometric tests assign to different authors are so closely related that it makes little sense, from a theatrical history perspective, they should be divvied up between collaborators.[39] Convincing contributions to attribution scholarship anchor data-driven approaches in an understanding of theatrical and historical context, as well as sensitive readings of dramatic works. Surely there must be agreement between statistical methods and more traditional literary approaches for an authorship theory to be deemed secure?

The *New Oxford Shakespeare* team relied on another statistical method to attribute parts of the *Henry VI* trilogy to Marlowe, involving 'Word Adjacency Networks' (WANs). This is a particularly complicated method that many readers might consider too cunning to be understood; its roots are in electrical engineering. The WAN practitioners claim that the 'choice, the frequency, and (crucially for our method) the relative placing of function words' appear to be 'an unconscious set of preferences specific to an author'.[40] They treat an author's choice of words in a sentence as if it functioned like their choice of letters in a word. An author might be more likely than another author to follow the word 'one' with the word choice 'with' for instance. Content words are completely ignored, but it could be argued that function words are dictated by such content words to create meaningful sentences.[41] In *Collocations and N-grams* the word 'devoid' is consistently followed by 'of'. One of the attractive aspects of function-word analysis is that these markers are supposedly less likely to be seized on by other dramatists, meaning they can offer insights into authorial individuality. But can the fact that authors habitually pinched phrases from each other affect these statistical results? After all, such phrases will almost certainly repeat function words as well as content words. In recycling phrases from Marlowe plays, Shakespeare would inevitably reproduce the sequencing and placement of Marlowe's function words. Take for example the word combination we saw earlier in this book, 'all that treasure dry who hoards up wealth is base who spends it brave earth breeds gold so I tread but on my slave',[42] shared between Thomas Dekker's *The Wonder of a Kingdom* and John Day's *The Parliament of Bees*. This is a stunning illustration of conscious imitation by Day: he lifts a huge stretch of words verbatim from Dekker. The choice and order of the function words placed in bold tell us nothing about Day's unconscious preferences but would be treated as evidence for common authorship by the WAN practitioners. This is just one example of the ways borrowed phrases can affect a method that relies on the idea that the choice of function words is specific to an author. Does this mean that the WAN method is found wanting? The vast number of repeated word combinations in plagiaristic works would likely affect such data-driven methods.

What exactly makes an authorship marker 'unconscious' anyway? How can we tell without travelling back in time and perching in an author's mind as he sits down at his writing desk? As one critic objects: 'it's not clear that words like *bar, dare, given, enough* or *might* are really devoid of meaning, and would not be attached to particular characters or dramatic circumstances'.[43] Such theoretical considerations might be considered airy-fairy if the WAN method succeeds in identifying authors with a high success rate. However, although the authors claim that their method attributes plays with 93.6 per cent accuracy, replications of the method have had much less success, suggesting that this technique is even less reliable than approaches that are sensitive to play genre.[44] Either way the Zeta and the WAN methods frequently disagree on the authorship of scenes. They fail to agree on as many as fourteen scenes in *Henry VI Part Three*.

Such statistical studies abandon the meaning of words in early modern plays, a genre containing multiple characters, each of them speaking with individualised voices, from the more dignified manner of high-status characters to the colloquial exchanges of low-status characters. Social interaction and attitude affect vocabulary choices, such as the second person pronouns 'thou' or 'you',[45] but it's only by reading the plays closely that we can identify dramatic context. This is impossible for methods that treat words as mere items to be counted.[46] It's also notable that statistical tests conducted by researchers outside of the *New Oxford Shakespeare* team have led to entirely different findings. In the previous chapter we saw that Discriminant analysis successfully identified Shakespeare as author of all his plays with three exceptions, one being *Love's Labour's Lost* and the others being plays widely held to be co-authored: *Henry VI Part One* and Shakespeare and George Wilkins's Romance play *Pericles*. The second and third parts of *Henry VI* were assigned to Shakespeare with 91 per cent confidence.[47] These results suggest Shakespeare's sole authorship of the second and third plays in the trilogy, but that *Henry VI Part One*, which we'll explore in more detail later, is co-authored. Another method, which examines all words in early modern plays rather than just function words or content words, succeeded in distinguishing the plays of Marlowe and Shakespeare and was awarded the prestigious Calvin Hoffman Prize in 2003. This research team concluded that Marlowe couldn't have authored any of Shakespeare's plays.[48]

Have you ever noticed, when reading, say, a novel, or perhaps your own writing, that the same phrase is repeated within a few pages or even paragraphs? What does this tell us about the ways an author's memory functions? It's an interesting phenomenon that can also be found in early modern plays. Moving away from single words and returning to how authors grouped their words together, intuition would have us believe that Shakespeare is more likely to repeat himself than passages written by his co-authors. Control tests on Shakespeare's sole-authored and co-authored plays confirm this.[49] Sole-authored Shakespeare plays, such as *Richard III* and *Romeo and Juliet*, feature many phrases repeated between scenes, such as 'how fares our loving', which can be found in 3.1.96 and 5.5.35 of the earlier play, than co-authored plays such as *Titus Andronicus* and *Edward III* (1593). This gives us a snapshot into Shakespeare's associative memory in the midst of writing his plays, the ways he links particular phrases to characters or situations. On this basis *Henry VI Part Two* is much closer to the sole-authored Shakespeare plays than the collaborative works in terms of the number and nature of phrases repeated across the play. In the opening scene of *Henry VI Part Two*, which has been attributed to Marlowe, the Cardinal Beaufort, speaking of Gloucester, stresses that '**he is the next** of blood / And heir apparent to the crown' (1.1.149–50). In a scene attributed to Shakespeare in the third act, Margaret warns her husband that Humphrey 'is near you in descent, / And, should you fall, **he is the next** will mount' (3.1.21–2). The phrase 'he is the next' serves the same purpose in the Cardinal's and Margaret's speeches. This cluster of words seems to have been triggered in Shakespeare's brain by the similar context of Margaret's warning. Phrases repeated between scenes also include such examples as the string of ten words 'Cold news for me for I had hope of France', followed by four separated words: 'as I' with 'fertile England' in 1.1.237–8 and 3.1.88–9. No similar examples can be found in any of Shakespeare's co-authored plays. These findings run counter to claims that large parts of *Henry VI Part Two* are detachable or distinct in terms of style.

It's useful to look at phrases in *Collocations and N-grams* shared between *Henry VI Part Two* and Marlowe's *Edward II*, his closest play in terms of genre. *Edward II* is usually dated later than *Henry VI Part Two* and *Henry VI Part Three*, so the matches with scenes that the *New Oxford Shakespeare* team attribute to Marlowe could be considered either Marlovian self-repetition or examples of Marlowe borrowing from Shakespeare. In *Henry VI Part Two* 1.1 contains only one unique match with Marlowe's play, the short phrase, 'lordly peers', which can be found in Suffolk's opening speech, 'In sight of England and her **lordly peers**' (1.1.11), and in Gaveston's speech in Marlowe's play: 'Farewell base stooping to the **lordly peers**' (1.1.18). The communicative context is different: Suffolk is giving a formal speech in which he delivers Margaret to Henry, whereas in Marlowe's play Gaveston is reading a letter from the King. There's not a single match unique to Marlowe's play in *Collocations and N-grams* with the following scene, which the Zeta method gives to Marlowe, nor with 4.3, 4.6, 4.8–10, or 5.2. There are no unique Marlowe matches with 1.4 or 4.7 either, which the WAN method assigns to him. There are, however, ten unique phrases (around a third of all unique matches between the plays) in the third act of *Henry VI Part Two*, attributed most confidently to Shakespeare according to both methods, such as when Margaret's venom towards Gloucester is delivered in a tumble of hexameter lines amid a pentameter speech: 'We know the time since he **was mild and** affable' (3.1.9). The phrase is repeated in Marlowe's play in a regular pentameter line: 'Thou seest by nature he **is mild and** calm' (1.4.387). The wording is similar but the verse rhythm of these speeches is different; there's no speech in Marlowe's canon approaching Margaret's polemic, which is stuffed from the crown to the toe with images of animals and horticulture. The longest unique match between these plays features in a scene not assigned to Marlowe. We find it in the character Young Clifford's speech 'To quell **the rebels and their complices**' (5.1.210) and in King Edward's line in Marlowe's play: 'Have at **the rebels and their complices**' (2.2.264). The match with *Henry VI Part Two* closely corresponds to Shakespeare's tinkering with another line from *Edward II*, 'Thou com'st from Mortimer **and his complices**' (3.1.153), in *Richard II*: '**To** fight with Glyndŵr **and his complices**' (3.1.43). The *Richard II* example reveals parallelism of thought shared with *Henry VI Part Two* because it embraces the word 'To', placed in the first position of the verse lines, while the verbs, 'fight' and 'quell', are practically interchangeable. The pattern of unique matches doesn't support a theory of Marlowe repeating himself. It seems more likely that Marlowe borrowed from Shakespeare's play as a whole.

Edward II is the highest-ranked Marlowe play in the spreadsheet for *Henry VI Part Two* at position three, but the top five plays all belong to the history genre. Marlowe's play shares less unique matches with *Henry VI Part Two* than does George Peele's *Edward I* (1591). The next Marlowe play in the list is *The Massacre at Paris* in eleventh place, although the murky memorial origins of that play are a problem. The third Marlowe play to appear in this spreadsheet is *The Jew of Malta*, which nears sixtieth in the list. There are only nine unique phrases between these plays and most of them are dissimilar when it comes to dramatic context. Barabas manipulates his daughter, Abigail: 'Daughter, a word more: kiss **him, speak him fair**' (2.3.239). The First Gentleman's plea to Suffolk is genuine:

'My gracious lord, entreat **him, speak him fair**' (4.1.122). This scene in *Henry VI Part Two* features extensive wordplay on William de la Pole's name, with puns on 'pole', 'pool', and 'kennel, puddle, sink' (4.1.71–3), as well as 'Walter' and 'water' (4.1.36), characteristic of Shakespeare's 'fascination with the material possibilities of words' but unmatched in any of Marlowe's plays.[50] The longest unique phrase between these plays is found in a scene not attributed to Marlowe according to either the Zeta or WAN methods: Barabas says to Ithamore, '**Come on, sirrah,** / **Off with your** girdle' (4.1.146–7), which is closely echoed by the Beadle in *Henry VI Part Two*: '**Come on, sirrah, off with your** doublet quickly' (2.1.154). It makes sense that 'a young dramatist just beginning his career was influenced by the established playwrights of the time, many of whose plays he had doubtless absorbed as an actor'.[51]

We can compare these shared phrases to some genuine examples of Marlowe repeating himself. He links the adjective 'desperate' with the verb 'run' and the phrase 'the thickest throng' in *Tamburlaine the Great, Part Two*, when the title character prepares his son Celebinus for battle: 'But then **run desperate** through **the thickest throngs**' (3.2.139). In *Dido, Queen of Carthage*, Aeneas recounts the fall of Troy: '**desp'rate** of my life / **Ran** in **the thickest throng**' (2.1.210–11). This instance of self-repetition is far more complex than the examples we find in the *Henry VI* plays: although the phrase 'the thickest throng' isn't distinctive to Marlowe, the fact that he brings in additional words to perform similar duties offers us insights into a single author's thought processes and his verbal formulae. Another unmistakable authorship marker can be found in the repetition of the phrase 'rend not my heart' in *Doctor Faustus* and *Edward II*. Faustus prepares for damnation: 'Ah, **rend not my heart** for naming of my Christ' (5.2.81). In *Edward II*, Gaveston asks, 'Is all my hope turned to this hell of grief?', to which Edward responds: '**Rend not my heart** with thy too-piercing words' (1.4.116–17). Reading the repeated phrase in context, we find accompanying religious lexis through the invocations of 'hell' and 'Christ'. We might note too the convergence of thought in the word choices 'naming' and 'words'. Marlowe was prone to repeating striking images and phrases, as we can see in Dido's belief that Aeneas will '**make me immortal with a kiss**' (4.4.123). Faustus, having had his wish for Helen of Troy to be his paramour granted, repeats this sequence of six words verbatim: 'Sweet Helen, **make me immortal with a kiss**' (5.1.91). Here Marlowe recycles phraseology to serve a much more powerful dramatic purpose, indeed for the most famous scene in his canon. Marlowe innovates while improving on his own material. It's debatable whether the same can be said for the phrases shared between the *Henry VI* plays and *Edward II*.

Could Marlowe's presence in the Folio's *Henry VI* plays have been obscured by a thorough Shakespearian revision of *The Contention between York and Lancaster* and *The True Tragedy of Richard Duke of York*? As we'll see in later chapters, a theory of revision doesn't chime with the evidence for Shakespeare's revision of other writers' work elsewhere. The most sustained examination of these texts remains that conducted by the scholar Alfred Hart in a book-length study. Hart showed that, if Shakespeare revised material originally written by Marlowe, he rendered that material indistinguishable from his vocabulary in terms of the much larger proportion of new words; prefixes and suffixes most commonly found in his plays as opposed to Marlowe's; and in terms of adjectival compounds and those ending in a present or past participle, which Shakespeare employed around 50 per cent more frequently than Marlowe. Shakespeare must also have revised Marlowe's lines, which rarely feature an unstressed syllable at the end, so assiduously as to produce verse alien to any of Marlowe's acknowledged plays. He diluted the use of classical allusions, which feature far more frequently in Marlowe's plays than early Shakespeare's, with *Edward II* having as many as the first two *Henry VI* plays put together.[52] That Shakespeare often collaborated with fellow dramatists is now beyond question. But the evidence for Marlowe's co-authorship of *Henry VI Part Two* and *Henry VI Part Three* seems shaky.[53]

If new attribution theories are to be believed, Marlowe must have been remarkably busy writing plays in the last years of his life. It's recently been proposed that Marlowe co-authored *The Taming of the Shrew*, with Marlowe largely responsible for the subplot, and

Shakespeare the 'taming plot' involving Katherina and Petruchio. This conclusion rests on the method known as 'microattribution'.[54] This game of dominoes-like technique, which gives small passages of plays (usually just 173 words, the length of Aaron's speech we saw earlier) to whichever author shares the most verbal links according to database searches, hasn't been endorsed by any specialist outside of the *New Oxford Shakespeare* team. Criticisms of the method include the following: small fragments of text don't represent the linguistic elements which make up a play; the numbers for verbal links are far too small for reliable results; reproductions of the method have assigned the same segments to entirely different authors. One critic finds the attribution of parts of *The Taming of the Shrew* to Marlowe on this basis 'absurd, since the sample size is too small to prove anything: any other passage as tiny as 173 words could be chosen at random for the comparison and would produce different results', elaborating that 'Lines from Katherina's speech in the final scene, famous for its misogyny, are compared with a passage from act 1, an exchange between the young Lucentio and his servant Tranio, to reach the not exactly surprising conclusion that they have nothing in common'. It's hardly surprising that 'lines like "Or so devote to Aristotle's checks / Or Ovid be an outcast quite abjured" resemble passages in *Doctor Faustus* more than "Thy husband is thy lord, thy life, thy keeper"'.[55] Many of the matches claimed for Shakespeare occur in scenes from co-authored plays that attribution scholars agree weren't written by him. According to the analysis of twenty-one lines from the Induction of the play, Shakespeare has nine matches with plays first performed in 1576–94, as opposed to Marlowe's four, which makes Shakespeare the likeliest candidate for the authorship of those lines.[56] But there are issues here: some word associations can be found in scenes given to George Peele in *Titus Andronicus* and shouldn't count as hits for Shakespeare. Similarly, matches with scenes in *Henry VI Part One* are counted as hits for Shakespeare,[57] even when those scenes aren't generally believed to have been written by him. The decision to treat many matches with the second and third parts of the *Henry VI* trilogy as anonymous inevitably impacts the number of parallels, or hits, recorded for Shakespeare, even if he were sole author of those plays. Disagreements in a field for which published works often read like acid-laced Elizabethan pamphlets (Thomas Nashe would have loved it) are inevitable. But such inconsistencies present real problems for a method that claims to tell authors apart according to handfuls of matches in tiny textual fragments. It's widely accepted in science that the smaller the sample size the smaller the power.[58] Control tests reveal that unique phrases aren't sprinkled consistently across small stretches of sole-authored plays.[59] Would numerous authors spring up, like roses newly washed with dew, if this technique was applied consistently across plays for which we're certain of the author?

The *New Oxford Shakespeare* team summarise what they consider to be anomalies in *The Taming of the Shrew*: the play has the 'highest concentration of *has* in verse before *Othello*, the highest concentration of *does* in verse before *Twelfth Night*'; its 'two contractions 'rt (for *art* or *wert*) are not matched until *Timon of Athens*; its two examples of contractions involving 're for *are* have no parallel frequency before *Measure for Measure*'.[60] They also observe that the play has the lowest ratio of syllabic *-ed* and *-eth* verb endings in the canon, words such as 'desired' or 'seemeth', which are somewhat old-fashioned markers, and that its frequency of redundant *do* (as in 'I do commend you') is the lowest in Shakespeare's canon.[61] The team propose that the play is co-authored, but they don't check where these markers are located according to scenes considered to be by 'Shakespeare' and 'not Shakespeare' by E. K. Chambers,[62] whom they cite as an authority for divvying up this play. *The Taming of the Shrew* is the only play considered by Chambers, a brilliant but conservative scholar when it came to authorship matters, to be collaborative. Chambers gave Shakespeare the Induction, 2.1.1–38, 115–326, 3.2.1–129, 151–254, 4.1.3, 5, and 5.2.1–181, and the rest of the play to an unidentified author. However, the results often conflict with Chambers's divisions of authorship: the word *does* in verse lines features overwhelmingly in scenes he gave to Shakespeare. That said, the *New Oxford Shakespeare* team's observations are of great value: rather than suggesting dual authorship, could these anomalies reveal that the text first published in the Folio was copied out by a later hand? This hand need not have belonged to an author. Either way, evidence for stylistic markers more commonly found in plays dating from the 1600s hardly supports a theory of Marlowe's co-authorship.

Chambers observed that Shakespeare's conjectured collaborator used 'feminine' endings 'in much the same proportion (17%) as Shakespeare (19%)'.[63] A year after Chambers made this observation, there was a revelation: only Shakespeare could have reached a frequency as high as 17 per cent.[64] In other words the only known playwright who could have co-authored the play with Shakespeare was Shakespeare himself! Another scholar has pointed out that the 'statistically registerable metrical differences between the two divisions' of *The Taming of the Shrew* 'are in fact negligible' and 'certainly do not offer any support for the collaboration theory'.[65] Shakespeare takes an experimental approach to gendered rhymes in this play. In both 'Shakespeare' and 'non-Shakespeare' scenes male characters employ 'feminine' rhymes (rhyming words in which the final syllables are unstressed) when their status in the play becomes uncertain,[66] whereas Marlowe tends to reject 'feminine' rhymes, indeed, 'feminine' endings in general, in his plays.

The evidence for Shakespeare's characteristic verse style and use of rhyme is buttressed by the evidence for Shakespeare's individuality when it comes to his favourite phrases. The spreadsheet for plays sharing large numbers of phrases with *The Taming of the Shrew* in *Collocations and N-grams* reveals that Shakespeare plays figure prominently: *As You Like It* and *Richard III* feature in the top four plays. There's little to link the language of the play to Marlowe, whose *Tamburlaine the Great, Part One* is ranked thirty-fifth, followed by *Edward II* at eighty-eighth. It's hard to reconcile the paucity of links with the theory that Marlowe was author of the bulk of the play's subplot.

The textual history of *The Taming of the Shrew* is difficult to disentangle, particularly due to its relationship with the anonymous play, *The Taming of a Shrew*, which was published in May 1594. Was *The Taming of a Shrew* a source play for Shakespeare? Or could it be an adaptation of Shakespeare's comedy pieced together from memory? Philip Henslowe records a performance of *The Taming of a Shrew* at Newington Butts on 11 June 1594. Could it have been Shakespeare's play, written originally for Pembroke's Men, that was revived on that date? Was *The Taming of the Shrew* originally titled *The Taming of a Shrew*? The compilers of the 1623 First Folio might have swapped *'a'* for *'the'* to distinguish the text from an adaptation masquerading in bookstalls as Shakespeare's comedy. This would account for why the publisher Nicholas Ling transferred the rights of *The Taming of a Shrew*, rather than *The Taming of the Shrew*, to John Smethwick in 1607, which led to the inclusion of Shakespeare's play, rather than the text printed in 1594 under the title *The Taming of a Shrew*, in the Folio.

Textual complexities extend to Marlowe's canon: 'Marlowe is often assumed to have an oeuvre that is authorially and textually well-defined and neatly delimited'.[67] And yet almost all of Marlowe's plays are suspected of corruption or of containing other hands, with only *'Edward II*, published in quarto in 1594', providing 'a well-founded ascription to Marlowe on the title page' and giving us 'access to that object of Marlovians' desire, a sole-authored dramatic text'.[68] It's worth remembering, however, an earlier observation that Marlowe's borrowings from other dramatists, particularly his room-mate Kyd in *Edward II*, amounted to plagiarism, and 'exceeds anything found in the most corrupt play of that period'.[69] The idea that Marlowe's canon provides a firm stylistic signature for stylometric analysis is questionable.

The exchange of critiques and rejoinders in authorship studies must seem as dizzying to readers as the extreme verge Edgar imagines for Gloucester in *King Lear*. But that shouldn't divert attention away from the substantive criticisms of stylometry. Given that several new stylometric methods are so controversial and that these research conclusions seldom tally with long-standing methods proven to be reliable, the attribution of parts of Shakespeare plays to Marlowe should be taken with a healthy sprinkle of sodium. The external evidence conflicts with some of these claims as well: 'there is a circumstantial reason why Marlowe in particular had no involvement in the writing' of *The Taming of the Shrew* '(or of *1 Henry VI*): because he was not in England at the time'.[70] We might remember that during the winter of 1591–92 Marlowe was in Flushing, where he was arrested for allegedly counterfeiting coins.[71] The difficulties that some statistical methods face in telling Marlowe apart from other playwrights are testament to his powerful influence on Elizabethan drama, an influence that would haunt Shakespeare throughout his writing career. While Shakespeare sought to emulate Marlowe in his earliest plays, to 'bombast out a blanke verse' in Marlowe's accomplished manner, he also saw opportunities to distinguish himself from his predecessor through more flexible verse, more nuanced rhetoric, and an overall suppler dramatic style.

4

Thomas Kyd

Twisting and perhaps twisted, Marlowe's life was a branch hewed before it had a chance to grow straight. The branch of Thomas Kyd's life (1558–94) was fatally intertwined.[1] Referred to as a 'Cockney dramatist' by the first editor of his collected works,[2] Kyd was baptised in the church of St Mary Woolnoth, Lombard Street on 6 November 1558. He was the son of Anna Kyd and Francis Kyd. His father was warden of the Company of Scriveners (professional scribes) from 1580 and Kyd likely engaged in his father's trade before turning his neat hand to writing plays. He attended Merchant Taylors' School from 1565 onwards, where he was taught by the formidable scholar and educationalist Richard Mulcaster, whose pupils also included such luminaries as Thomas Lodge, Lancelot Andrewes, and Edmund Spenser. Mulcaster was a big advocate of performing Latin drama at the school, alongside music and games, which no doubt helped prepare Kyd for a dramatic writing career.

When did Kyd embark on this career? Thomas Dekker, in his pamphlet *A Knight's Conjuring* (1607), offers us some clues. Dekker links Kyd with several major poets and actors of the Elizabethan period:

> In another companie sat learned *Watson*, industrious *Kyd*, ingenious *Atchlow*, and (tho hee had bene a Player, molded out of their pennes) yet because he had bene their *Lover*, and a Register to the Muses, Inimitable *Bentley*: these were likewise carowsing to one another at the holy well, some of them singing Pæans to *Apollo*, som of them *Hymnes* to the rest of the Goddes.

Judging by this testimony, Kyd had written roles for the actor John Bentley, who was a member of the Queen's Men between 1583 and 1585. So Kyd appears to have been among the playwrights for the leading company of the period, probably debuting in the early to mid-1580s. Kyd was also employed by Ferdinando Stanley, Lord Strange, for whom he served as secretary as well as a playwright with Strange's Men. Kyd is twice praised in Francis Meres's compilation *Palladis Tamia: Wit's Treasury* (1598), first as a notable English writer, where his name appears alongside Robert Greene, George Peele, and others, and secondly as one of the finest English tragic poets, alongside Christopher Marlowe, Peele, Ben Jonson, George Chapman, Shakespeare, and others. In his eulogy on Shakespeare published in the First Folio Jonson gamely placed 'sporting Kyd' (l. 30) among Shakespeare's peers. Kyd enjoyed a high reputation among his contemporaries. Dekker's and Jonson's epithets, 'industrious' and 'sporting', suggest his canon was much larger than the three surviving plays now widely acknowledged as his and that he may have written comedies.

Kyd is traditionally recognised as the sole author of *The Spanish Tragedy*, an immensely popular revenge play, the *Gone with the Wind, Titanic*, or *Avengers: Endgame* of the Elizabethan period, performed by the likes of Strange's Men and possibly Pembroke's Men. His Turkish tragedy *Soliman and Perseda* belonged to Pembroke's Men until at least 1597, although we can't be sure for which company Kyd wrote his play.[3] He also wrote *Cornelia* (1594), a translation of Robert Garnier's French drama *Cornélie* (1573). Kyd seems to have been responsible for a lost *Hamlet* (1588) play, which preceded Shakespeare's version by around a decade and might also have been in the repertory of Pembroke's Men.[4] His non-dramatic work includes a translation of Torquato Tasso's *Padre di Famiglia* known as *The Householder's Philosophy* (1588). That some of Kyd's plays were associated with Pembroke's Men raises the tantalising possibility that Shakespeare had acted in them.

We saw earlier that Kyd's life was racked and ruined when he was caught up in the 'Dutch Church Libel' controversy alongside his London room-mate Marlowe. After Kyd was released from imprisonment, possibly suffering from the pangs of torture, he sought patronage in desperate hopes of evading the icy fingers of poverty. In the dedication to the Countess of Sussex in *Cornelia* he alludes to the bitter times and broken passions he's endured. There are moments within the text itself when Kyd veers wildly from his source and expresses such bone-aching sadness that we hear his personal voice:

> The cheerful cock, the sad night's comforter,
> Waiting upon the rising of the sun
> Doth sing to see how Cynthia shrinks her horn
> While Clitie takes her progress to the east,
> Where wringing wet with drops of silver dew
> Her wonted tears of love she doth renew.
> The wand'ring swallow, with her broken song,
> The country wench unto her work awakes,
> While Cytherea, sighing, walks to seek
> Her murdered love transformed into a rose
> Whom (though she see) to crop she kindly fears,
> But (kissing) sighs, and dews him with her tears.
> Sweet tears of love, remembrancers to time;
> Time past with me that am to tears converted,
> Whose mournful passions dull the morning's joys,
> Whose sweeter sleeps are turned to fearful dreams,
> And whose first fortunes, filled with all distress,
> Afford no hope of future happiness. (3.1.1–18)

When Kyd writes like this, the breath catches in the throat. We feel all his pain, his sense of utter dejection and futility, all the physical and mental torture he has undergone, compressed into a single speech delivered by his heroine. It's a moment of stunning poetry. In the same dedication to the Countess of Sussex he promises another tragedy, called *Portia*, which, like *Cornelia*, would most likely have been a closet drama written to be printed rather than performed in the public theatres. This work never appeared: Kyd died in 1594 at the age of thirty-five. He was buried on 15 August in St Mary Colechurch, which was destroyed in the Great Fire of London in 1666, meaning his grave is lost to posterity. His traditionally accepted plays are fragments of an explosive career, particles that have sometimes caught the light of scholarly inquiry, his brilliance having the potential to brim like a thousand stars, yet all too often occluded by the daunting shadows of better-known contemporaries.

That Kyd influenced Shakespeare has long been recognised. But the extent of those influences has been severely underestimated in comparison to Shakespeare's relationship with Marlowe. The connections between Kyd and Shakespeare can be traced in Jonson's coupling of *The Spanish Tragedy* and Shakespeare and Peele's *Titus Andronicus* in his Induction to *Bartholomew Fair* (1614): 'He that will swear *Jeronimo* or *Andronicus* are the best plays' (Induction.123–4). Shakespeare and Peele's tragedy, like Kyd's most famous play, is written in the Senecan mode. No other author exerted as wide or deep an influence on Elizabethan literature as Seneca.[5] Seneca's tragedies were translated into English between 1557 and 1581 and flourished at the Inns of Court. But it was Kyd who refined the Roman tragedian for the commercial stage, emphatically proclaiming Seneca as his dramatic ancestor.[6] Senecan influences are patent in *The Spanish Tragedy*, especially through Kyd's use of the Ghost of Andrea and the allegorical figure of Revenge, who 'serve for Chorus in this tragedy' (1.1.91) and divide the play's acts with commentary on the action. Here Kyd follows Seneca's division of acts separated by allegorical or supernatural choruses that often bellow for revenge. Kyd's device of having Revenge and the ghost of Andrea watch over events follows the Senecan Chorus, which 'casts a shadow of fatality over the unwitting characters'.[7] Kyd's drama, like Seneca's, follows a providential design: divine, supernatural, or allegorical figures have a say in a play's events. Kyd's play also conforms to the idea of the *theatrum mundi*, the world as a theatre, in which the figure of Revenge serves as both a cosmic playwright and a spectator viewing his own creation.[8] In Seneca choric figures sometimes intervene in the play's action: the Chorus in *Thyestes* scolds the villainous Atreus, who serves up his brother's children at a cannibalistic banquet. Seneca's choruses get sucked into the tragic vortex, transitioning from a seemingly objective viewpoint at the beginning of a play to engaging directly with characters and their downfalls. Once the Senecan chorus joins the action, the world of a play is destined to crumble under the awesome weight of tragedy.[9] In Kyd's play the choric figure of Revenge eventually intervenes, fulfilling his promise and avenging Andrea's death.

Early in his career Shakespeare was deeply impressed by Kyd's ingenious framing device, which helped him structure *The Taming of the Shrew*, a play that, despite generic differences, has considerable similarities with Kyd's tragedy. These similarities include encouraging the audience in the theatre to view the play's action through the eyes of onstage audiences, and the use of commentators outside the main action of the play.[10] In the Induction to Shakespeare's play Christopher Sly is woken from a drunken slumber by a Lord who dupes him into believing that he has merely dreamt he's a tinker (a mender of utensils) but is in fact a nobleman. The gambit works: Sly starts speaking in more dignified verse rather than colloquial prose and even uses the royal 'we'. This Lord also gets his pageboy Bartholomew to dress as a beautiful young woman and claims that he is Sly's wife. Again the trick works spectacularly and Sly hastens to get the boy between his newfound posh sheets. A group of travelling actors turns up and Sly watches them perform, although he ends up falling asleep again. This echoes Kyd's choric commentator Revenge, who falls asleep during the drama, much to Andrea's dismay. All the events in the shrew-taming narrative of Shakespeare's comedy therefore form a play-within-a-play, while Hieronimo avenges the murder of his son Horatio at the hands of Lorenzo and Balthazar by casting his adversaries in a tragedy and arranging their deaths on stage. In Kyd's play the onstage courtly audience clap along before realising that the bloodshed is real. Kyd's drama is deliciously metatheatrical, relying self-consciously on the *theatrum mundi* for its very foundations, while Shakespeare's play could be considered something of an 'insult comedy'. Like an intrepid stand-up comedian, Shakespeare pokes fun at contemporary audiences just as Kyd's protagonist disparages the courtly audience at the end of *The Spanish Tragedy*.

In *The Taming of the Shrew* the Christopher Sly framing narrative is on the same plane as the audience's reality, which means that the taming plot involving Katherina and Petruchio is distanced.[11] It's difficult to believe that perceptive Elizabethan audience members would follow Sly in seeing the play's events as instructive, a manual on how to tame a wife. Audiences might have laughed at Sly's desire for the disguised pageboy, or Katherina's submission to Petruchio's absurd whims. But, watching the play at the theatre during the afternoon, they might also have recognised that, like Katherina, they were going along with the idea that the sun was the moon and that boys in drag were beautiful young women. Philip Sidney elaborates on the necessity for audiences to collaborate with actors and playwrights in his *Defence of Poesy*, or *Apologie for Poetry*, which was published after his death in 1595:

> you shall have Asia of the one side, and Afric of the other, and so many other under-kingdoms, that the player, when he comes in, must ever begin with telling where he is, or else the tale will not be conceived? Now you shall have three ladies walk to gather flowers, and then we must believe the stage to be a garden. By and by we hear news of shipwreck in the same place, then we are to blame if we accept it not for a rock.

The metatheatricality of *The Taming of the Shrew* was tangible in Michael Bogdanov's 1978 production for the Royal Shakespeare Company. Before the play began, a drunkard wandered into the theatre, destroyed the set, and berated a steward. Some audience members clambered to the nearest phone box to tell the police that a madman was causing chaos in the auditorium. The man was soon wrestled to the ground, however, then stripped and bathed, and audiences realised that he was in fact Jonathan Pryce in the role of Sly and that the steward was Paola Dionisotti. The actors doubled as Petruchio and Katharina, the play-within-a-play representing Sly's dream of revenge over the member of staff who'd defeated him.

Both Kyd and Shakespeare's plays explore theatrical illusion, but Shakespeare draws attention to artifice for chiefly comic purposes. It must be said though that Kyd, as Shakespeare would do after him, toys with generic conventions through exploiting the dramatic potential of mixing comedy and tragedy. This cocktail sparkles in a moment of literal 'gallows humour' when the servant Pedringano mocks his executioner on the scaffold, having been duped into believing that an empty box, delivered by a Page, contains his pardon:

DEPUTY
Why, wherefore stay you, have you hope of life?
PEDRINGANO
Why, ay.
HANGMAN
As how?
PEDRINGANO
Why, rascal, by my pardon from the king.
HANGMAN
Stand you on that? then you shall off with this. *He turns him off.*
(3.6.105–8)

As one authority puts it, the 'innovative nature of Kydian comedy' represents 'a radical generic experiment'.[12] It's an experiment that has been underappreciated, especially given that dramatists like Marlowe, Greene, and Shakespeare followed his example.

Christopher Sly's line in *The Taming of the Shrew*, 'Go by, Saint Jeronimy' (Induction 1.7), is a barefaced allusion to Hieronimo's much-parodied line, 'Hieronimo beware, go by, go by' (4.6.31). On the page this speech is pretty mundane, suggesting it caught attention through some kind of spectacular, potentially lunatic gesture by the actor playing Kyd's protagonist. Shakespeare draws extensively from Kyd's hunting imagery: both plays make great use of metaphors drawn from falconry, with wording too similar to be coincidental.[13] Kyd's dramatic language in *The Spanish Tragedy* is sometimes labelled bombastic. He has been dismissed as a rhetorician rather than a poet, with T. S. Eliot calling him an 'extraordinary dramatic (if not poetic) genius'.[14] Yet even in his earliest surviving play, Kyd's fusion of verse permeated by horticultural and hunting imagery and colloquial, naturalistic dialogue, as well as the fluidity of linguistic register with which he conveys a wide range of dramatic voices, resembles early Shakespeare's style. Compare the haunting verse of Hieronimo,

Where shall I run to breathe abroad my woes,
My woes, whose weight hath wearièd the earth?
Or mine exclaims, that have surcharged the air
With ceaseless plaints for my deceased son?
The blustering winds, conspiring with my words,

At my lament have moved the leafless trees,
Disrobed the meadows of their flowered green,
Made mountains marsh with spring-tides of my tears,
And broken through the brazen gates of hell.
Yet still tormented is my tortured soul
With broken sighs and restless passions,
That wingèd mount, and, hovering in the air,
Beat at the windows of the brightest heavens,
Soliciting for justice and revenge.
But they are placed in those imperial heights
Where, countermured with walls of diamond,
I find the place impregnable, and they
Resist my woes, and give my words no way. (4.1.1–18)

to Kyd's choppy prose, crammed with wit and craning audience
necks as the Page reveals the intrigue plot:

My master hath forbidden me to look in this box, and
by my troth 'tis likely, if he had not warned me, I should
not have had so much idle time, for we men's-kind in
our minority are like women in their uncertainty: that
they arc most forbidden, they will soonest attempt – so
I now. [*Opens the box.*] By my bare honesty, here's nothing
but the bare empty box! Were it not sin against secrecy,
I would say it were a piece of gentlemanlike knavery.
I must go to Pedringano, and tell him his pardon is in this
box, nay, I would have sworn it, had I not seen the contrary.
I cannot choose but smile to think how the villain will
flout the gallows, scorn the audience, and descant on the
hangman, and all presuming of his pardon from hence.
Will't not be an odd jest, for me to stand and grace
every jest he makes, pointing my finger at this box: as
who would say, 'Mock on, here's thy warrant'? Is it not
a scurvy jest, that a man should jest himself to death?
Alas poor Pedringano, I am in a sort sorry for thee, but
if I should be hanged with thee, I cannot weep. (3.5.1–19)

Like Shakespeare, Kyd has characterisation at the forefront of his mind
as he toys with different mediums and affords his roles distinct voices.
And, like Kyd, Shakespeare would employ the play-within-a-play
device in *A Midsummer Night's Dream*, *Love's Labour's Lost*, and,
most famously, for revenge purposes in *Hamlet*. Shakespeare's memory
of *The Spanish Tragedy* might have been refreshed in the late 1590s.

Imagine that you are a book buyer in 1602. As you peruse the latest offerings, your eyes are drawn to a quarto edition of Kyd's play. Nothing striking about that. It's a hugely popular drama and has been printed several times. But wait, this edition is something different. It boasts that the play is 'Newly corrected, amended, and enlarged with new additions of the Painters part, and others'. Who was responsible for enlarging the play? At first glance the answer seems obvious: Philip Henslowe's diary records payments to Ben Jonson in 1601 and 1602 for 'new adicyons for Jeronymo'. But there are good reasons to suspect that the surviving additions are not those referenced by Henslowe. John Marston satirised the 1602 Fourth Quarto additions in his *Antonio and Mellida* (1599) and *Antonio's Revenge* (1600). In the most famous addition to Kyd's play Hieronimo, grieving over the murder of his son, commissions a painter to paint him a groan or a sigh. In Marston's hands in *Antonio and Mellida* this impossible request makes for great parody as his character Balurdo asks a painter to paint him 'Uh', which the painter interprets as a drunken belch. Marston's parody in the late 1590s suggests the additions were well known long before Henslowe's payments to Jonson. In *Cynthia's Revels* (1600) Jonson criticises those who believe '"that the old *Hieronimo*", as it was first acted, "was the only best, and judiciously penned play of Europe"' (Praeludium.166–7), which suggests revisions predating Henslowe's payments. The additions don't resemble Jonson in terms of psychology or poetry. Internal and external evidence would seem to rule Jonson out as their author.

It was the Romantic poet Samuel Taylor Coleridge who first pointed out that the Fourth Quarto additions bear no trace of Jonson's style but are very like Shakespeare, and they do indeed closely resemble Shakespeare in terms of vocabulary and verbal parallels.[15] Shakespeare's company almost certainly performed *The Spanish Tragedy*, with Richard Burbage receiving high praise in the leading role, the sort of role that could pop the buttons off his doublet as he grew fat with revenge.[16] It would make sense for Shakespeare to contribute to a revision of this blockbuster tragedy for the Chamberlain's Men. In a remarkable turn of events major authorship scholars on all sides of various battlelines now agree that

Shakespeare had a hand in these additions. The evidence suggests not only that Kyd's tragedy influenced Shakespeare's early plays but that Shakespeare collaborated posthumously with Kyd in the late 1590s. In one great moment Hieronimo delivers a bitterly ironic speech following the death of Horatio, pondering why the loss of a son might lead a father to madness when he could as easily 'melt in passion o'er a frisking kid' (Addition3.15). Is this line a tender allusion to Shakespeare's dramatic predecessor, an irresistible opportunity to play on his pun-worthy surname?

Shakespeare's revision could have helped shape the writing of *Hamlet* at the turn of the century. Kyd's influence might go far deeper than Shakespeare's use of *The Spanish Tragedy* as a model, given that he's often associated with a lost *Hamlet* play of the late 1580s. Kyd, like Shakespeare, lacked a university education, meaning that he was open to criticism from university-educated playwrights such as Greene and Thomas Nashe. Nashe seems to attack Kyd in his preface to Greene's pamphlet *Menaphon* (1589), which has led some to identify Kyd as the author of the so-called *Ur-Hamlet*.[17] Nashe alludes to 'the Kidde in Aesop' who has left 'the trade of *Noverint*' (meaning a scrivener, Francis Kyd's occupation) and now meddles 'with Italian translations', as Kyd had done with Tasso. Nashe claims that Kyd bleeds Seneca 'line by line' in order to 'affoord you whole *Hamlets*'. He scoffs at the opening of *The Spanish Tragedy* when Kyd 'thrusts Elisium into hell' during Andrea's account of his descent into the lower world. Nashe also claims that Kyd is prone to 'bodge up a blanke verse with ifs and ands', which parodies a line from *The Spanish Tragedy*: 'What, villain, *if*'s and *an*'s?' (2.1.77). Although Nashe refers to 'a sort of shifting companions', he often adopted the plural form even when a specific sneer was aimed at an individual. If we eliminate the writers Nashe speaks favourably of in the same preface, there's no one else who fits the description Nashe gives.[18] The earliest recorded performance of the lost *Hamlet* took place at Newington Butts on 9 June 1594 when the Admiral's Men and Shakespeare's company were performing there. Two years after the record of its performance, Kyd's schoolfellow Thomas Lodge alluded to the old *Hamlet* in his *Wit's*

Misery (1596): 'looks as pale as the vizard of the ghost which cried so miserably at the Theator like an Oyster wife, Hamlet, revenge'. We glean from this account that, unlike Shakespeare's other sources, this lost *Hamlet* play featured a ghost, an important innovation that had a major impact on Shakespeare's play. The scholar Gary Taylor has attempted to assign the play to early Shakespeare. He infers that the ghost in the lost *Hamlet* 'engaged directly with the play's living characters – as Seneca's ghosts do not, as Kyd's ghost does not'.[19] But the ghost of Pompey in Kyd's *Cornelia* visits and speaks to the terrified heroine.[20] It's hardly outside Kyd's wheelhouse for a ghost to demand revenge from a protagonist. There's a history of plays long attributed to Kyd being reassigned to Shakespeare. Kyd's reputation seems unable to withstand the commercial appeal of Shakespeare's name. This even extends to the case of a lost play.

Going back to Kyd's surviving work, *Soliman and Perseda* anticipates Shakespeare's *Romeo and Juliet* and *Othello*: it's an innovative tragedy of love. As is characteristic of Kyd's drama, the play bristles with intrigue: at its conclusion, the heroine, Perseda, vows revenge against the Turkish emperor, Soliman, for executing her lover. Unaware that he's fighting Perseda, who is disguised as a man, Soliman mortally wounds the woman he loves. He claims a kiss before she dies. He then realises that Perseda's lips are poisoned. It is a fatal kiss and a brilliant play that deserves more critical attention and would do well on the modern stage. Here Kyd expands the story of the play-within-a-play from *The Spanish Tragedy*, drawn from Henry Wotton's *A Courtly Controversy of Cupid's Cautels* (meaning craftiness), which was published in 1578 by an acquaintance of Kyd's father. Shakespeare remembered the moment in Kyd's play when Basilisco climbs a ladder but is pulled down by the servant Piston and made to swear an oath. In *King John* the Bastard alludes to Kyd's braggart in the line 'Knight, knight, good mother, Basilisco-like' (1.1.244), and there are touches of Basilisco in Shakespeare's characterisation of Falstaff.

Shakespeare's use of a handkerchief in *Othello* resembles *Soliman and Perseda*, in which Kyd places similar emphasis on the lost love token of a gold chain. In *Othello*, Shakespeare was harking back to the genre of so-called 'Turk plays', or plays with 'Turk motifs', which included: Marlowe's *Tamburlaine* plays; Greene's *Alphonsus, King of Aragon* (1587); Peele's *The Battle of Alcazar* (1588); and indeed *Soliman and Perseda*. However, while Turkish villains take centre stage in these plays, the threat of Turkish violence comes to nothing when the fleet is dispersed in *Othello*.[21] Shakespeare glances expertly at past dramas to pull the rug from under audience members' feet. He also seems to have had *Cornelia* in mind when writing *Julius Caesar*. The plays traverse the same period of Roman history and it's possible that Shakespeare's Brutus and Cassius were inspired by Kyd's.

Considerable attention has been paid to similarities between early Shakespeare and Kyd's room-mate Marlowe's style. It might surprise readers to discover that, in several respects, early Shakespeare is much more similar to Kyd. Kyd's rates for 'feminine' endings range from 1.2 per cent in *The Spanish Tragedy* to 10.2 per cent for *Soliman and Perseda*.[22] Kyd is unique among Shakespeare's predecessors in making such liberal use of these endings. Was Shakespeare inspired by Kyd's verse? We've seen that Shakespeare had a higher rate of use for compound forms than many of his contemporaries, including Marlowe. This aspect of Shakespeare's lexicon might also stem from Kyd, who was in turn influenced by the French poet Robert Garnier's fondness for fusing words together. *The Spanish Tragedy* contains such forms as 'ever-glooming' (1.1.56) and 'stately written' (5.1.152). *Soliman and Perseda* has a striking number of new compounds, the text bursting with inventions like 'cloud-compacted' (2.1.90) and 'marrow-burning' (5.2.14). *Cornelia* gives us 'flaxen-haired' (1.1.59), 'thorny-pointed' (2.1.269), and 'fire-darting' (5.1.179). The impact of Kyd's language on Shakespeare's style was like an engineering brick through a window. Their feathers are of more similar hues than has been acknowledged. Far from being stuffy and bombastic, Kyd was experimenting with language in daring and unique ways among Shakespeare's dramatic forebears.

Collocations and N-grams offers us never-before-seen insights into Kyd's influence on Shakespeare's language. Several Shakespeare plays are ranked highly in the spreadsheet for *The Spanish Tragedy*, which was probably first printed in 1592. The spreadsheet ranks all other plays in the database compared to Kyd's tragedy according to numbers for unique phrases. *Richard III* is ranked tenth and Shakespeare's contributions to *Titus Andronicus* are ranked fifteenth. Although *Soliman and Perseda* wasn't as popular with audiences and readers as *The Spanish Tragedy*, it seems to have been a favourite of Shakespeare's. In the spreadsheet for Kyd's Turkish tragedy, likely printed in the same year as *The Spanish Tragedy*, one-fifth of the top twenty plays are by Shakespeare: *The Comedy of Errors*, *The Two Gentlemen of Verona*, *Henry V*, and *Troilus and Cressida*. The highest-ranked play in the spreadsheet for *Cornelia* is *Julius Caesar* at fourteenth, which might support the idea that Shakespeare read Kyd's liberal translation when working on his Roman tragedy, although setting could also be a contributing factor to these numbers. These eyelid-wrenching findings suggest that Shakespeare owes as great a debt, if not a greater, to Kyd's language than he does to Marlowe's.

Richard III has been styled 'a study in Kydian methods',[23] and we can see the significant influence that *The Spanish Tragedy* exerted on that play through close reading of shared phrases in *Collocations and N-grams*. Shakespeare seems to have been deeply conscious of Kyd's dramatic language in 2.3 of *The Spanish Tragedy*, a conversation between the King of Spain, the Portuguese ambassador, and Don Cyprian. Shakespeare recalled the King's speech 'Endeavour you **to win your daughter's** thoughts. / If she give back, **all** this **will come to naught**' (2.3.49–50), for Richard's confrontation with Queen Elizabeth, '**To win your daughter**' (4.4.271), and for a speech delivered by a Scrivener, a character who likely shared Kyd's occupation: 'Bad is the world, and **all will come to nought**' (3.6.13). The King and the Scrivener's speeches provide the final rhyming couplets for their respective scenes. Did Shakespeare remember Kyd's cue lines for the actors playing Horatio, Bel-Imperia, and Pedringano? He remembered another passage during the gruesome play-within-a-play, when Balthazar delivers the lines, 'Fair queen of beauty, let not favour die, / But **with a gracious eye** behold his grief' (5.4.56–7). Shakespeare switches up the context for this unique phrase in

Richmond's speech on the eve of battle: 'Look on my forces **with a gracious eye**' (5.5.62). Shakespeare was conscious of Kyd's storehouse of phrases relating to warfare, as can be seen in Richard's command '**The rest march on** with me' (4.4.469), which echoes the Spanish King's command to his army: '**The rest march on**, but ere they be dismissed, / We will bestow on every soldier' (1.2.129–30). Shakespeare was particularly fond of the intrigue plot involving Pedringano: Clarence notes that his brother, the scheming Richard, promised '**That** he **would labour my delivery**' (1.4.241). In Kyd's play Lorenzo falsely promises that he will save Pedringano from the gallows. Pedringano reminds him of this oath: '**That** you **would labour my delivery**' (4.1.33). In *Titus Andronicus*, Shakespeare echoed the earlier moment when Pedringano is caught by the Watch: 'To **bring the murdered body** with us too' (3.3.45). Just as Lorenzo frames Pedringano for the murder of Serberine, Aaron and Tamora frame Titus's sons Martius and Quintus for the murder of Bassianus: 'Some **bring the murdered body**' (2.3.300). Kyd's Lorenzo must have had a profound impact on his Elizabethan contemporaries. He's the first Machiavellian villain in Elizabethan drama,[24] providing the template for Aaron and many other Shakespearian villains, as well as Marlowe's Barabas.

Curiously, Shakespeare had Lorenzo's devilish speeches firmly in mind when writing his comedy, *The Taming of the Shrew*. Katherina's father's line 'I will be very **kind and liberal**' (1.1.98), echoes Lorenzo's duplicitous speech to Pedringano: 'thou shalt find me **kind and liberal**' (2.1.84). Lorenzo fears that Serberine will give the game away and make it known to Hieronimo that he murdered his son: 'This **is that damnèd villain** Serberine' (3.2.74). In Shakespeare's comedy Vincentio asks: 'Where **is that damnèd villain** Tranio' (5.1.111). Lorenzo is a frightening villain, but he's also characteristic of Kyd's innovative blend of comic and tragic materials. It's remarkable that 'a man should jest himself to death' (3.5.17) and Pedringano's execution reveals a 'sensationally lethal turn' in Lorenzo's knavery, which provokes an 'oddly mixed response – of amusement and horror, revulsion and admiration'.[25] Kyd's influence on Shakespeare wasn't limited to heavy tragedy. He paints beautiful dramatic chiaroscuros and Shakespeare recognised that the lighter moments in Kyd's works afforded opportunities to engage and entertain audiences.

Intriguingly, two of the top Shakespeare plays in the spreadsheet for *Soliman and Perseda* are early comedies: *The Comedy of Errors* and *The Two Gentlemen of Verona*. Shakespeare seems to have been particularly attuned to Kyd's romantic language. Valentine speaks of **'the sweet glances of** thy honoured love' (1.1.4). Kyd's Basilisco speaks of **'the sweet glances of** many amorous girls' (1.3.2–3). Valentine uses similarly inflated, lovey-dovey language in the line, '**To her whose worth** makes other worthies nothing' (2.4.164). Perseda accuses her lover, Erastus, of cheating on her with Lucina: '**To her whose worth** will never equal mine' (2.1.135). Shakespeare's Proteus renounces his love for Julia: 'So the remembrance of **my former love** / **Is** by a newer object quite forgotten' (2.4.192–3). Perseda tells Erastus that 'all **my former love is** turned to hate' (2.1.154). Near the conclusion of Shakespeare's play Thurio says of Silvia: '**I** claim her **not, and therefore she is** thine' (5.4.133). Here he is echoing the moment Erastus grieves over the loss of his lover's gold chain: '**I** kept it **not, and therefore she is** lost' (1.5.73). Despite the generic differences between these plays, they both revolve around love triangles, albeit a fatal one in Kyd's play.

Shakespeare must have returned to *Soliman and Perseda* when he wrote *Othello*. After murdering Perseda, Soliman asks: 'Was she not constant?' (5.4.97) and 'Was she not chaste?' (5.4.99). These questions are affirmed by Brusor. This moment anticipates the dialogue between Othello and Iago: Shakespeare inverts the exchanges, with Iago responding to Othello's descriptions of Desdemona's 'wit and invention' (4.1.186) and 'so gentle a condition' (4.1.189) with such refrains as 'She's the worse for all this' (4.1.187) and 'Ay, too gentle' (4.1.190). Shakespeare once again scrutinised the comic elements of Kyd's dramas, even when composing a dark tragedy like *Othello*. He was especially influenced by the witty servant, Piston. In a turning point for Iago's intrigue plot, Montano says to the drunken Cassio, '**I pray you, sir, hold your hand**' (2.3.146). This line uniquely parallels Piston's exchange with Erastus: '**I pray you, sir, hold your hands**, and,

as I am an honest man' (1.5.62–3). In Shakespeare's mind, Piston's speech provoked the repetition of the word 'honest' in relation to Iago throughout *Othello*. Iago echoes Piston later in the same scene: '**As I am an honest man**' (2.3.260). Iago is a brilliant, Machiavellian villain whose lineaments can be traced in part to Kyd's Lorenzo, but he's also a comedian, a savage practical 'Joker in the Pack', as the poet W. H. Auden labelled him.[26] *Collocations and N-grams* proves that Shakespeare was deeply aware of Kyd's dramatic language throughout his career. Like a necromancer Shakespeare summons lines from Kyd's dramas to fulfil purposes of genre and characterisation. Kyd's influence on Shakespeare's style has been largely considered in tragic terms, especially the refinement of Senecan rhetoric for the stage. Kyd's flights of rhetorical devices such as *polyptoton*, *antanaclasis* (the repetition of a word with different meanings in each case), and *antimetabole* (the transposition of words repeated in successive clauses) more closely approximate early Shakespeare than do the works of university-educated playwrights. However, Kyd's greatest impact on Shakespeare is surely the hybrid nature of his plays, his willingness to interrogate genres, to weave together strands of tragedy and black comedy and kick aside binding traditions with a heavy boot. It's high time that Kyd was regarded as much more than just a Senecan disciple.

Scholars since the late nineteenth century have attributed several anonymous plays to Kyd. *The Collected Works of Thomas Kyd*, which has been described as an 'ambitious project' that confirms Kyd's 'place as a pioneering and prolific dramatist, not just as the author of the blockbusting *Spanish Tragedy* and a couple of other plays',[27] adds three plays to his sole-authored canon. These are *The True Chronicle History of King Leir*, a chronicle history play with Romance elements; *Arden of Faversham*, a true-life crime drama written in Kyd's distinctive mixture of tragedy and black comedy in which bumbling hired assassins finally get the job done; and *Fair Em, the Miller's Daughter of Manchester*, a comedy in part about William the Conqueror falling in love with a picture on a shield and in part about the daughter of a miller feigning blindness and

deafness to avoid numerous suitors. All three plays have important links to Shakespeare. *Fair Em* was inspired by Kyd's source
A Courtly Controversy of Cupid's Cautels and aroused Robert
Greene's ire in strikingly similar terms to Nashe's attack on Kyd.[28]
The comedy was catalogued as Shakespeare's in the library of
Charles II. The evidence for Kyd's authorship of these plays includes
similarities in verse style, idiosyncratic stage directions, vocabulary
choices and repeated phrases, distinctive use of sources, and overall
dramaturgy.[29]

King Leir was likely written in the late 1580s. A performance
of the play took place in April 1594 at the Rose Theatre, where
the Queen's Men and Sussex's Men were performing. So far
as we know, it wasn't printed until 1605. Shakespeare's name
is given special prominence on the title page of the 1608 First
Quarto edition of *King Lear*, probably to differentiate the tragedy as clearly as possible from its dramatic predecessor.[30] *King
Leir* provided an important source for Shakespeare's drama. Were
Shakespeare's two greatest tragedies, *Hamlet* and *King Lear*, adaptations of works by Kyd? Like all of Shakespeare's sources for *King
Lear* the older play ends happily, with the King restored to his
throne. Audiences would have been familiar with this dramatisation of the Lear myth and its happy conclusion, or at least with
other analogues, including the chronicle accounts of Geoffrey of
Monmouth and Holinshed, as well as *Gesta Romanorum* and *Brut*.
Shakespeare's play departs strikingly in its devastating conclusion
with Lear's heart breaking as he holds the corpse of his daughter
Cordelia in his arms. Here Shakespeare makes ingenious use of a
play that anticipates his own not only as source material but also
to subvert audience expectations. He elaborates themes and verbal
cues in Kyd's text: Shakespeare keeps the kneeling competition
between the King and his daughter, but whereas this moment
is comically absurd in the older play, Shakespeare recognised its
potential to heighten pathos. In scene 19 of *King Leir* divine thunder saves Leir and his companion Perillus from a Messenger who
has been hired to murder them, a dangerous inversion of the 'Don't
shoot the messenger' sentiment. They attribute this storm to 'The

King of heaven' (19.294), as is characteristic of Kyd, who likes to transform pagan concepts into Christian ones. Shakespeare's Lear similarly attributes the 'dreadful pother o'er our heads' to 'the great gods' (3.2.49–50). But while divine justice is accomplished in Kyd's providential world, Shakespeare plunges us into a tragic universe in which 'All' is 'dark and comfortless' (3.7.82) and 'As flies to wanton boys, are we to the gods. / They kill us for their sport' (4.1.38–9). The heavens listen to Leir's prayers but reject those uttered by Shakespeare's Lear.

King Leir exercised a profound influence over Shakespeare's dramas long before the older play was available in print. Shakespeare didn't need to wait for the publication of the 1605 edition of *King Leir* to write his tragic version. He seems to have imbibed its verbal details, themes, and elements of characterisation like a weary traveller hitting the bar, probably drawing on the phenomenal aural memory he needed as an actor-dramatist. The moment in scene 19 of the old play when the Messenger first comes across his victims Leir and Perillus, who are asleep, 'Now could I stab them bravely while they sleep' (19.30), looks forward to the murder of Clarence in *Richard III*: 'What, shall I stab him as he sleeps?' (1.4.98). It also anticipates Hamlet's speech when he stumbles upon his villainous uncle Claudius praying: 'Now might I do it pat, now a is praying, / And now I'll do't, and so a goes to heaven' (3.3.73–4). The old play gave Shakespeare a vivid tableau to work with. The would-be murderous Messenger's speech in *King Leir* 'thou **shalt never wake until** dooms**day**' (19.174) closely resembles the Second Murderer's line in the same scene of *Richard III*: 'Why, he **shall never wake until** the great judgement **day**' (1.4.100). Shakespeare places the King's companion Perillus's words, ''Tis shame for **them that were the cause thereof**' (14.27), in the mouth of his main villain in *Richard III*: 'God pardon **them that are the cause thereof**' (1.3.313). Shakespeare also remembered Perillus's line, '**The King hath dispossessed himself of** all' (8.1), when he wrote Salisbury's speech several years later in *King John*: '**The King hath dispossessed himself of** us' (4.3.23). He again recalled scene 19 when the Bastard tells Hubert in that play that he's damned '**if thou didst this deed** of death' (4.3.118), which echoes Leir's warning and offers a cue for the divine thunderclap: 'Swear not by hell, for that stands gaping wide / To swallow thee an **if thou do this deed**' (19.189–90). Did Shakespeare always plan to adapt this play?

In the spreadsheet for *King Leir* in *Collocations and N-grams*, the playwright and scribe Robert Yarington's lamentably plagiaristic play *Two Lamentable Tragedies* (1595) tops the list. This is an important link with Kyd because Yarington was apprenticed to Kyd's father. Kyd's authorship of *King Leir* could help to explain Yarington's intimate familiarity with its language. Did Yarington have access to Kyd's manuscripts? Could he have been involved in copying out Kyd's plays? *Soliman and Perseda* is ranked twentieth and was probably written by Kyd around the same time. *King Lear* appears in second position but several earlier Shakespeare plays also feature fairly high in the rankings: *King John* is at position seventeen and *Henry IV Part One* and *Richard II* at thirty-four and thirty-six respectively.

Unsurprisingly, lines from the old play were at the forefront of Shakespeare's mind when he wrote *King Lear*. He remembered another speech delivered by the Messenger in the brilliant scene 19, '**my** sweet queen willed me for to **show** / **This letter to them ere I** did the deed' (19.34–5), for Kent, who also serves as an envoy:

> **My** Lord, when at their home
> I did commend your highness' **letters to them,**
> **Ere I** was risen from the place that **showed**
> My duty kneeling, came there a reeking post. (2.2.203–6)

Perillus, very much the model for Shakespeare's Kent, asks the King: '**What should you need** to give me any **more**?' (10.75). Shakespeare alters the context of this line for the moment when Regan spites her father: 'I dare avouch it, sir. What, fifty followers? / Is it not well? **What should you need** of **more**?' (2.2.410–11). The verbal echoes in *King Lear* are of a similar quality to those found in Shakespeare's much earlier works. As is the case with the plays traditionally given to Kyd, Shakespeare seems to have known *King Leir* throughout his career, possessing an intimate familiarity with its verbal details that is testament to his capacious memory.

On Valentine's Day 1551 the county of Kent was rocked by a sensational murder. A former mayor and controller of the Port of Faversham named Thomas Arden was butchered in his home by hired assassins, his own wife, and her lover. With a napkin held over his face, he was strangled, beaten with an iron, and his throat was cut. On that cold wintry night his corpse was dragged outside, only to be discovered during a frantic search by the townspeople. The murder weapons were poorly hidden and, alongside hair and traces of blood found in the house, pointed to the site of Thomas's demise and the shocking identity of his murderers. It was only a matter of time until a playwright seized on this juicy story. *Arden of Faversham* was published in 1592 by Edward White, who also published Kyd's *The Spanish Tragedy* and *Soliman and Perseda* and owned the rights to *King Leir*. One authority on Kyd notes that the 'quick succession' of *The Spanish Tragedy*, *Soliman and Perseda*, and *Arden of Faversham* 'is intriguing' and speculates that the reason why these plays 'were published by the same stationer around the same time may be that Kyd sold White the manuscripts'.[31] The play was printed by Edward Allde, who also printed *Soliman and Perseda* and owned rights to the title of *King Leir* in 1624. Could *Arden of Faversham* have belonged to Pembroke's Men? If so, might Shakespeare have acted in it? Others have gone further and suggested that Shakespeare had a hand in writing the play. The domestic tragedy has edged into his canon in recent times. Readers might be surprised to learn though that *Arden of Faversham* has been given solely to Kyd since 1891 and that a consensus of scholars from all over the world recognised him as sole author in the twentieth century.[32] Such a wide-ranging, globetrotting consensus is unique in the history of the field. In the twenty-first century a battery of modern statistical tests based on phraseology, vocabulary, and verse style would seem to validate the attribution solely to Kyd. Biographical and historical evidence aligns the play more closely to Kyd than rival authorship candidates.[33] Along with the attribution of parts of the *Henry VI* plays to Marlowe, the authorship of *Arden of Faversham* has caused huge academic rifts. The question of who wrote this domestic tragedy could be considered the most important in the field of early modern authorship attribution studies. Whether Shakespeare had a hand in it or not, the play is fundamental to understanding his development.

The widely held belief during the twentieth century that Kyd was the play's sole author was dislodged in 1963 when a scholar named MacDonald Jackson gave parts of the play to Shakespeare. What can ongoing arguments about the play's authorship tell us about how Shakespeare is positioned in comparison to his fellow Elizabethan playwrights? These debates will help us further explore the striking similarities between early Shakespeare and Kyd, which are so considerable that leading scholars have had difficulties distinguishing their work. For several decades Jackson has rejected the evidence for Kyd's authorship of *Arden of Faversham*. Parallels with Kyd are considered examples of 'cliché' and those with Shakespeare to be 'poetry'. Kyd's imagery is 'characteristically confused', his writing a mere 'tissue of inert expressions and other men's inventions',[34] while Shakespeare's poetry has a 'vividness and concreteness never on display in Kyd's plays'.[35] Such evaluative, aesthetic approaches are usually avoided in attribution studies. *Arden of Faversham* is considered a co-authored play with an older dramatist who was probably not Kyd. Shakespeare is alleged to have been responsible for the middle portion of the play: scenes 4–8 and at least parts of scene 9.

One piece of evidence adduced for Shakespeare is that compound adjectives in *Arden of Faversham* more closely resemble his early plays than those of dramatists such as Marlowe, Greene, or Peele.[36] Yet none of the compound forms considered to be of Shakespearian quality, such as 'hollow-eyed' (2.46) and 'dry-sucked' (3.103), can be found in scenes 4–9. Neither are they beyond Kyd's capacity. In fact such forms occur less frequently in *Arden of Faversham* than they do in *Soliman and Perseda*. Some supposedly Shakespearian forms, such as compound adjectives formed with a present participle in *Arden of Faversham*, feature more often in the middle scenes. There are five in scenes 4–9 and just four in the rest of the play. Does this pattern suggest that different authors were responsible for these portions? Looking at Kyd's *The Spanish Tragedy*, there's a much greater disparity: three-quarters of such forms as 'ever-glooming' (1.1.56), 'never-killing' (1.1.69), and 'neighbour-bounding' (1.2.51) cluster in the play's opening two scenes. Evidently, authors didn't pepper these forms with steady hands across their solo plays. The argument that these markers provide evidence for Shakespeare's co-authorship, as opposed to Kyd's sole authorship, would surely be deemed inadmissible in a court of law.

Since Shakespeare's part authorship was first proposed, there have been considerable advances in technology. We can now uncover minute details of poetic texts and establish similarities between anonymous plays and those of authorial candidates. One method applied to the question of *Arden of Faversham*'s authorship involves using a database called *Literature Online*, or *LION*. The so-called '*LION* method' tests speeches or scenes for verbal parallels and works out exactly how many times they can be found in other plays of the period. This method has highlighted numerous parallels between Shakespeare plays and the fantastic scene 8 of *Arden of Faversham*, which dramatises a quarrel between Alice Arden and her lover, Mosby. Parallels with that scene are recorded only if they can be found no more than five times in drama of the period 1580–1600. Eight rare phrases shared with Kyd's three traditionally accepted plays were discovered, far fewer than found for Shakespeare plays. The result: Shakespeare is considered the more likely author of this scene. But is the case really closed? Objections can be raised. This method involves an element of subjectivity and is open to human error. A researcher chooses the phrases, images, or word combinations they consider to be of best use for determining authorship. They pluck the feathers that seem most colourful. They then punch that phrase into a search bar and the database lists any other works in which it can be found.

In several respects the scene duplicates an earlier quarrel between Alice and Mosby in the opening of the play, not attributed to Shakespeare. This repetition of similar scenes creates a structural rhythm in the play closely resembling *The Spanish Tragedy*.[37] Scene 8 begins with a paranoid Mosby alone on stage before Alice enters and a battle of the sexes ensues. Mosby is concerned that his accomplices will betray him. He decides to eliminate them: 'And then am I sole ruler of mine own' (8.36). Here he recalls Lorenzo in *The Spanish Tragedy*:

> And better 'tis that base companions die,
> Than by their life to hazard our good haps.
> Nor shall they live, for me to fear their faith:
> I'll trust myself, myself shall be my friend. (3.2.115–18)

Mosby's schemes are remarkably similar to those hatched by Lorenzo. He uses his sister, Susan, as bait, just as Lorenzo matches his sister Bel-Imperia with Balthazar to fulfil his Machiavellian schemes. Mosby dangles the carrot of his sister's hand in marriage, pitting rivals in love Michael and Clarke against each other, just as Lorenzo pits Pedringano and Serberine against each other. Mosby and Lorenzo make optimum use of intermediaries to despatch sinister business. They then make sure that these goons are themselves eliminated. Although scene 8 of *Arden of Faversham* has been given to Shakespeare on aesthetic grounds, it finds its closest counterpart with 2.1 of *Soliman and Perseda*, in which the lovers quarrel when Perseda accuses Erastus of adultery. In the study using the *Literature Online* database,[38] the matching words and ideas shared between Alice's image, '**To forge** distressful **looks to wound** a breast' (8.55), and Perseda's lines, '**Ah, how** thine eyes **can forge** alluring **looks**, / **And** feign deep oaths **to wound** poor silly maids' (2.1.119–20), count as a hit for Kyd but with a rather prejudicial-sounding footnote claiming that Kyd's image 'is confused'.[39] Both passages concern the idea of forging (meaning to contrive or design) deceitful looks. These speaking looks have the power to betray and wound lovers. The list of matches between scene 8 of *Arden of Faversham* and other plays excludes the parallel structure in Perseda's torrent of questions: 'What are thy **looks** but like the cockatrice, / That seeks **to wound** poor silly passengers?' (2.1.163–4). Nor does this study register the match between Perseda's speech and Mosby's sexist line, '**Ah, how** you women **can** insinuate / **And** clear a trespass with your sweet-set tongue!' (8.145–6). Matches with Shakespeare are recorded in the first line of Mosby's speech, 'Disturbèd thoughts **drives me from** company' (8.1), but no mention is made of a phrase shared with *The*

Spanish Tragedy, '**drive me from** this place' (1.4.99), even though it's unique among plays first performed between 1580 and 1600. Shakespeare gains a hit for the phrase '**Feebles my body by** excess' (8.4), which matches *Henry VI Part Two*'s contextually dissimilar line 'his old **feeble body**' (5.5.17). But there's a closer parallel with *The Spanish Tragedy* that gets neglected: 'Thus hath he ta'en **my body by** his force' (2.1.130).

For Mosby's line 'But **what** for that I may **not trust** you, Alice' (8.39) a match is recorded with Shakespeare but a parallel of wording and thought with Kyd's earlier villain, Lorenzo, is left out: 'But to **what** end? I list **not trust** the air' (3.4.78). The same grouping of words is employed to emphasise the paranoia of these schemers. Two lines of the quarrel scene, '**You** have supplanted Arden **for my sake** / **And** will extirpen me' (8.40–1), seem to have been missed out entirely. They give us another distinct match with Kyd's play in terms of verse structure and the congruence of word choices: '**You** (gentle brother) forged this **for my sake,** / **And** you, my lord, were made his instrument' (4.4.64–5). The parallel of both thought and language between Alice's line 'conceal **the rest,** for 'tis too **bad**' (8.62) and *Soliman and Perseda*'s '**The rest** I dare not speak, **it is** so **bad**' (5.2.50), is missed. In both passages the characters stress that intrigue must be concealed. According to this study Shakespeare is the only playwright with rare links to Alice's speech, 'But **I** will dam that fire **in my breast** / **Till** by the force thereof my part consume' (8.48–9). The method fails to register a rare hit with another powerful female role, Bel-Imperia in *The Spanish Tragedy*, suggesting not only the same author's thought process but the very timbre of his verse: 'But how can love find harbour **in my breast** / **Till I** revenge the death of my beloved' (1.4.64–5).

The list of rare parallels doesn't include the match between Alice's line 'And spoke **as smoothly as an** orator' (8.127) and Kyd's *Cornelia*, '**as smoothly as a**' (4.2.14), even though that sequence of words can't be found in any other play of the period. Links between Mosby's speech '**sweet**-set tongue! / **I will forget** this quarrel, gentle Alice' (8.146–7) and Shakespeare are recorded. But a striking thought-parallel, in which another male character forgives a female

in *Soliman and Perseda*, is overlooked: **'sweet** love, abandon fear, /
I will forget thy former cruelty' (2.1.66–7). The method also fails to
identify the convergence of thought and wording shared between the
line '**Till then my** bliss is **mixed with bitter** gall' (8.163), and lines
in *Soliman and Perseda*, 'A sweet renown, but **mixed with bitter**
sorrow' (2.Prologue.23), and *The Spanish Tragedy*: '**Till then my**
sorrow never shall be spent' (2.4.123). Although the method appears
to afford all candidate authors an equal opportunity for sharing
verbal links with a target passage, an element of unconscious bias
might very well have played a role in this study. Either way significant matches with Kyd are missed.[40] It's also questionable whether
many of the parallels with Shakespeare were worth recording: passages sharing single words or even just synonyms are included in his
totals.

Arden of Faversham probably predates all of Shakespeare's plays.
Was he immersed in its language because he acted in it? In terms
of numbers for shared phrases the play fits neatly into the pattern of Shakespeare's borrowings from plays written by Kyd. In fact
Shakespeare shares more links with *The Spanish Tragedy*, *Soliman
and Perseda*, and *King Leir* than he does with *Arden of Faversham*.
There's not a single Shakespeare play in the top twenty for the
Arden of Faversham spreadsheet in *Collocations and N-grams*,
with *Richard III*, that Kydian study, featuring in twenty-first position. This statistical fact undermines the idea that Shakespeare par-
ticipated in the writing of *Arden of Faversham*: every Shakespeare
play of the Elizabethan period commonly regarded as collaborative, including *Henry VI Part One*, to which, as we'll see shortly,
Shakespeare contributed only a few scenes, *Titus Andronicus*, and
Edward III, features several other Shakespeare plays in the top
twenty. Top of the list for the *Arden of Faversham* spreadsheet
is *Soliman and Perseda*. No other play of the early modern period
shares as many unique matches with *Arden of Faversham*. If this
were the Grand National, Kyd would be a safe horse on which to
bet. Rather than admitting the possibility of Shakespeare borrowing
from Kyd, many prefer to see Shakespeare's actual hand in the play.
It seems that, in some eyes, to quote *Arden of Faversham*, giving

the play to Shakespeare as opposed to Kyd is equivalent to swapping 'a raven for a dove' (8.96).[41]

Distinguishing authorship from influence remains an obstacle, despite advances in technology. The first scene given to Shakespeare in *Arden of Faversham* features abundant distinct matches with Kyd of a wholly different order to Shakespeare's borrowings from Kyd. They embrace additional words serving similar semantic and syntactic functions and reveal complex modes of expression. Arden's companion, Franklin, reassures him that his cheating wife will either atone or die: **'If neither** of these two do haply fall, / **Yet let your comfort be'** (4.24–5). This speech shares a peculiar turn of words with *The Spanish Tragedy* when Hieronimo tells himself that his miseries will ease or he will die: **'If neither, yet let** this **thy comfort be'** (4.7.18). Left alone on stage, Franklin exclaims: 'Ah, what a hell is **fretful jealousy!'** (4.39). The unique match with Kyd's *Cornelia* is all the more significant given that Kyd departs from his source in the line, 'Opposing of thy **fretful jealousy'** (5.1.387). Later in this scene the servant Michael delivers an earlobe-tugging speech imagining the hired ruffians, Black Will and Shakebag, murdering him: **'Methinks I hear** them ask where Michael is, / And pitiless Black Will **cries, "Stab the slave!"** / The peasant will **detect** the tragedy' (4.78–80). Here the author recycles Kyd's language from two speeches in *Soliman and Perseda*: 'Then **stab the slaves'** (3.5.24) and **'stab** in **the** Marshal, / Lest he **detect** us unto the world' (5.2.127–8). The author of this scene also draws from the verbal fabric of a speech delivered by Hieronimo when he remembers finding his son's murdered body: **'methinks I hear** / His dismal **outcry** echo in the air' (5.4.107–8). Michael has had a **'fearful dream that troubled me'** (4.92). Kyd's Cornelia also has an ominous dream (Kyd loved prophetic dreams and visions, no doubt inspired by Seneca and Garnier) and laments 'The **fearful dream's** effects **that trouble me'** (2.1.209). Michael, caught in an impossible situation as the murderers enlist his aid to get rid of his master, despairs: 'Ah, harmless Arden, how, how **hast thou misdone**, / That thus **thy** gentle **life** is levelled at?' (4.186–7). Hieronimo cries: 'O poor Horatio, what **hadst thou misdone** / To leese **thy life** ere life was new begun?' (2.4.90–1).

Do these links help us enter the same author's verbal storehouse, to witness the goods of his mind?

The most striking match with Kyd occurs when Franklin is woken up by Michael's terrified howls: '**What dismal outcry calls me from my** rest?' (4.87). If Shakespeare authored this scene, he might very well have remembered Hieronimo's famous line, '**What outcries** pluck **me from my** naked **bed**' (2.4.63). It was frequently parodied in plays of the period (think: 'Do I feel lucky?', 'I'll be back', 'I'm flying, Jack!') and Shakespeare seems to have remembered it when Titania awakes in *A Midsummer Night's Dream*: '**What** angel wakes **me from my** flow'ry **bed**?' (3.1.122). Frederick Boas, whose edition of Kyd's works has inflicted lasting damage to the dramatist's critical reputation by painting him as a dull workman in relation to Marlowe's luminescence,[42] claimed that the 'imitation' in *Arden of Faversham* is 'so transparent that it is almost sufficient of itself to prove that Kyd could not have written the anonymous play'.[43] Other critics have argued that Kyd was simply reproducing, in his own dramatic voice, an incident from his earlier play. Modern methods reveal that there's nothing transparent about the echo here: this single line shares no fewer than four unique matches with two of Kyd's acknowledged plays. If Shakespeare were responsible for this line, he must have not only recalled Hieronimo's famous speech but also a later one in which he describes finding his son's corpse: 'His **dismal outcry** echo in the air' (5.4.108). He must have also remembered Hieronimo's question, 'Oh, was it thou that **call'dst me from my** bed?' (2.4.78). More, he must have remembered the line-opening phrase in *Soliman and Perseda*: '**What dismal** planets guides this fatal hour?' (1.6.78). Shakespeare's debts to Kyd are far more pervasive than has been acknowledged. But there's no comparable example of Shakespeare echoing so many speeches from Kyd's plays in the space of a single line. Franklin's speech and the play as a whole are imbricate with Kyd's distinct word combinations. It's not enough to amass examples of shared language and attribute a speech or scene to whichever author shares the most matches. An additional step is required: it's only through looking closely at similarities between the works of candidate authors that we can be sure a contested play fits into what we might expect for verbal borrowings. Maybe Franklin's line affords opportunities for tackling the prickly difficulty of distinguishing authorial borrowing from self-borrowing.

The attribution board for the *New Oxford Shakespeare*, of which MacDonald Jackson was a member, decided to include the play in their edition of Shakespeare's works. Jackson's work has been supplemented by other scholars adopting statistical approaches. The same issues with stylometric analysis that bedevil claims for Marlowe's co-authorship of the *Henry VI* plays apply also to *Arden of Faversham*. The 2009 Zeta study gave the verdict that '*Arden of Faversham* is a collaboration; Shakespeare was one of the authors; and his part is concentrated in the middle portion of the play'.[44] We've seen that these methods have been heavily criticised and the content-word tests don't actually give scene 8 to Shakespeare.

Other statistical studies of vocabulary run counter to the Shakespeare attribution, placing *Arden of Faversham* squarely in Kyd's canon.[45] Statistical analysis, like literary analysis, can aspire to objectivity. But it too relies on interpretation. The methods used in the 2009 Zeta study are extended in the *New Oxford Shakespeare* with the gaze-grabbing pronouncement that it's 'impossible to reconcile the results we have found with a belief that Shakespeare had no hand in *Arden of Faversham*, thus the play takes its rightful place in the canon of his works'.[46] But the results for scenes that the team give to Shakespeare often point to Kyd, calling this conclusion into doubt. The *New Oxford Shakespeare* function-word tests assign the supposedly Shakespearian scenes 4–8 to Kyd and locate Shakespeare's hand in passages that nobody gives to him. These approaches based on single words stripped of meaning fail to agree. Can we place faith in these stylometric methods? No matter the questionable readings of results (those pointing towards Kyd's authorship go unmentioned in the conclusion to this study), eyebrows might tilt at the fact that this method fails to identify Shakespeare as author of *Richard III* or Kyd as author of *Soliman and Perseda*.[47]

What about more traditional techniques? Could they help us work out how many hands lie behind the play? The scholar Philip

Timberlake endorsed the attribution to Kyd because the play averages 6.2 per cent 'feminine' endings, which he compared to Kyd's similarly high percentages.[48] These results tally with Kyd's traditionally accepted plays as well as *King Leir*'s 10.8 per cent and *Fair Em*'s 6.5. Scenes given to Shakespeare in *Arden of Faversham* average 6.4 per cent 'feminine' endings, while his conjectured co-author averages a strikingly similar percentage of 6.1. Both results would be too high for any known Elizabethan playwright except Kyd or Shakespeare. The first scene given to Shakespeare, scene 4, runs to 103 verse lines. This makes it a 'long scene' suitable for analysis. Scene 4 has a low figure for 'feminine' endings of 0.9 per cent, which fits into Kyd's range but is anomalous for Shakespeare, who consistently employed 'feminine' endings in scenes of over one hundred verse lines more frequently than his contemporaries, Kyd included.

The idea of Shakespeare's hand in *Arden of Faversham* has proved irresistible for many scholars. Has it blinded them to the evidence for Kyd's sole authorship? One leading expert in early modern verse originally attributed the play solely to Kyd. Persuaded by the 2009 study arguing for Shakespeare's part authorship, this scholar cut up portions of the play according to a theory of collaboration. Scenes 4 to 8 are now handed to Shakespeare because, among other pointers, there are lots of run-on lines in them. And yet there are fewer run-on lines in these scenes than in *Cornelia*.[49] Can such results really be taken as evidence for Shakespeare's authorship rather than Kyd's?

A recent study points out that *Arden of Faversham* is consistent and distinct in terms of style and so it was likely the product of a single author's hand. Divided authorship is considered unlikely because dispersed rhymes are found throughout the play.[50] It's long been noted that Kyd employs whimsical rhyme schemes, seemingly at random in his verse.[51] Take for example the *aca* scheme, a rhyming couplet broken up by an unrhyming word. In *Arden of Faversham*, Dick Reede says: 'I am now bound to sea. / My coming to you was about the plot of ground / Which wrongfully you detain from me' (13.11–13). In *Soliman and Perseda*, Erastus's rhyming dialogue is similarly broken up by an unrhyming word ('would') when he asks Perseda:

> Why when, Perseda, wilt thou not assure me,
> But shall I like a mastless ship at sea
> Go every way and not the way I would?
> My love hath lasted from mine infancy. (1.1.1–4)

Kyd enjoys rhyming the pronouns 'thee' and 'me' with polysyllabic words ending -cy, -ny, -ty, and -ry. We can see this in the following passage from scene 8 of *Arden of Faversham*:

> Whose beauty and demeanour far exceeded thee.
> This certain good I lost for changing bad,
> And wrapped my credit in thy company.
> I was bewitched – that is no theme of thine!
> And thou unhallowed hast enchanted me. (8.89–93)

The lovers' quarrel in *Soliman and Perseda* also features this unusual mix of blank verse and complicated rhyme:

> Couldst thou abuse my true simplicity,
> Whose greatest fault was overloving thee?
> I'll keep no tokens of thy perjury.
> Here, give her this; Perseda now is free. (2.1.150–3)

Instead of admitting the possibility of Kyd's sole authorship and analysing his rhyming patterns, it has been concluded on this basis that Shakespeare wrote *Arden of Faversham* alone. This contradicts the historical evidence and isn't supported by any statistical studies of the play. The absence of the domestic tragedy from the First Folio (indeed, any subsequent Folio) argues against Shakespeare's sole authorship. What words count as rhymes anyway? Recorded combinations like 'wavering' and 'one as he', 'here awhile' and 'talked their fill', and 'lay' and 'stage', some as many as twelve lines apart, aren't reliable. And repeated words such as 'die' and 'die' and 'me' and 'me' are examples of the rhetorical device *epistrophe*.[52] The play's rhymes have been compared to *The Taming of the Shrew* as a drama written close in date (Shakespeare's comedy was likely written at least two years after *Arden of Faversham* however), with the dispersion of words and phrases like 'comedy / very meet / of frenzy' in these plays considered similar.

Yet the use of rhyme in *Arden of Faversham* is far closer to *Soliman and Perseda* than it is to Shakespeare's play: *Soliman and Perseda* shares the *aca*, *aaa*, and *acaa* schemes with Kyd's other plays and these are the exact patterns that recur in *Arden of Faversham*. *The Taming of the Shrew* shares only the first pattern and it's used much less frequently than in *Arden of Faversham*.[53] The character of these rhymes is also very different; none of them couples pronouns with the kind of multisyllabic words we find in Kyd. Similarly, many of the speeches in *King Leir* look like blank verse but are in fact controlled by rhyme.[54] For all their stylistic similarities, Kyd and early Shakespeare's approaches to rhyme are rather different. If the quirky use of rhyme in *Arden of Faversham* suggests a single author, it's Kyd, not Shakespeare, and indeed not any other known Elizabethan playwright. The great mobility of Kyd's rhyming forms was likely influenced by the choric odes in works by Robert Garnier. Genuine rhyming patterns in *Arden of Faversham* might help us to distinguish Kyd and early Shakespeare's stylistic feathers. Internal evidence tends to be interpreted in Shakespeare's favour. Too often Kyd is dismissed or bypassed altogether. Is *Arden of Faversham* an example of Shakespeare bias? Is there a more interesting story to tell about how Shakespeare was deeply influenced by his tragic predecessor? The stakes are high. The implications of expanding Kyd's canon are that he is properly recognised as a major Elizabethan dramatist alongside Shakespeare and Marlowe, whose plays traverse a wider range of genres and themes.

Unlike *Arden of Faversham*, *Henry VI Part One* is widely held to be a Shakespeare collaboration. In or around 1591 Shakespeare wrote two history plays dealing with the Wars of the Roses, the factious rivalries between competing houses in fifteenth-century England. These plays, glossily titled *The Contention between York and Lancaster* and *The True Tragedy of Richard Duke of York*, might have been Shakespeare's first forays into dramatic writing. They were likely written for Pembroke's Men, the company named on the title page for the later play. On 3 March the following year, the rival company Lord Strange's Men put on a play at the Rose Theatre called 'Harey the vi'. Box office receipts show it was a smash hit. The production was celebrated by Thomas Nashe in his 1592 pamphlet *Pierce Penniless His Supplication to the Devil*:

How would it have joyed brave Talbot, the terror of the French, to think that after he had lain two hundred years in his tomb, he should triumph again on the stage and have his bones new embalmed with the tears of ten thousand spectators at least (at several times), who, in the tragedian that represents his person, imagine they behold him fresh bleeding!

Shakespeare had nothing to do with the original 'Harey the vi' play, which was commissioned to duplicate Pembroke's Men's offerings, dramatising a similar subject with the leading role, Lord Talbot, possibly designed for the star actor Edward Alleyn.

When Strange's Men collapsed in 1594 the book of 'Harey the vi' made its way into the possession of Shakespeare's company, Lord Chamberlain's Men. Shakespeare added three scenes: 2.4, the famous rose plucking scene that links the play to his two *Henry VI* plays as a serial about the Wars of the Roses; 4.2, in which Talbot is confronted by the General of Bordeaux; and 4.5, in which Talbot begs his son John to leave the battlefield. The three *Henry VI* plays appear as a trilogy in the First Folio, with the first part acting as an awkward prequel that is often inconsistent with the other plays in terms of plot and characterisation, *The Phantom Menace* of the Shakespeare canon if you will. Readers have long puzzled over the fact that 4.5 and 4.6 are strikingly similar scenes: Lord Talbot urges his son to leave the battlefield, the characters speaking almost the same lines at times. Is this a case of Shakespeare's immature craftmanship? This baffling doppelgänger effect can be explained by Shakespeare's revision. He rewrote the scene known as 4.6 in the First Folio, just as some of the passages added to the 1602 edition of *The Spanish Tragedy* were probably designed to replace parts of the original. The Folio compilers neglected to delete the older scene in *Henry VI Part One*, meaning that here, as one editor of the play put it, we see Shakespeare 'in the very act of beautifying the plumage' of another dramatist's work.[55]

If Shakespeare had nothing to do with the play known as 'Harey the vi' performed at the Rose, who were its original authors? Thomas Nashe likely had good reason to puff this play. He's widely credited as being responsible for Act 1 because of verbal links to his known works; his fondness for grammatical inversions, the device known as *hyperbaton* seen in the very first line of the play, 'Hung be the heavens with black' (1.1.1); and his distinctly un-Shakespearian vocabulary choices among other similarities.[56]

So who wrote Acts 2 to 5, minus Shakespeare's scenes? Marlowe has been touted but that's historically improbable given he was embroiled in a counterfeiting scheme in the Netherlands when the play was written. We're looking for a writer with a very similar lexicon to Marlowe, but who uses 'feminine' endings at a higher rate and compound adjectives with a frequency and inventiveness indistinguishable from Shakespeare.[57] Enter Thomas Kyd. If we compare the rate for compound forms in Acts 2 to 5 of *Henry VI Part One*, one every 602 words, we find that it is remarkably close to *The Spanish Tragedy*'s average of one every 601 words. Additional evidence for Kyd's authorship involves statistical analysis of all words in plays, as opposed to just function words or content words, which classifies these scenes in *Henry VI Part One* as his. Quantitative study of shared phrases shows that Acts 2 to 5 of *Henry VI Part One* fit into what we might expect from Kyd.

Kyd appears to have been responsible for writing many of the scenes involving Joan of Arc. Act 5 scene 3, in which Joan conjures spirits, resembles Marlowe's *Doctor Faustus*, with the *New Oxford Shakespeare* team claiming that Marlowe is clearly the author of this scene.[58] It's no surprise that Kyd and Marlowe shared lots of phrases: they also shared a room and Kyd was tortured because the authorities couldn't distinguish their writing. Beyond the conjuration of spirits, however, Joan's speech differs from Marlowe and verbal links with Kyd are of a much higher quality. Joan's line, 'I'll **lop a member off**' (5.3.36), uniquely parallels *Soliman and Perseda*: 'They **lopped a collop off my** tenderest **member**' (4.2.15). The connection with Joan's speech is of particular interest given that the reference to 'collop' (a piece of meat) is repeated by Joan's father in another scene that appears to have been written by Kyd: 'God knows, thou art **a collop of my** flesh' (5.6.18). The repetition of this peculiar phrase provides a closer textual connection between *Henry VI Part One* and *Soliman and Perseda* than any play in Marlowe's canon.

Joan's offer of sacrifice, 'Where I was wont to **feed you with my blood**' (5.3.35), gives us a hit with the heroine of *Cornelia*: 'Come, wrathful Furies with your ebon locks, / And **feed yourselves with mine** enflamèd **blood**' (5.1.342–3). The almost identical wording, combined with the analogous context of a female character appealing to supernatural forces, is highly distinctive in Elizabethan drama. Joan can be traced to Kyd's other strong-willed female characters, such as Bel-Imperia, Perseda, and possibly Alice Arden, who use intrigue, disguise, and deception for vengeful purposes. Kyd contributed greatly to the process of carving out more space for women in tragic narratives, laying foundations for Shakespeare's female roles, such as Margaret of Anjou in *Richard III*.[59]

Shakespeare's additions to this play afford us fascinating insights into his engagement with the work of other Elizabethan playwrights. He takes seeds from the older 2.5, in which the play's original audiences would have been introduced to Mortimer, who is imprisoned in the Tower of London, and his nephew Richard Plantagenet, and makes sure they sprout in the Temple Garden scene. From a single speech telling Mortimer that Richard has been summoned from the Temple, Shakespeare creates the most brilliant moment in the play.[60] Shakespeare also prepares the audience for Talbot's downfall by confronting him with an ominously powerful opponent in the General of Bordeaux for 4.2. He adapts the rhymed couplets in Kyd's 4.6, which are written in run-on lines designed to convey immediacy but which have the unfortunate effect of obscuring their rationale. Kyd's dramas are littered with enjambed rhyming couplets, whereas Shakespeare tends to treat his couplets as self-contained units, the first line raising an issue that's settled by the second line.[61] The enjambed rhymes in 4.7 when Talbot mourns his son's death before perishing himself are identical in manner to those found in 4.6 and are unlike Shakespeare's couplets in 4.5:

Where is my other life? Mine own is gone.
O where's young Talbot, where is valiant John?
Triumphant death, smeared with captivity,
Young Talbot's valour makes me smile at thee.
When he perceived me shrink and on my knee,

His bloody sword he brandished over me,
And like a hungry lion did commence
Rough deeds of rage and stern impatience. (4.7.1–8)

Talbot's narration of his son's death has been considered Shakes-pearian on the grounds that it reveals psychological poignancy.[62] Does this preclude Kyd as a candidate? *The Spanish Tragedy* is full of poignant speeches in which Hieronimo mourns the death of his son Horatio. Following his success with the father–son relationship in *The Spanish Tragedy*, it makes sense that Kyd would be commissioned by Strange's Men to write the scenes deal-ing with the deaths of Talbot and his son. This is the very moment lauded by Nashe, who rarely shied away from promoting works in which he had a hand. The rhyming habits in Talbot's speech are strikingly similar not only to 4.6 but also to the remainder of 4.7 when the character of Sir William Lucy enters and provides an elegiac tribute to Talbot, a titular ancestor of Lord Strange. It's a moment of dramatic arse-kissing. The speech must have been part of the original 'Harey the vi' play performed by Strange's Men. Neither the internal nor external evidence suggests Shakespeare wrote Talbot's speech.

Other scenes are also up for grabs. Although 4.3 and 4.4 are some-times given to Shakespeare, they differ from his style in several respects. The opening sixteen lines of 4.3 display an older author's habits, bulging with *-ed* inflections, often given syllabic value in Kyd's plays: 'discoverèd' (4.3.6), 'promisèd' (4.3.10), 'Renownèd' (4.3.12), and so on. York uses the word 'cornets' (meaning a company of cavalry, or a troop of horsemen) in the line 'Doth stop my cornets' (4.3.25). Shakespeare never uses it during character dialogue in any of his plays. He sometimes employs this word in stage directions, but with a very different meaning: a cornet is also a brass instrument of course. The word appears in almost identical dramatic situations in Kyd's plays: during the General's speech in *The Spanish Tragedy* when he relates news from the war against Portugal, 'Did with his cornet bravely make attempt' (1.2.42), and in *Cornelia* when the Messenger delivers a speech reporting on a battle: 'Thrice did the cornets of the soldiers' (5.1.198).

In this scene Sir William Lucy enters and pleads with York to 'send some succour to the distressed lord' (4.3.30). Lucy is sometimes considered a Shakespearian character designed to honour Sir William Lucy of Charlecote who served as sheriff of Warwickshire during Henry VI's reign.[63] But Sir William Lucy can be found in both Edward Hall's *The Union of the Families of Lancastre and York* (1548) and Raphael Holinshed's *Chronicles*. These chronicles report that he rushed to join a battle but arrived too late and was killed with an axe by his wife's Yorkist lover. Did Kyd simply draw the name from this burningly memorable account in his source materials? York and Lucy's exchanges are written in Kyd's seemingly random fluctuations between rhymed and unrhymed lines, as in York's couplet, 'vexation almost stops my breath / That sundered friends greet **in the hour of death**' (4.3.41–2), which uniquely echoes *Soliman and Perseda*: 'Even **in the hour of death**' (5.4.96). York weeps '**cause I cannot** aid the man' (4.3.44), while Cornelia mourns: ''**cause I cannot** dry / Your ceaseless springs' (2.1.3–4).

Lucy is then left alone on stage to voice his concerns about England to the audience. He says: 'Thus while the vulture of sedition / Feeds in the bosom of such great commanders' (4.3.47–8). Lucy's imagery recalls classical figures like Prometheus and Tityus. The author of this speech 'constructs an image that is intelligible to groundling and noble alike' in *Henry VI Part One*, whereas a university-educated dramatist such as Marlowe might have been more inclined to include the Greek names. Around two-thirds of all classical allusions in this play are concentrated in Act 1, attributed to university-educated Nashe. Including the names of the mythological figures 'would distract his audience from the main purpose of the speech, which is to foreshadow that the factious English nobility, not the might of France, will be responsible for the loss of the dead king's French conquests'.[64] The author presses this point home in 4.7 when the French acknowledge that 'Had York and Somerset brought rescue in, / We should have found a bloody day of this' (4.7.33–4). Tityus's fate is transferred to the Duke of Castille at the conclusion of *The Spanish Tragedy*. Kyd also draws from the myth in *Cornelia* without explication: 'Or his whose soul the vulture seizeth on' (1.1.204). Similarly, the Chorus in *Cornelia* speak of 'Spiteful Hate' that 'pecks' the 'breast' (4.2.233) and makes 'souls' as 'sore / As Prometheus' ghost' (4.2.238–9), an allusion more closely resembling Lucy's than any other Elizabethan drama. In terms of style and dramaturgy Lucy's speech can't be detached from the text in the same way as Shakespeare's three scenes. Lucy's lines 'Who now **is** girdled with a waste of iron / And **hemmed about** with grim destruction' (4.3.20–1) anticipate the phrasing of a stage direction in the non-Shakespearian 4.6: '*John* **is hemmed about** *by French soldiers*' (4.6.0.1 SD). Again the evidence suggests that Lucy's dialogue belongs to the original 'Harey the vi' play. This phenomenon is characteristic of plays associated with Kyd, which often echo dialogue in stage directions.[65] When Bedford says that the French Dauphin and Joan Pucelle did 'Leap o'er the walls for refuge in the field' (*1H6*, 2.2.25), he's echoing the earlier direction: '*The French soldiers leap o'er* **the walls in** *their shirts*' (2.1.39.1 SD). In Elizabethan drama this direction is distinctive to *Soliman and Perseda*: during the thrilling ending to Kyd's play '*Perseda comes upon* **the walls in** *man's apparel*' (5.4.15.2 SD) and challenges Soliman to combat. Kyd's plays have a different printer provenance from *Henry VI Part One* and consensus holds that the Folio text originated in a manuscript not yet finalised by the prompter for performance. These stage directions are authorial.

Lucy's speech linking two scenes in which he pleads to separate characters is a brilliant moment of staging, the author playing fast and loose with sense of place and scene division.[66] This is classic Kydian craftsmanship. These scenes reveal, as one expert writes of *The Spanish Tragedy* and *Soliman and Perseda*, Kyd's 'emphasis on haste', the action forming 'a causal sequence. The causality of the action rather than a precise duration is expressed through the apparent temporal juxtaposition of the different scenes.'[67] Lucy disrupts scenic illusion and, like Revenge and the Ghost of Andrea, casts an ominous shadow over other characters in the play before getting involved in the tragic events himself. The great scholar and editor John Dover Wilson pointed out that 'In the first scene of Part II Gloucester gives a list of those who had shed their blood in

France to preserve what Henry V had won, and overlooks the name of Talbot altogether'. Gloucester does, however, list Somerset and York, 'who are represented in' 4.3 and 4.4 of 'Part I as factious traitors responsible for Talbot's death'.[68] These fundamental differences between the traitorous Somerset and York of *Henry VI Part One* and the celebrated figures in Shakespeare's *Henry VI Part Two* suggest Shakespeare wasn't responsible for 4.3 and 4.4 of the first part. His revision was limited to the three scenes of the play that help us recognise him as a man of the theatre, not above contributing to other playwrights' works. Such an undertaking would have been perfectly normal in Elizabethan theatre.

Over the centuries Shakespearians have been more inclined to view him as a writer occasionally paid to 'tinker and repatch old plays',[69] even when the evidence, unlike that for *Henry VI Part One*, points strongly towards simultaneous collaboration. Another chronicle history play, *The Reign of King Edward III*, was printed in 1596 with no author mentioned on its title page. *Edward III* has been attributed to Shakespeare on purely internal grounds since 1760.[70] The play is now universally acknowledged as an early Shakespeare collaboration. Shakespeare might have contributed to it at the end of 1593, not long after finishing *Richard III*, during a short period spent working for the company Derby's Men after Pembroke's Men collapsed. *Titus Andronicus* was also played by Derby's Men according to its 1594 quarto. Shakespeare wrote scenes 2 and 3, the Countess episode, which conjures memories of King Edward's wooing of Lady Jane Grey in *Henry VI Part Three*. He also contributed scene 12, in which the nobleman Audley meditates on death and Prince Edward is taunted by French heralds, which looks ahead to the taunting of the English King by the French Dauphin in *Henry V*. Shakespeare was commissioned to write scenes for which he was considered the ideal contributor. This pattern of writing earlier scenes and a later one could be an attempt by Shakespeare and his co-author to ensure some kind of stylistic continuity; it's a pattern that recurs in *Titus Andronicus*. The play draws from Holinshed's *Chronicles* and Jean Froissart's *Le Premier Volume de Froissart de Chroniques de Frances* (1513), with Shakespeare taking account of William

Painter's *The Palace of Pleasure* (1566) for the episode in which King Edward develops an adulterous fascination with the Countess of Salisbury (when quite frankly he should be going into battle with the French). It's been suggested that Shakespeare replaced Froissart's story of a now lost 'Ur-Countess' episode with the version found in Painter.[71] But couldn't Shakespeare have simply consulted both sources when he wrote his scenes? Given that Painter's *The Palace of Pleasure* was available as a source for over two decades, it's far easier to conclude, as an earlier scholar put it, that 'the dramatist merely followed the order of events that Froissart had established, and selected only certain details from Painter for the Countess scenes'.[72] The Countess episode is referred to in scenes attributed to Shakespeare's co-author: the King of France says that Edward 'th'other day was almost dead for love' (6.156) and Edward feels the need to justify that he is 'No love-sick cockney' (8.101). Do these references suggest that the authors worked together from a single plot scenario?

There seems to be some hesitance to acknowledge *Edward III* as an early co-authored play by Shakespeare.[73] *Edward III* is typical of simultaneous collaboration, in which one writer might allude to episodes written by their co-author, without necessarily having access to the details of those episodes beyond the plot outline. The theory that Shakespeare revised an older play seems weaker than for other plays Shakespeare is believed to have revised: Shakespeare's portions of *Edward III* are far more extensive than in the likes of *The Spanish Tragedy* and *Sir Thomas More*. While the thought of Shakespeare guiding younger dramatists in his later co-authored plays has become acceptable, it seems there's an unwillingness to accept Shakespeare himself being guided in earlier collaborations. The apologist narrative of Shakespeare as reviser tallies with E. K. Chambers's claim that Shakespeare was responsible only for scene 2 from the entrance of King Edward, echoed in editions of this play.[74] Yet there is a remarkable shift in language right from the beginning of the scene.[75] The whole rhythmic structure of the verse is of a different order in the Countess's opening speech:

Alas, how much in vain my poor eyes gaze
For succour that my sovereign should send.
Ah, cousin Montague, I fear thou wants
The lively spirit sharply to solicit
With vehement suit the King in my behalf.
Thou dost not tell him what a grief it is
To be the scornful captive to a Scot,
Either to be wooed with broad untunèd oaths
Or forced by rough insulting barbarism.
Thou dost not tell him, if he here prevail,
How much they will deride us in the North,
And, in their vile, uncivil, skipping jigs
Bray forth their conquest and our overthrow
Even in the barren, bleak and fruitless air. (2.1–14)

Provocative insults aimed at the Scottish in this scene prick the eye and ear. The Countess describes the 'confident and boist'rous boasting' (2.75) Scots as 'Vile, uncivil' (2.12). Is this a case of editors trying to absolve Shakespeare by denying him these passages? A letter written by the diplomat George Nicolson in 1598 complains of such negative depictions of the Scottish on stage, which could 'stir the King and country to anger thereat'. It would take a brave publisher to risk having his nose or ears slit by printing the play during James's reign. This is a compelling explanation for why the play wasn't included in Shakespeare's First Folio.

Thomas Kyd has been proposed as Shakespeare's co-author since the late nineteenth century, when attention was first drawn to the striking similarities between the Mariner's account of the naval Battle of Sluys in scene 4 and the General's account of a battle with the Portuguese in *The Spanish Tragedy*, which Kyd modelled partly on the Messenger's account of the Battle of Thapsus in Robert Garnier's *Cornélie*.[76] Just as Shakespeare appears to have been considered the ideal author for certain episodes, Kyd was certainly the ideal choice to compose such retrospectively related action. The evidence for Kyd's authorship of the non-Shakespearian portions of the play is powerful, ranging from Kyd's engagement with sources such as Seneca and Garnier; verse style; vocabulary; and Kyd's distinct phrasing. All these tests link the non-Shakespeare portions of *Edward III* to Kyd's sole-authored plays as well as the scenes attributed to him in *Henry VI Part One*. These portions also reveal Kyd's habit of interspersing complicated rhyme forms in his blank verse. The very opening lines of the play provide a great example. Edward tells Artois that

> banished though thou be
> From France thy native country, yet with us
> Thou shalt retain as great a seigniory:
> For we create thee Earl of Richmond here.
> And now go forward with our pedigree. (1.1–5)

This use of interrupted rhyme contrasts with Shakespeare's Countess scenes, which, befitting love poetry, employ rhyming couplets. Again we see stylistic differences between the playwrights' use of rhyme.

Kyd's portions of the play closely resemble the 'misfit' Kyd scenes in *Henry VI Part One*, which are unlike Shakespeare's 'autumnal and pessimistic' sole-authored history plays in their 'comparative optimism and jingoism'.[77] Did Shakespeare remember the disparate tones of these collaborative efforts when he came to write *Henry V*? Shakespeare's incorporation of a Greek chorus in *Henry V* casts a shadow over what appears, on the surface, to be a jingoistic, pro-war play concluding in a happy marriage. Like the choric figures of Exeter and Lucy in Kyd's portions of *Henry VI Part One*, the Chorus in *Henry V* foretells England's downfall, reminding the audience that 'oft our stage hath shown' (Epilogue.13) the disasters of Henry VI's reign. The providential design of Kyd's dramas, influenced mainly by Seneca's tragedies, dovetailed with the providentialism of the chronicle history materials these writers were consulting.

Shakespeare recalled his early collaborations with Kyd and engaged particularly closely with *The Spanish Tragedy*, the lost *Hamlet*, *Soliman and Perseda*, and *King Leir* when he embarked on his great tragic run. Much attention has been paid to Shakespeare's borrowings from university-educated playwrights like Marlowe. The time has come to recognise the remarkable extent to which Shakespeare was also arrayed with his fellow non-university-educated dramatist's feathers.

5

Robert Greene

From county Kent, paradise of gentlemen and commoners alike, to the sprawling metropolis of early modern London, borne by the wings of historical knowledge we now make our way to the second most populated place in Elizabethan England: Norwich. There were around twelve thousand people residing in this cathedral city, far fewer than in London, which would swell to a staggering population of two hundred thousand by 1600. Dedicated to the slayer of dragons who served as patron saint, St George's, Tombland, had been largely rebuilt in the thirteenth century. Tombland means 'empty space', which might evoke theatrical connotations for some readers. This is fitting because on 11 July 1558 the future playwright Robert Greene (1558–92) was baptised in that pretty flint church.[1] Greene's parentage is uncertain: he was the son of either a saddler or an innkeeper. Either way he hailed from Norwich and had humble beginnings. He must have attended the Norwich Grammar School, one of the oldest schools in the country, traceable from as far back as the eleventh century, before being entered as a sizar at St John's College in Cambridge.

In the 1580s Greene established his literary reputation as a writer of pamphlets before turning his hand to also writing for the commercial stage. In the first-person pamphlet *The Repentance of Robert Greene* (1592) he claims that he married a gentleman's daughter but deserted her when she bore him a child; he settled in London while she went back to Lincolnshire. Greene had a son named Fortunatus by a mistress who was the sister of a notorious criminal named

Cutting Ball. Greene's death on 3 September 1592, at the age of thirty-four, preceded his son's by almost a year. Greene had the double misfortune of an infamous death, which was announced by a literary rival. Gabriel Harvey attributed Greene's demise to 'a surfeit of pickle herring and Rhenish wine' in *Four Letters and Certain Sonnets* (1592). A 'fatal banquet' indeed with strong insinuations that Greene's ending mirrored a life of debauchery. Harvey also claimed that Greene was buried in a churchyard near Bedlam (a hospital for mentally ill patients) on 4 September, but no record of this burial has been discovered. Do unsuspecting feet tread over his bones today, his remains now far from green beneath the earth? It's tempting to try and piece out the imperfections of available documentary evidence through Greene's biographical claims in his pamphlets. Stanley Wells is right to point out though that 'Greene was so much a master of the journalistic skill of turning anything that happened to him into copy for the printers that it is difficult to distinguish between fact and fiction in his writings'.[2]

The generic range of Greene's literary output is startling: Romances, pastoral works, as well as repentance and so-called cony-catching pamphlets teeming with trickery. If Greene's name is mentioned at all today, however, it's usually in relation to *Greene's Groatsworth of Wit* and is often met with judgemental frowns or an ironical squirm of the eyebrow. This pamphlet has overshadowed Greene's reputation as an Elizabethan playwright through invidious comparisons between his plays and those of Shakespeare. Did Shakespeare engage with the diatribe that provides the first reference to him as an actor-dramatist in London? Might Shakespeare have lampooned Greene in the role of Falstaff, a sleazy, parasitical titan of a man? Or did Shakespeare respond to Greene's attack in *The Comedy of Errors* when Dromio of Ephesus tries to help his master, Antipholus, get into his own house? Antipholus asks for a crow (or crowbar), which befuddles his servant, who struggles to picture a crow without feathers. Would Shakespeare's audience have been in on the joke? Is this a winky-nudgy point that Shakespeare had every right to enter the profession as a playwright, that he was not, as Greene put it, a mere 'upstart crow'? Shakespeare would use Greene's *Pandosto* (1588) as a source for *The Winter's Tale*. In doing so he made a conscious decision to versify Greene's prose Romance. Was this a riposte to Greene's criticism of Shakespeare's early verse style? Shakespeare triumphs over Greene, but Greene in turn triumphs over Shakespeare, his criticism continuing to tread on Shakespeare's metrical feet long after his death.[3]

Although Greene is recognised as a prolific pamphleteer, his significant place in the rise of commercial drama hasn't been properly recognised. Greene's traditionally accepted surviving plays are *Alphonsus, King of Aragon; Friar Bacon and Friar Bungay* (1589); *James IV* (1590); and *Orlando Furioso*. He co-authored *A Looking-Glass for London and England* with Thomas Lodge. Greene's dramas are particularly notable in their inventive use of theatrical effects, his skilful blending of materials, groundbreaking mingling of plots and subplots, and his creation of new genres. Greene 'demonstrated clearly to his contemporaries', as one rare admirer put it, 'what manifold potentialities lay ready to be exploited by anyone who refused to be bound by the conventions of existing *genres*, and who set out in a new spirit of freedom to interweave dramatic types of the greatest diversity'.[4] Greene seizes on innovations in machinery, making as much use of the stage as theatrical exigencies will allow, especially when presenting magic. His plays are also highly entertaining, packed with intrigue plots and ingenious disguises.

In what is likely his first play, *Alphonsus, King of Aragon*, Greene aimed to capitalise on the bone-shuddering success of Marlowe's *Tamburlaine the Great*. The London theatrical scene was 'a system of community of ideas' in which 'Greene was entirely at home. Of this we have abundant evidence in his often displayed ability to feel the popular pulse, and to make himself a part of every growing movement.'[5] The heroical Romance *Alphonsus, King of Aragon* showcases the visual nature of Greene's theatre. It opens with the striking theatrical device of Venus being '*let down from the top of the Stage*' (Prologue SD).[6] A chair draws Venus upwards at the end of the play. Greene makes maximal use of stage machinery and properties. Later in the play there's another example of Greene's spectacular stagecraft in the direction: '*Let there be a Brazen Head set in the middle of the place behind the stage, out of the which cast flames of fire, drums rumble within'* (4.1 SD). Stagehands must have employed pyrotechnics to depict fire emanating from this brazen head. Greene, like Shakespeare after him, always had staging possibilities firmly in mind when composing his plays, sniffing out spectacle at any opportunity. Sometimes Greene's cues for visual theatre strain credulity. Some of his effects are so daring they might not yet have been achievable on the commercial stage.[7] Greene's imagination was colossal, difficult to constrain. It often strides beyond the limits of playing spaces, his effects prompting companies to innovate in ways that must have snatched at the throats of awestruck audience members.

Friar Bacon and Friar Bungay, with its fusion of a love story between Prince Edward, the Earl Lacy, and the beautiful daughter of a gamekeeper named Margaret, as well as popular traditions concerning Roger Bacon's magical skills, is by far Greene's most popular play. Stanley Wells notes that the 'terms in which Prince Edward speaks of the beautiful Margaret of Fressingfield' at the beginning of the play 'have a lyric grace that looks forward to Florizel's descriptions of the supposed shepherdess Perdita' in Shakespeare's *The Winter's Tale*.[8] Prince Edward tells his companion, Lacy, the Earl of Lincoln,

> that her sparkling eyes
> Do lighten forth sweet love's alluring fire;
> And in her tresses she doth fold the looks
> Of such as gaze upon her golden hair:
> Her bashful white, mix'd with the morning's red,
> Luna doth boast upon her lovely cheeks;
> Her front is beauty's table, where she paints
> The glories of her gorgeous excellence;
> Her teeth are shelves of precious margarites,
> Richly enclos'd with ruddy coral cleeves.
> Tush, Lacy, she is beauty's over-match,
> If thou survey'st her curious imagery. (1.1)

Greene is a master of assembling stock ingredients with melodic charm. The play also validates Thomas Nashe's observation in *Have with You to Saffron Walden* (1596) that Greene was his 'crafts master' at 'plotting Plaies'. Greene weaves together two distinct plots: the love triangle of Prince Edward, Lacy, and Margaret with the account of Friar Bacon and his magical endeavours. Some have gone so far as to suggest that Greene invented the double plot, distinct from plays with comic subplots, while others have proposed multiple structural components in this play.[9] Uncertainties over the configurations of Greene's dramatic narrative attest to the play's admirable intricacies, its ambitious dramatic structure, its expertly constructed scenes. The play also affords several opportunities for stunning visual theatre, most notably in Greene's ingenious reuse of the brazen head prop as well as magical battles that conjure thoughts of scenes from the *Harry Potter* franchise.

In one of the play's better-known scenes Bacon is exhausted by his labour and asks his servant, Miles, to wake him if the brazen head speaks. Miles doesn't find the head's statements 'Time is' and 'Time was' sufficient to alert his master: 'Well, Friar Bacon, you have spent your seven years' study well, that can make your head speak but two words at once' (4.1). The head expands its vocabulary and says, 'Time is past' (4.1). A hand clutching a hammer appears and smashes the head into pieces: '*A lightning flashes forth, and a hand appears that breaks down the Head with a hammer*' (4.1 SD). Again, as in *Alphonsus, King of Aragon*, Greene takes advantage of striking stage effects. Earlier in the play the friar invites Prince Edward to look into a magical glass, through which he can see Margaret and Lacy in Fressingfield. Here we have a 'split' scene in which Prince Edward and Bacon stand on the inner stage and 'look directly in the glass' (2.3) while Margaret and Friar Bungay enter the outer stage. This moment is testament to Greene's skilled stagecraft, the simultaneous scenes taking place miles apart in Oxford and Fressingfield. Such scenes, ferocious in their daring, anticipate Shakespeare's craftsmanship, like when Iago co-ordinates the eavesdropping scheme in *Othello*, rendering his intended victims, Cassio and Othello, the observed and the observer.

The biblical play *A Looking-Glass for London and England* pours comic and tragic matter into an aggressive shaker. Greene once again takes full advantage of stage effects, such as ascending and descending allegorical figures and bursts of fireworks when characters leap into flames or find themselves struck by lightning bolts, as in the stage direction: *'Lightning and thunder, wherewith REMILIA is strucken'* (2.1 SD). At one point in this play Jonah is thrown overboard and swallowed by a whale. In Lodge, Greene found a Garfunkel to his Simon.[10] Lodge was the son of Sir Thomas Lodge, who became Lord Mayor of London in 1562. He went on to take his BA at Trinity College, Oxford, in 1577 and his MA there four years later. He was closely associated with the Stanley family: a page to Henry Stanley and his son, William Stanley, Lodge spent his salad days in the Stanley household. He entered Lincoln's Inn in April 1578 but shook a defiant fist at his family's wishes, turning that hand to writing literature rather than becoming a lawyer. *Rosalind: Euphues' Golden Legacy* (1590) is his most famous work; it inspired Shakespeare to write *As You Like It*. Lodge would later pursue a medical career in London and France. He took refuge abroad as a Catholic recusant before going back to London. Plague brought an end to his rainbowed life in 1625.

Greene's extraordinary generic range can also be seen in *James IV*, for which he drew from a tale by Italian writer Giraldi Cinthio and again fused comic matter with darker material. This innovative drama defies categorisation and looks forward to the tragicomedies of John Fletcher and Francis Beaumont, particularly in its comic ending, which seems particularly dark in light of Greene's exploration of courtly corruption and King James's villainy. It also looks forward to Shakespeare's later plays, which are similarly difficult to pigeonhole in terms of genre, the ambiguous endings of works like *Measure for Measure* (1603). In *James IV*, Greene exploits the opportunity to experiment with male actors playing female characters disguised as boys. Queen Dorothea disguises herself as a male to escape her husband, who has murder on the brain. She's taken in by Sir Cuthbert Anderson, whose wife falls in love with her. This relationship recalls the exploration of cross-dressing heroines in Renaissance Italian works as well as the dramas of John Lyly. It also looks forward to Shakespeare's comedies, such as *The Two Gentlemen of Verona*, *As You Like It*, and *Twelfth Night*.

That Greene's reputation as a playwright in his own time was greater than it is today can be gleaned from the fact that *Orlando Furioso* is the only traditionally accepted play of his not featuring his name or initials on the First Quarto title page. However, in the pamphlet *A Defence of Cony-catching* (1592) Greene is charged with selling the play first to the Queen's Men and then to the Admiral's Men: 'Master R.G., would it not make you blush – if you sold *Orlando Furioso* to the Queen's players for twenty nobles, and when they were in the country, sold the same to Lord Admiral's men, for as much more?' Greene was desperate for money: the wolf was clawing at his door, its howls rising in pitch, affronting Greene's ears. But Greene was no mere hack writer jumping from company to company, churning out work just to survive without consideration of artistic merit. Evidence suggests that Greene intended all his plays originally for the Queen's Men. He was a leading dramatist for the leading company of the 1580s. He was one of the most important playwrights of his day, a fact obscured by the ravages of time and critical opinion.

Like *James IV* in particular, *Orlando Furioso* is a difficult play to classify, consisting of elements of chivalric Romance but also revenge tragedy. *Orlando Furioso* fits into the vogue for presenting stage madness, as seen in plays such as *The Spanish Tragedy* and probably the lost *Hamlet* play. It looks ahead to Shakespeare's exploration of madness as a dramatically effective voice for grief and tragedy. *Orlando Furioso* reveals the growing Senecanism of Greene's plays, perhaps in the wake of Kyd's big-splash dramas. Greene skilfully absorbs, interrogates, and parodies growing trends in Elizabethan drama, such as Senecan influences and the presentation of Machiavellian villains. In a pioneering study of the reception history of the Italian diplomat and philosopher Niccolò Machiavelli in Tudor culture, Ateukin in *James IV* is labelled 'a fox' who later 'shows himself to be a repentant coward'. Rather than being a 'Marlowesque villain', he's regarded as an ancestor of similar figures in works by Beaumont and Fletcher.[11] In *Orlando Furioso*, Greene presents another repentant Machiavellian villain in Sacrapant. He begins the play with a thirst for blood and ambition:

> Sacrapant must have Angelica,
> And with her Sacrapant must have the crown:
> By hook or crook I must and will have both.
> Ah sweet Revenge, incense their angry minds,
> Till, all these princes weltering in their bloods,
> The crown do fall to County Sacrapant! (1.1)

By the end of the play, he is overcome with remorse:

> O, that's the sting that pricks my conscience!
> O, that's the hell my thoughts abhor to think!
> I tell thee, knight, for thou dost seem no less,
> That I engrav'd the roundelays on the trees,
> And hung the schedules of poor Medor's love,
> Intending so to breed debate
> Between Orlando and Angelica:
> O, thus I wrong'd Orlando and Angelica! (5.1)

So, at a time when villains such as Marlowe's Barabas were cursing their enemies on stage while in the very throes of agonising death (boiled alive in a cauldron, a trap of his own making), Greene was presenting Machiavellian figures who anticipated the likes of Shakespeare's Edmund in *King Lear*. Like his dramatic forebears, Edmund acknowledges in Shakespeare's tragedy that 'The wheel is come full circle' (5.3.170) and means to do some good 'Despite of my own nature' (5.3.240). Greene's repentant Machiavels complicate audience perceptions of villainy, breaking the wood for Shakespeare to carve out his villains, the heaps of contradictions made all the more human by their redeeming features, just as Shakespeare's heroes often reveal darker characteristics.

Did Shakespeare beautify himself with Greene's dramatic language? Or did he consider Greene's phrases vile? According to *Collocations and N-grams*, there's little indication that *Alphonsus, King of Aragon* influenced Shakespeare. The top plays are dominated by other works attributed to Greene, as well as Marlowe's *Tamburlaine* plays, which are ranked eighth and ninth. From the beginning to the very end of Greene's career, Marlowe's influence infected him like a disease. He repeatedly went back to the likes of the *Tamburlaine* plays and *Doctor Faustus*, duplicating, interrogating, subverting, and mocking Marlowe. This long wrestling match is reflected in the results for all of Greene's plays. The top Shakespeare play for *Alphonsus, King of Aragon* is *The Two Gentlemen of Verona* in thirty-fourth place, followed by *Richard II* at fifty-fourth. In the spreadsheet for *Friar Bacon and Friar Bungay* comparing that play to all others of the period for phrases found nowhere else, we find that *Richard III* is ranked fifteenth, followed by *The Merry Wives of Windsor* at position thirty-three. The most striking phrase shared between *Friar Bacon and Friar Bungay* and Shakespeare can be found in *Twelfth Night*: Prince Edward has sent Lacy to woo Margaret by proxy. But Lacy has fallen in love with her himself. Edward rages: 'Did I **unfold the passions of my love**' (3.1). In *Twelfth Night*, Duke Orsino sends the disguised Viola to woo Olivia on his behalf: 'O then **unfold the passion of my love**' (1.4.24). *The Two Gentlemen of Verona* fares better in the spreadsheet for *James IV* in twenty-third position. *The Taming of the Shrew* follows at thirty-one. But none of the matching phrases between these plays is particularly striking: the image of 'beauteous looks' can be found in *James IV*, *Friar Bacon and Friar Bungay*, and *The Taming of the Shrew*, but it also recurs in Thomas Dekker's *Old Fortunatus* (1599). Shakespeare doesn't seem to have been drawn to the language of *Orlando Furioso*: his *King John* is ranked a lowly eighty-first in the spreadsheet for that play. The Orlando of Greene's play and the Orlando of *As You Like It* share some similarities. They both post love poems on trees, which echoes Ludovico Ariosto's epic poem *Orlando Furioso* (1516) and John Harington's English translation (1591). Love is indeed a kind of madness in these works. And yet *As You Like It* is ranked ninetieth in the spreadsheet for *Orlando Furioso* and Greene's play is ranked even lower at position 164 for Shakespeare's comedy. It's ironic that for all the talk of plagiarism surrounding Shakespeare and *Greene's Groatsworth of Wit*, the results in comparison to the plays of Marlowe and Kyd contrast severely.

The unsure boundaries of Greene's canon have long hampered an appreciation of him as a playwright who helped to define Elizabethan drama. Several anonymous plays have been associated with him, and fresh evidence suggests that the tragedies *Locrine* (1591) and

Selimus (1591) should be admitted into his canon. The latter play seems to have been another collaboration between Greene and Lodge.[12] The attribution of parts of *Selimus*, a Queen's Men play, to Lodge has important implications for our understanding of the company origins of *A Looking-Glass for London and England*. Despite his deep-rooted associations with the Stanley family, Lodge was clearly willing to write for companies other than Strange's Men,[13] so *A Looking-Glass for London and England* was probably written for the Queen's Men too.

Locrine dramatises the tale of the Trojan founders of England and Troynovant, the name given by early chroniclers to London. Brutus divides his kingdom among his three sons, which, as in *King Lear* and other early modern plays, has inevitably dreadful consequences. The play has a long history of being attributed to Greene on textual and bibliographical grounds, its distinct use of comedy, richness of classical allusions, and its verse style.[14] The tragedy was described as 'Newly set forth, overseen and corrected, By W.S.' when it was published by Thomas Creede in 1595, which led to its inclusion by Philip Chetwinde in Shakespeare's 1664 Third Folio. Creede was responsible for publishing Greene and Lodge's *A Looking-Glass for London and England* in 1594, Greene's *James IV* in 1598, and *Alphonsus, King of Aragon* in 1599. The title-page attribution to 'W.S.' is seldom taken as serious evidence for Shakespeare's hand.

Potential red herrings abound when it comes to this play: a manuscript note written by George Buc in a surviving copy of the 1595 quarto identifies *Locrine* as a play called *Estrild*, written by Charles Tilney, who was executed in 1586 for attempting to assassinate Elizabeth I and replace the monarch with her Catholic cousin, Mary, Queen of Scots. Buc claims that he made the dumb shows (miniplays largely acted in mime) for this play. But *Locrine*'s spectacular dumb shows are intensely characteristic of Greene in the language of stage directions and dramaturgy; they can't be detached from the remainder of the play. The framing device involving the goddess Atè most closely resembles *James IV*, in which dumb shows also serve as an instructive part of the choric narrative.

Although there's evidence of a revising hand in the surviving text, 'W.S.' is almost certainly not Shakespeare, for whom there's little indication he had even read or seen, let alone revised, *Locrine*. The one stretch of text that we can attribute with confidence to this mysterious 'W.S.' is the play's Epilogue, which was apparently new in 1595 as it refers to the thirty-eighth year of Elizabeth I's reign (a slight inaccuracy as Elizabeth ascended the throne in 1558). Atè enters and concludes the play:

> Lo! Here the end of lawless treachery,
> Of usurpation and ambitious pride,
> And they that for their private amours dare
> Turmoil our land, and set their broils abroach,
> Let them be warnèd by these premises.
> And as a woman was the only cause
> That civil discord was then stirrèd up,
> So let us pray for that renownèd maid,
> That eight and thirty years the sceptre swayed
> In quiet peace and sweet felicity;
> And every wight that seeks her grace's smart,
> Would that this sword were pierced in his heart. (Epilogue.1–12)

This is an archaic verse style. The triple repetition of the *-ed* inflection in 'warnèd', 'stirrèd', and 'renownèd' thrums the ear. The monotonous thud of ten-syllable lines is utterly unlike Shakespeare, especially during his more lyrical phase around 1595. This seems to be the work of an older-generation playwright sharing Shakespeare's initials, perhaps even older than Greene. Although *Locrine* fits into Greene's stylistic habits in practically every respect, there are some very minor differences: the play features more *-ed* and *-eth* words than other Greene plays. Could Greene have revised an older, lost play by Tilney?[15] It's far more likely that Greene was wholly responsible for *Locrine*, which was revised by an even more old-school playwright who peppered the text with archaisms. The evidence is plain to see in the style of this Epilogue and the title-page attribution.

Journalists took to the field when new evidence for Greene's authorship of *Locrine* was first publicised in the autumn of 2020. The narrative fixated on Greene's 'sneering dismissal of William Shakespeare' and the suggestion 'that his young contemporary was a plagiarist', lending a delicious irony to the fact that new research 'attributed to him a play – a revenge tragedy no less – that appeared under Shakespeare's name in the Third and Fourth Folios' of 1664 and 1685.[16] Whilst *Greene's Groatsworth of Wit* has served to link Shakespeare and Greene for ever, the attribution of *Locrine* to Greene provides another link through Chetwinde's misattribution of the play to Shakespeare, along with the inclusion of several other non-Shakespearian dramas, in the Third Folio. The 'expanded' Greene canon shows him to have worked almost exclusively for the Queen's Men playing company, so the context of theatrical competition becomes even more important when comparing these dramatists. In comparison to Shakespeare's debts to Marlowe and Kyd there's very little evidence of so-called 'plagiarisms' from Greene's dramatic language. Yet Shakespeare would go on to adapt several plays associated with the Queen's Men, such as *The Famous Victories of Henry V* (1586) and *The Troublesome Reign of King John* (1589). The attribution of *Locrine* to Greene strongly suggests that the tragedy belonged to that company.[17] In working for competing companies Greene and Shakespeare could be considered rival playwrights. Greene was evidently a far more commercially attractive dramatist than has been recognised, with playing companies such as Lord Strange's Men attempting to take advantage of successful elements of his dramaturgy in plays such as *Fair Em* and the sequel to *Friar Bacon and Friar Bungay*, titled *John of Bordeaux* (1591). Here we witness the 'commercial strategy of the companies', which was 'to duplicate the popular offerings of their competitors'.[18]

Selimus, like *Alphonsus, King of Aragon*, features 'Turk motifs'. The play tells the tale of the Ottoman Sultan, Selim I, also known by such ominous titles as Selim the Grim or Selim the Inexorable, so not the kind of bloke you'd go to the pub with. As is characteristic of Greene's approach to dramatising history, staged events flirt heavily with inaccuracies. The 1594 quarto, again printed by Creede, tells us that 'it was playd by the Queenes Majesties Players'. A second edition of *Selimus* printed in 1638 lists the play's author on its title page as 'T.G.'. It has been proposed that the initials on the title page might be an 'unlucky misprint for R.G.'.[19] Passages from the play were attributed to Greene in the verse compilation *England's Parnassus* (1600), providing firm external evidence for Greene's hand in the play.[20] Could the misprint on the title page of the second edition be down to a conflation of its authors' initials: 'T.L.' and 'R.G.'?

Links between *Selimus* and Shakespeare plays, especially *Titus Andronicus* and *King Lear*, have long been noted.[21] *Selimus* is ranked twenty-fifth in the spreadsheet for *Titus Andronicus* in *Collocations and N-grams*. But the verbal echoes in *King Lear* are faint: Greene and Lodge's play is ranked low at 253. None the less, these three plays are tied together by moments of horrific violence. The most harrowing moment in *Selimus* is when Acomat (son of Bajazet) plucks out the eyes of Aga (a messenger to Bajazet) and lops off his hands in portions most securely given to Lodge. There are clear similarities between Aga's violent torture and that endured by Gloucester in *King Lear*, the sensationalised violence used for entertainment purposes, a form of morose delectation that can still be found in the horror genre today. Shakespeare's possible borrowings from *Selimus* go well beyond the aesthetics of violence though. They touch upon the very heart of Shakespeare's conceptualisation of tragedy. Aga's lament, 'Thou shouldst have slain me, barbarous Acomat, / Not leave me in so comfortless a life; / To live on earth, and never see the sun' (ll. 1423–5), anticipates Gloucester's unbearable suffering: 'All dark and comfortless. Where's my son, Edmund? / Edmund, enkindle all the sparks of nature / To quite this horrid act' (3.7.82–4). Acomat responds to Aga with an order to have his hands lopped off. Regan's response to Gloucester is even more devastating: she reveals to Gloucester that his own son, Edmund, has betrayed him. Regan confirms that the characters in the play are operating in a Senecan universe in which, as Gloucester puts it, 'Love cools, friendship falls off, brothers divide; in cities, mutinies; in countries, discord; in palaces, treason; and the bond cracked 'twixt son and father' (1.2.106–9). The brutality of *King Lear* is effectively showcased in Peter Brook's 1971 film version: a barren world of howling winds and hissing snakes of snow. Shakespeare engaged closely with an episode in Philip Sidney's *Arcadia* (1590) when he composed the Gloucester plotline. But it seems likely that he also remembered the devastating betrayal of Bajazet, Emperor of Turkey, by his son to create the tragic universe of his bleakest play. This idea is supported by the unique match between Bajazet's offer to comfort Aga, '**Give me thy arm**; though thou hast lost thy hands' (l. 1582), and the moment when Edgar guides his blind father: '**Give me thy arm**' (4.1.73).

Selimus has stronger links with Shakespeare's *King John* than it does with *King Lear*: it's ranked forty-third out of all plays in *Collocations and N-grams* for unique phrases shared with *King John*. In Shakespeare's history play, Arthur escapes the horrific tortures endured by Aga and Gloucester when Hubert gives in to Arthur's pleas, refusing to burn the boy's eyes out. Shakespeare returned to that earlier sequence when he composed Gloucester's blinding. The image of eyes can be found in one of the unique matches between these plays: Bajazet says, 'Why, thus must Selim blind his subjects' **eyes**, / **And strain** his own to weep for Bajazet' (ll. 2003–4), while King John speaks of 'that idiot, laughter' which can 'keep men's **eyes** / **And strain** their cheeks' (3.3.45–6).

Shakespeare had an eye on Greene's plays, which must have influenced his stagecraft and approach to dramatic genres. Although Greene's dramas showcase a brilliant imagination and an expert approach to plotting, there's scant verbal evidence to suggest that Shakespeare took inspiration from his writing style. Did Shakespeare deliberately avoid copying Greene's dramatic language in the wake of the *Groatsworth of Wit* attack? Either way the Romance elements of plays by Shakespeare, as well as dramatists such as Fletcher and Beaumont, would be quite different if not for Greene's contributions to Elizabethan repertoires. Shakespeare's tragic plays would also be quite different if not for Greene's influences on the evolution of that genre. Greene's feathers, far more colourful than often credited, helped the works of later playwrights to take flight.

6

George Peele

We wing our way back to London. The year 1556 was like many others during the period: thwarted usurpation attempts and the air thick with the stink of burning martyrs. Perhaps the ghostly scent of garlic, sold nearby during the medieval period, still lingered in attenders' imaginations when George Peele (1556–96) was baptised on 25 July at St James Garlickhythe.[1] He was the son of James Peele, a writer of two treatises on the practice of bookkeeping and clerk of the grammar school Christ's Hospital in Newgate, which was founded by Edward VI and where Peele was educated. In 1571 Peele entered Broadgates Hall, which became Pembroke College, Oxford. Three years later he removed to Christ Church. It was here that Peele first turned his hand to dramatic writing: a translation of a play by the Greek tragedian Euripides. He was awarded his BA in 1577 and his MA followed two years later.

In 1580 Peele married Ann Cooke, the daughter of an Oxford merchant, and he moved back to London the following year. Alongside writing for the commercial stage in London, Peele followed in his father's footsteps by contributing to Lord Mayor's shows; other poet-dramatists such as Thomas Dekker, Anthony Munday, Thomas Middleton, and Ben Jonson would in turn follow in his footsteps. Peele was even entrusted with the arrangement of two Latin plays by the academic dramatist William Gager at Christ Church, despite having left the college several years earlier. Peele's non-dramatic works include *The Tale of Troy*, a retelling of the fall of Troy drawing from the works of Ovid, William Caxton, and John Lydgate, first published in 1589, and *The Honour of the Garter*, written to celebrate the Earl of Northumberland's installation as a Knight of the Garter in 1593. Despite his career as a courtly poet and a writer of pageants and plays, Peele died in poverty in 1596. The cause of his death was the pox according to Francis Meres's testimony, hinting at a debauched life not dissimilar to Robert Greene's. Buried on 9 November, Peele's reputation among contemporaries such as Greene, Meres, Dekker, and Thomas Nashe as a formidable poet and scholar subsequently gave way to a reputation for waywardness. One story in circulation has him attending a posh dinner and insulting a witty gentlewoman sitting next to him. When the lady leaned forward at the table, Peele apparently let out a huge fart, drawing the eyes and flaring the nostrils of all other dinner guests. Peele nudged the lady's elbow and reassured her in a loud voice that he'd say he was responsible. Such jesting accounts were often attached to famous figures during the period, and claims of Peele's riotous living are open to scrutiny.[2] Either way these tales contribute to a picture of Elizabethan playwrights who worked hard but played even harder.

Like his fellow university-educated dramatist, Greene, with whom he was closely associated, Peele was eclectic, writing plays in a variety of genres as well as embracing hybrid dramatic forms with widespread arms. His acknowledged surviving canon is made up of the pastoral *The Arraignment of Paris*, which was written mostly in heroic couplets and as we've seen was performed by the Children of the Chapel; *The Battle of Alcazar*, a feast of violence and bombast performed by Lord Admiral's Men; *David and Bathsheba* (1590), which, like Greene and Thomas Lodge's *A Looking-Glass for London and England*, drew from an Old Testament source (in this case, II Samuel); the history plays *The Troublesome Reign of King John*,[3] which was written for the Queen's Men playing company, and *Edward I*; the comic Romance *The Old Wife's Tale* (1592), again written for the Queen's Men; and *Titus Andronicus*, which he co-wrote with Shakespeare.

He's been described as 'the most neglected yet the most versatile of all the major Elizabethan playwrights',[4] but fairly little has been written about Peele's influence on Shakespeare. Yet Shakespeare seems to have recalled the Chorus in Peele's dramatisation of the 1578 Battle of Alcácer Quibir in *The Battle of Alcazar*, which adds a sense of the epic to the play's action in much the same way as is achieved by Shakespeare's use of the Greek Chorus in *Henry V*. That Shakespeare had *The Battle of Alcazar* in mind when composing his *Henry IV* and *Henry V* plays is suggested by Pistol's ranty misrememberings of Peele's play and Marlowe's *Tamburlaine*. The impulse to parody thrummed through Peele's veins and he often undercuts Marlovian rhetoric, something we also see in Hotspur's deluded heroism in the *Henry IV* plays.[5] It's also possible that Shakespeare recalled the tyrant Muly Mahamet's command, 'A horse, a horse, villaine a horse' (5.1.1288),[6] in *The Battle of Alcazar* for Richard's far more famous request at the Battle of Bosworth in *Richard III*.

Shakespeare might have been influenced by Peele's use of the framing device in *The Old Wife's Tale*, a play that has attracted more attention than many of Peele's other efforts and has been described as 'a delicate and delightfully inconsequential fantasy' that 'gently satirises chivalric romances'.[7] The play begins with three servants lost in the woods, who are rescued by a blacksmith. He invites them to stay at his cottage, in which his wife tells them a fairy tale. The metatheatricality of this play, with its incorporation of the device of a play-within-a-play through storytelling, resembles Shakespeare's *The Taming of the Shrew* and in particular the choric role of John Gower in *Pericles*. Peele's weaving of contrasting elements and motifs certainly anticipates Shakespeare's late Romance plays. *The Old Wife's Tale* has been called 'the most ingeniously constructed play of its time, without any true precedent or descendant', and although 'other playwrights tried to imitate it, no one managed to do so', Shakespeare included.[8] The play is testament to Peele's skilled craftsmanship, his integration of narrative and visual theatre, his seamless stitching together of plot strands while making full use of properties to stage the numerous locations traversed in the play.[9]

Peele's nationalistic plays like *Edward I* helped pave the way for Shakespeare's popular history dramas. Peele can be credited with not only recognising potential in dramatising English history but also blending his treatments with motifs more commonly associated with Roman tragedy. Dramatists like Kyd and Shakespeare followed suit, while Greene blends Senecanism with British history in *Locrine*. Peele's visual theatre resembles Greene's and is characteristic of plays in the Queen's Men repertory, whereas Shakespeare places more emphasis on auditory techniques, inviting audiences to use their imaginations through imagistic verse. There are significant correspondences between *The Troublesome Reign of King John* and *Richard II*, which Shakespeare wrote not long before adapting Peele's play in his *King John*. Peele's drama seems to have lingered at the back of Shakespeare's consciousness, certain moments and snatches of dialogue often surfacing in his pelagic thought processes. Echoes of *The Troublesome Reign of King John* have been traced in earlier Shakespeare plays, such as *Henry VI Part Three* and *Richard III*, suggesting that Shakespeare was intimately familiar with the drama before he adapted it.[10]

Let's go back to the treasure trove that is *Collocations and N-grams*. Suddenly the influence of *The Troublesome Reign of King John* on Shakespeare's dramatic language bursts to the surface like a shark spotting an unfortunate seal. Peele's play is divided into two spreadsheets because it was split into two plays when first published, even though it hardly exceeds the average length for an Elizabethan drama. The vogue for two-part plays was likely kickstarted by the success of Marlowe's *Tamburlaine*. In the spreadsheet for the first part, *King John* is unsurprisingly ranked in first place. But *Love's Labour's Lost*, *Richard III*, and *Richard II* cluster in eleventh to thirteenth place. *King John* is ranked third place in the spreadsheet for the second part, suggesting that Shakespeare attended more closely to the earlier scenes of his source play, which chimes with his use of source materials in general. *Richard III* is in seventh place. Peele's habit of repeating his favourite phrases has an impact on the rankings: his *Edward I* is ranked sixth in the spreadsheet for the first part and *The Battle of Alcazar* is ranked fifth in the spreadsheet for the second part, followed by *The Arraignment of Paris* in twelfth position and *Edward I* in thirteenth.

The contrast in results for some of Peele's other plays is as sharp as a Damascus sword. The highest-ranked sole-authored Shakespeare play for *The Arraignment of Paris* is *Troilus and Cressida*, positioned thirty-fifth. Peele's play revolves around the Trojan prince Paris, so shared phrases between these plays are probably due to similarities in subject matter. *Richard II* is the top-ranked sole-authored Shakespeare play in the spreadsheet for *The Battle of Alcazar*, in nineteenth position, suggesting that Shakespeare had Peele's drama in mind when he composed that play. Shakespeare plays don't figure prominently in the spreadsheet for *The Old Wife's Tale*, with *Romeo and Juliet* ranked thirty-ninth. It's interesting, however, that the first two acts of *Pericles* are ranked ninth. Are these links due to George Wilkins's hand as Shakespeare's co-author on *Pericles*? Wilkins is widely held to have authored these specific acts.[11] Wilkins was a neighbour of Shakespeare's and an innkeeper, probably a euphemism for a pimp. He was a violent man, especially towards women, one of whom he once kicked in her pregnant belly. Peele seems to have shaped Wilkins's creative process in different ways than he did Shakespeare's. The evidence suggests that the major contribution Peele's sole-authored plays made to Shakespeare's output wasn't in the genres of either biblical plays or Romances, but most certainly in the immensely popular genre of chronicle history.

In *Richard III*, Shakespeare remembered Peele's dramatic language in *The Battle of Alcazar* relating to military conflict: Clarence speaks of his father York, who 'Blessed his three sons **with his victorious arm**' (1.4.231). In Peele's play Don de Menysis, governor of Tangier, speaks to the captains: 'To aide this Moor **with his victorious armes**' (3.3.871). Shakespeare also remembered Peele's language of courtly protocol in *Edward I*, such as Longshanks's speech, 'Ladies **by your leave, / How doth** my Nell' (10.1454–5), which Shakespeare recycles in Queen Elizabeth's query: 'Master Lieutenant, pray you **by your leave, / How doth** the Prince' (4.1.13–14). Richard pretends his wife is ill: 'Anne, **my queen, is sick**, and like to die' (4.2.59). Richard's phraseology uniquely echoes Peele's play: 'Nobles **my Queen is sick**' (21.2321).

The matching phrases between *Richard III* and *The Troublesome Reign of King John* are even more extensive: Buckingham says of Hastings, '**And in good time, here comes the sweating** lord' (3.1.95). This speech seems to have been triggered by Pembroke's association of that lengthy phrase with the verb 'sweat' in the second part of Peele's play: '**And in good time, here come the** war-men all, / That **sweat**' (3.25–6). Lady Anne's lamentation over the coffin of her father-in-law, '**That makes us wretched** by the **death** of thee' (1.2.18), echoes Viscount Meloun's death: '**That made us wretched** with his **dying** tale' (5.60). Shakespeare was evidently conscious of the language of Peele's play right from the beginning of his career, as shown by the striking match between the line in *Henry VI Part Three*, 'Sham'st **thou** not, **knowing whence thou art extraught**' (2.2.142), and the first part of Peele's history: 'And when **thou knowest** from **whence thou art extraught**' (1.398). Shakespeare never used that word, 'extraught', the past participle of 'extracted', again. As the ghosts of dramatic predecessors danced around his desk, flitting in unison with candlefire and pitching long shadows on his chamber walls, Shakespeare resummoned Peele's play when he got to work on *Richard II*. Bolingbroke commands the execution of Bushy and Green, who '**stained the beauty of** a fair queen's cheeks' (3.1.14). Just as Shakespeare likens the kingdom to an unweeded garden, King John speaks of 'ambitious weeds' that can '**stain the beauty of** our garden plot' (13.90–1). Here Shakespeare seizes on not only words but imagery at the very heart of *The Troublesome Reign of King John* and, subsequently, *Richard II*. Bolingbroke pardons the Bishop of Carlisle in Shakespeare's play: '**So as thou liv'st in peace**' (5.6.27). Queen Eleanor advises her son to give up five French provinces: '**so** shalt **thou live in peace**' (4.166). The dramatic language of *The Troublesome Reign of King John* left a lasting impression on Shakespeare. Maybe he always had an eye on adapting the play? The connections between Shakespeare and Peele's play recall those of Shakespeare and *King Leir*. Shakespeare's relationship with Kyd involved not only influence but also perhaps direct collaboration. This also appears to be the case with Shakespeare and Peele. Was Peele Shakespeare's first co-author?

The attribution of parts of *Titus Andronicus* to Peele goes back to the early twentieth century and has been buttressed by multiple approaches.[12] There are distinct differences between the authors' styles that help us distinguish their portions of the tragedy. The scenes commonly given to Peele, the first act, 2.1, 2.2, and 4.1, average 1.8 per cent 'feminine' endings, an identical figure to *Edward I* that fits neatly into Peele's range in his sole-authored plays of 1.5 5.4. The high figure of 5.4 for *The Old Wife's Tale* is misleading: Philip Timberlake pointed out that Peele 'never attained over 2.7 per cent of feminine endings in 100 consecutive lines' and that the 'significance' of *The Old Wife's Tale* is 'considerably lessened by the fact that the blank verse occurs in short, scattered speeches and not in long passages'.[13] The percentage of 9.4 for Shakespeare's portions of *Titus Andronicus* once again reveals a fundamental difference between Shakespeare's verse and the plays of university-educated dramatists. In the first act of *Titus Andronicus* many of the characters speak with the same voice, using the same rhythm, and they often even repeat the same words or phrases. Peele doesn't individualise his characters in the same way that Kyd and Shakespeare do. There are also discernible differences in the playwrights' use of rhetorical schemes. Shakespeare's rhetorical figures often seem conversational, his dialogue mirroring real-life conversation, whereas Peele's rhetoric often feels a bit stiff, a bit formal.[14]

The differences between Peele and Shakespeare's styles are illustrated in two soliloquies delivered by Aaron, that villain in the mould of the murderous Muly Mahamet in *The Battle of Alcazar*. This is Aaron's first speech of the play:

> Now climbeth Tamora Olympus' top,
> Safe out of fortune's shot, and sits aloft,
> Secure of thunder's crack or lightning flash,
> Advanced above pale envy's threat'ning reach.
> As when the golden sun salutes the morn
> And, having gilt the ocean with his beams,
> Gallops the zodiac in his glistering coach
> And overlooks the highest-peering hills;
> So Tamora.

Upon her wit doth earthly honour wait,
And virtue stoops and trembles at her frown.
Then, Aaron, arm thy heart and fit thy thoughts
To mount aloft with thy imperial mistress,
And mount her pitch, whom thou in triumph long
Hast prisoner held fettered in amorous chains,
And faster bound to Aaron's charming eyes
Than is Prometheus tied to Caucasus.
Away with slavish weeds and servile thoughts!
I will be bright, and shine in pearl and gold
To wait upon this new-made empress.
To wait, said I? – to wanton with this queen,
This goddess, this Semiramis, this nymph,
This siren, that will charm Rome's Saturnine
And see his shipwreck and his commonweal's. (2.1.1–24)

This is a great example of Peele's distinctive vein, his emphasis on 'masculine' endings, largely end-stopped verse lines, and his voracious appetite for recycling elements of his idiom. The image of galloping the zodiac also appears in his poems, and the idea of being bound to eyes features in *Edward I*: 'Fast to those looks are all my fancies tied' (10.1629). Aaron's speech droops under weighty classical allusions, from the abode of the gods in Greek mythology, Olympus, to the Titan god of fire, Prometheus, and the Assyrian queen, Semiramis. Semiramis is also mentioned in a scene attributed to Shakespeare when Lavinia says disparagingly, 'Ay, come, Semiramis – nay, barbarous Tamora' (2.3.118). Was the link between this figure and Tamora, Queen of the Goths, made during the plotting phase? Either way the concentration of mythological and legendary figures in this single speech is unlike Shakespeare's more conversational-sounding soliloquies:

He that had wit would think that I had none,
To bury so much gold under a tree
And never after to inherit it.
Let him that thinks of me so abjectly
Know that this gold must coin a stratagem
Which, cunningly effected, will beget
A very excellent piece of villainy.
And so repose, sweet gold, for their unrest. (2.3.1–8)

While Peele's is a fine Machiavellian speech, his characters tend to employ the same generalised vocabulary, be they Roman villains or English heroes. Peele's characters are functional, they're types. The lineaments of later multifaceted schemers like Iago are perceptible in Shakespeare's speech. Aaron in 2.3 speaks in a far more flexible verse style. He could easily be chatting to us in the pub. Shakespeare's rhetoric is more subtle and his speech bristles with wordplay like the juxtaposition of 'repose' and 'unrest'. Shakespeare's Aaron, like his Richard III, is a seductive figure; we marvel at his villainy. Shakespeare uses the device of soliloquy as a means of creating an umbilical cord between his villain and the audience.

The attribution of the earlier speech to Peele is also supported by *Collocations and N-grams*. In the spreadsheet for 2.1 Peele's *The Old Wife's Tale* is ranked fifth. In the spreadsheet for the opening act of *Titus Andronicus*, *The Battle of Alcazar* is ranked in first place. This is powerful evidence of Peele's habit of self-repetition. In the spreadsheet for 4.1, the second part of *The Troublesome Reign of King John* is also ranked higher than any Shakespeare play at thirteen. Matches between 4.1 and Peele's plays include complex collocations of thought and language: when Titus asks his daughter who was responsible for her rape in the line, 'What Roman **lord** it was **durst do the deed**' (4.1.61), he's echoing the Monk's willingness to murder the King in the second part of *The Troublesome Reign of King John*: 'Why, I, my **lord**, **dare do the deed**' (6.136). When the identity of Lavinia's harmers is revealed, Marcus tries to calm his brother Titus down: 'To stir a mutiny in the **mildest thoughts** / And arm the **minds**' (4.1.84–5). In *Edward I*, Longshanks tries to pacify Nell: 'Leave these ungentle **thoughts**, put on a **milder mind**' (10.1681). Marcus Andronicus changes course and incites revenge: 'And see **their blood**, or **die with** this reproach', to which his brother responds: ''Tis **sure** enough' (4.1.93–4). This language of bloody violence uniquely echoes Peele's *The Battle of Alcazar*: 'For which as we are **sure** to **die**, / Thou Shalt paie satisfaction **with thy blood**' (5.1.1308–9). All that said, it's curious that while Shakespeare's *Richard III* is ranked highly at second position in the spreadsheet for Shakespeare's portions of *Titus Andronicus*, revealing his own habit of repeating favoured phrases, the first part of *The Troublesome Reign of King John* also features highly in tenth place. This could be testament to the influence of Peele's dramatic language on Shakespeare. Was Shakespeare especially conscious of his co-author's style when writing his scenes? Was he trying to achieve stylistic continuity? We've seen that Shakespeare borrowed heavily from Marlowe when writing Aaron's speech in 5.1, but it's also notable that Aaron's line 'Wherein **I** did **not some notorious ill**' (5.1.127) offers up a striking match with *The Troublesome Reign of King John*: 'How, what, when and where have **I** bestowed a day / That tended **not** to **some notorious ill**?' (8.81–2). The authors' divisions of labour suggest that Peele got the narrative ball rolling and then contributed the later scene in which Lavinia reveals the identities of her rapists. Shakespeare is left to kick that ball into touch. It's a pattern of co-authorship resembling *Edward III*.

Although Peele's and Shakespeare's styles are distinctly different, the authorship of 4.1 has recently come under scrutiny and attempts have been made to gift the scene to Shakespeare.[15] But the verse style tells a different story: 4.1 provides a suitable sample size of 123 verse lines and has a figure for 'feminine' endings of 1.5 per cent. This corresponds to the percentages for other sufficiently sized scenes: the first act has a lowly 1.9 per cent and the first scene of the second act has a figure of 2.4. The lowest figure for a 'long scene' attributed to Shakespeare in *Titus Andronicus* is for 5.2, which has 201 verse lines and a strict percentage of 5.4. The differences between figures for scenes attributed to Peele and Shakespeare pluck at the eyestrings.

The main evidence for doubting Peele's authorship of 4.1 is the so-called '*LION* method' invented by MacDonald Jackson.[16] According to this approach, 4.1 shares more phrases with Shakespeare than with Peele. The problem is that the Shakespeare works chosen for comparison were around 60 per cent larger than Peele's canon in terms of word count, giving Shakespeare a huge advantage. This error was inflated in later tests, with miscalculations resulting in a Shakespeare canon 85 per cent larger than it should have been.[17] The attribution of 4.1 to Shakespeare was swiftly embraced by the Shakespeare community, providing another cautionary tale for readers blindsided by purely data-driven approaches to matters of authorship. When it comes to favoured phrases, vocabulary, rhetoric, and verse style, the scene more closely resembles Peele than it does Shakespeare. As is characteristic of Peele's other scenes in the play, 4.1 is stuffed with classical references. Titus says, 'Ah, boy, Cornelia never with more care / Read to her sons than she hath read to thee / Sweet poetry and Tully's *Orator*' (4.1.12–14). He asks his daughter if she was 'Ravished and wronged as Philomcla was' (4.1.52). Having invoked 'Apollo, Pallas, Jove' and 'Mercury' (4.1.65), Marcus Andronicus swears revenge on Lavinia's harmers:

> My lord, kneel down with me; Lavinia, kneel;
> And kneel, sweet boy, the Roman Hector's hope;
> And swear with me – as, with the woeful fere
> And father of that chaste dishonoured dame
> Lord Junius Brutus sware for Lucrece' rape. (4.1.86–90)

The references come thick and fast, sticking to the text like gloopy syrup. Actors delivering these lines risk sounding as if they suffer from hypersalivation: Cornelia, Lucius Junius Brutus, Hecuba of Troy, Tarquin and Lucretia, Apollo, Pallas, Jove, Mercury, and Hector, these and many more are named in the space of just a hundred lines. This scene reads like the work of a university-educated playwright showing off his classical knowledge even at the risk of alienating audience members. The dense cluster of signals to learning seems un-Shakespearian.

When the *LION* tests are rerun with suitable canon sizes for these playwrights, the results point towards Peele. This might suggest a more dynamic collaboration between the dramatists than has been supposed. But the playwright Edward Ravenscroft claimed in 1687 to have it on good authority that Shakespeare merely revised the play:

> I have been told by some anciently conversant with the Stage, that it was not Originally his (Shakespeare's), but brought by a private Author to be Acted and he only gave some Master-touches to one or two of the Principal Parts or Characters; this I am apt to believe, because 'tis the most incorrect and indigested piece in all his Works, It seems rather a heap of Rubbish then a Structure.

The identification of the majorly successful commercial dramatist Peele as author of large portions of *Titus Andronicus* establishes that the play wasn't 'brought by a private Author'. Shakespeare is the play's principal author in terms of dialogue. He was responsible for the bulk of *Titus Andronicus*, his contributions extending well beyond 'some Master-touches to one or two of the Principal Parts or Characters'. Ravenscroft's scathing remark that the play is 'the most incorrect and indigested piece in all his Works' is subjective. Many would disagree with this evaluative claim. None of these anecdotal statements, which seem designed to promote Ravenscroft's adaptation, *Titus Andronicus, or the Rape of Lavinia*, as an improvement on the source play while catering to seventeenth-century tastes, holds weight. Why should we then believe the mysterious witness who supposedly claimed that the play 'was not Originally his (Shakespeare's)'?

The scholar Jonathan Bate highlights recent claims that 'the surviving (1596) text' of *Edward III* 'was Shakespeare's revision of an older play by another dramatist' as evidence in support of the 'idea that Shakespeare began his career as the reviser of existing plays', which 'is gaining increasing traction in twenty-first century scholarship'. He asks: 'Might he have done the same with *Titus*?' An alternative proposition is that Shakespeare collaborated directly with and therefore learned from more experienced dramatists at the beginning of his career. However, Bate finds it 'hard to imagine Peele, the older and more experienced partner, saying words to the effect of "I'll get you started, then you do the rest"'. He accepts 'powerful' arguments that 4.1 is stylistically more like Shakespeare than Peele.[18] But the revived case for Peele's authorship of 4.1 suggests simultaneous collaboration between the writers. As we'll see later in this book, this way of working together could account for why 3.2, the so-called 'fly scene', is absent from the 1594 quarto of *Titus Andronicus*. That scene first appeared in print in the Folio edition of *Titus Andronicus*. A head-scratching textual conundrum if ever there was one. How unusual would it be for Peele to take responsibility only for the opening scenes of the play anyway? Thomas Nashe claimed in his pamphlet *Nashe's Lenten Stuff* (1599) that he contributed 'but the induction and first act' of *The Isle of Dogs*. This wasn't an uncommon way of working, it seems. The idea of Shakespeare completing an unfinished play isn't supported by any evidence beyond Ravenscroft's dubious anecdote.[19] The disqualification of Peele as worthy of collaborating directly with Shakespeare flouts the historical evidence. Shakespeare would have learned a great deal from his more experienced co-author. *Titus Andronicus* has received a kinder critical reception in recent decades and often works brilliantly on stage, whether creatives choose to go down the road of slapstick comedy, brutal gorefest, or torture of the imagination, as in the Globe's 2023 production at the Sam Wanamaker Playhouse, in which candles were brutalised in inventive ways to represent each of the play's fourteen deaths. There have even been hauntingly beautiful productions over the years, such as Peter Brook's 1955 stylised attempt in Stratford-upon-Avon, starring Laurence Olivier and Vivien Leigh as father and daughter, or Yukio Ninagawa's depiction of ribbons of blood in 2006. But the beginnings of the play's critical restoration were partly dependent on the idea that Shakespeare was its sole author, as if co-authorship would fail to produce a unified plot or a great piece of theatre.[20] The revision theory pictures Shakespeare early in his career as 'a hired man, a jack of all trades: the bit-part actor who had found a niche for himself as a reformer of old plays' and 'cut his teeth as a writer in the role of overseer, improver, and new setter forth of old scripts'.[21] This harks back to misplaced theories that he was a plagiarist. It also seems symptomatic of a reluctance to acknowledge that Shakespeare, at the very beginning of his career, would have been the junior partner of co-authors such as Peele and Kyd. He was commissioned to revise the plays of his dramatic predecessors later in his career once he'd established himself.

There's little to no evidence that Shakespeare and Peele had read each other's portions of *Titus Andronicus*.[22] There aren't many distinct phrases shared between their respective contributions, suggesting simultaneous collaboration with both authors working from a single plot outline. The few similarities that can be found between Shakespeare and Peele's scenes tend to revolve around classical figures like Semiramis; the same can be said for allusions to the story of Tereus's rape of Philomel in Ovid's *Metamorphoses*. We can't be sure whether one dramatist or both were responsible for the author plot.[23] But it seems likely that Peele's approach to dramatic narrative and characterisation relied heavily on classical analogies, which are more frequent in his plays and the works of other university-educated playwrights than in Shakespeare. Shakespeare would have benefited from Peele's approach to plot and characterisation, particularly his emphasis on Senecan violence and the motif of revenge. *Titus Andronicus* takes these matters to the extreme. It's a bonkers play featuring mutilation and decapitation, and concluding with a mother being tricked into eating her own sons who have been baked in a pie. Even today the play has a reputation for causing audience members to faint, productions keeping fake blood suppliers in profit as litres are spilt during the quest for revenge. Shakespeare cleverly invokes the allegorical figure of Revenge when Tamora disguises herself in that role, as opposed to including a choric figure like in the plays of Kyd and Peele. He also builds on Peele's characterisation of Aaron by having him elicit some audience sympathy through the care he reveals towards his newborn son. Aaron is a much more complex character than Peele's villain, Muly Mahamet. He is at one with Shakespeare's other schemers, who often reveal redeeming traits that humanise them.

Peele's scenes provide the stimuli for Senecan revenge by setting the wheels in motion and later revealing the correct targets to Titus, whereas Shakespeare deals with the 'main action', the 'progress', as one academic writes of the genre, 'of this revenge, leading to the death of the murderers and often the death of the avenger himself'.[24] As a well-established, highly educated and versatile dramatist Peele was an ideal co-author for Shakespeare, and this collaboration seems to have inspired Shakespeare to refine the blend of Roman tragedy and chronicle history, as seen in Peele's plays, for *Richard III*. Shakespeare is unlikely to have written *Richard III* immediately after *Henry VI Part Three*.[25] Did Shakespeare work on *Titus Andronicus*, a play heavily influenced by Kyd's and Peele's approaches to revenge tragedy, before turning his hand to *Richard III*? This could help to explain why *Richard III* represents an advancement on Senecan tropes found in *Henry VI Part Three*. These tropes include the bloody violence pooling on the pages of works by Peele, Kyd, Greene, and Lodge. Such violence would return with a vengeance in later works by dramatists such as Middleton and John Ford.

In Shakespeare's *King John* we appear to have a genuine adaptation of an older play by Peele: *The Troublesome Reign of King John*.[26] This adaptation impacted Shakespeare's style in ways that transcend Peele's influence on Shakespeare's portions of *Titus Andronicus*. The two parts of Peele's play average 1.9 and 1.2 per cent 'feminine' endings respectively, as is typical of Peele's style. *King John* has an uncharacteristically low percentage of 4.9 for Shakespeare, though still much higher than Peele's usual averages. In adapting Peele's play Shakespeare engaged more closely with the older dramatist's writing than when he drew from a shared plot for *Titus Andronicus*. We can imagine Shakespeare scribbling furiously at his writing desk, the 1591 edition of *The Troublesome Reign of King John* at his elbow. Shakespeare wrote his play around 1596 for the Lord Chamberlain's Men, who sought to duplicate the earlier offerings of the Queen's Men company. This can also be seen in Shakespeare's *Henry IV* and *Henry V* plays, which recycle numerous plot elements from *The Famous Victories of Henry V*. We might think of Shakespeare as a modern screenwriter commissioned to pen a remake of an old classic produced by a now defunct studio. Shakespeare displays remarkable skills in memorisation of passages from earlier plays he might have seen or in which he conceivably acted. The key difference between the affinities shared by *King John* and the earlier play is that Shakespeare also duplicates several stage directions pretty much verbatim, suggesting reading knowledge rather than reliance on his aural memory. Shakespeare recycles the direction '**Enter** *the* **Shrive,** *&* **whispers** *the Earl of Sals.* **in the ear**' (1.67.2 SD) in *King John*'s '**Enter** *a* **Sheriff,** *who* **whispers** *Essex* **in the ear**' (1.1.43.1 SD). The stage directions shared between these plays are so exact they couldn't possibly be due to memory. The Sheriff in Peele's play has eight lines of dialogue, whereas in *King John* he doesn't speak at all and isn't shown exiting. Shakespeare must have deleted the Sheriff's dialogue but forgotten to delete the stage direction. Shakespeare's 'ghost' character offers us glimpses of Peele's ghostly presence. 'Remember me' we can imagine Peele saying as he crossed the threshold to literary eternity that same year.

In *King John* Shakespeare filches dialogue from *The Troublesome Reign of King John* shamelessly. His borrowings from that play in his earlier works pale in comparison. The First Citizen says: 'In brief, **we are the King of England's subjects.** / **For him and in his right we hold this town**' (2.1.267–8). Peele's First Citizen says: 'He that tries himself our sovereign, to him will **we** remain firm **subjects**; and **for him, and in his right, we hold** our **town**, as desirous to know the truth' (2.224–7). The words are largely the same, but Shakespeare transfers Peele's prose speech into the medium of verse. *King John*, a seldom-performed play, gives us a unique snapshot of Shakespeare's creative process in the mid-1590s: Shakespeare condenses Peele's long scenes and relegates dispensable moments to offstage events, speeding up and streamlining the play. Shakespeare's adaptation results in a less unified plot than can be seen in *Titus Andronicus*, however. Shakespeare doesn't explain why King John needs a second coronation. No motive is provided for the murder of King John. Hubert is given a direct instruction to kill Arthur but later seems to think he's only been tasked with blinding the boy.[27]

In following the source play so closely, practically scene by scene, it's inevitable that Peele would exert a considerable influence on not only Shakespeare's plot structure but also his language, metre, and overall dramaturgy. Shakespeare adapting Peele in *King John* is considerably different from Shakespeare collaborating with Peele in *Titus Andronicus*. *King John* once again reveals Shakespeare as a shrewd magpie capable of transforming the language, stagecraft, plots, and theatrical effects of his predecessors. Shakespeare was still engaging with and learning from Peele several years into his writing career, particularly when it came to his history plays, which might not have been possible were it not for the older dramatist's trailblazing efforts. To quote *Henry V*, Shakespeare's contributions to that popular genre could be considered 'borrowed glories' (2.4.79).

7

Thomas Dekker, John Marston, and Ben Jonson

The glass turns. Time passes. We slide over the years. This swift passage leads us to a playwright whose career spanned both the Elizabethan and Jacobean periods, intersecting with Shakespeare's dramatic trajectory at the turn of the century. Before shifting our attention fully towards the fascinating relationship between Shakespeare and Ben Jonson, we're greeted by two other major playwrights working during these periods. Jonson engaged in savage literary feuds but also co-authored plays with both men: Thomas Dekker (c. 1572–1632) and John Marston (1576–1634).

Little is known of Dekker's origins: his birth year was probably 1572. We can piece together the bones of conjecture because Dekker claims in the epistle dedicatory to his 1632 work *English Villainies* that he was aged thirty.[1] In all likelihood he spent his entire life in London. He had three daughters with his first wife, Mary, who died in July 1616. We know nothing of his parents or his education, although his works, demonstrating fluency in Latin and extensive knowledge of Ovid, Horace, and Virgil, suggest he was educated at a grammar school. Alongside writing plays, which seems to have been his principal occupation, he wrote pamphlets, poetry, pageants, and other public entertainments, such as *The Magnificent Entertainment Given to King James*, which he and Ben Jonson were commissioned to write in 1603, and satires like his 1606 commentary on city life, *The Seven Deadly Sins of London*. Like many of his contemporaries, but unlike Shakespeare, Dekker didn't have a consistent patron, nor did he have any shares in a theatre company. The result was that he spent much of his life in debt, for which he was imprisoned in 1598 and 1599. He was thrown back into jail from 1612 to 1619. He appears to have been buried at St James, Clerkenwell, on 25 August 1632. That church has a dramatic history in every sense of the word: in the twelfth century the parish clerks of London would perform biblical plays nearby. Dekker's widow, Elizabeth, renounced the administration of his estate the following month. And so Dekker died as he lived: in debt.

Dekker embarked on a career as a dramatist during the 1590s. The first record of him as a playwright can be found in Philip Henslowe's diary in 1598. Excluding the fact that he landed in jail, it was in some ways an auspicious year for young Dekker. He was praised alongside Shakespeare, Michael Drayton, George Chapman, and Jonson by Francis Meres as a tragic writer, suggesting he had begun writing plays several years earlier. Dekker was an astonishingly productive dramatist, having a hand in over forty plays written between 1598 and 1602. He was often commissioned to doctor scripts and was labelled sneeringly as a 'dresser of plays about the town' by Jonson in his *Poetaster* (3.4.261). Dekker was a freelance, offering his services for the Admiral's Men, Worcester's Men, Chamberlain's Men, and the Children of Paul's. He wrote in collaboration with such dramatists as Drayton, Jonson, Henry Chettle, Robert Wilson, William Haughton, John Day, Richard Hathway, Anthony Munday, Thomas Heywood, Wentworth Smith, Thomas Middleton, and John Webster. All but a handful of these plays are lost, which has, as one scholar laments, 'significantly reduced his visibility to subsequent centuries'.[2]

Dekker's surviving unassisted plays are *The Shoemaker's Holiday* (1599), written for the Admiral's Men and depicting cultural tensions in Elizabethan London; another Admiral's Men play, *Old Fortunatus*, based on the German legend of Fortunatus who had an inexhaustible purse (we can see the appeal of that story to Dekker); *Satiromastix*, which, as we saw earlier, satirises Jonson and was performed both by the Chamberlain's Men and the Children of Paul's; *Blurt, Master Constable* (1601),[3] a comedy written for the Children of Paul's; *2 Honest Whore* (1605), a sequel to an earlier collaboration with Middleton, written for Prince Henry's Men; and *The Whore of Babylon* (1606), an anti-Catholic play also produced by Prince Henry's Men.

Dekker was attuned to the popular pulse. He thrived in the genre of city comedy. Writing for geographically specific audiences, Dekker developed a style that mirrored the everyday speech of the London streets, his 'mostly homespun' verse 'setting off the idiosyncratic and colloquial pungency of the prose' in *The Shoemaker's Holiday*,[4] a play set against the backdrop of Henry V's French wars performed around the same time as Shakespeare's *Henry V*. Dekker would further contribute to the development of this genre characterised by contemporary urban subject matter in his collaboration with Webster, *Westward Ho!* (1604), which resembles the concluding act of Shakespeare's *The Merry Wives of Windsor* by depicting the triumph of virtuous citizen women over jealous husbands and unwanted suitors.[5] Shakespeare didn't write London comedies, although *The Merry Wives of Windsor* can be considered a relative of the genre and *Measure for Measure* stages the urban world of Vienna in a manner that feels Dickensian at times. Shakespeare might have earned his money there, but he wasn't inspired to write a comedy zoning in on London life as he knew it. *Collocations and N-grams* gives us little indication that Shakespeare attended to the frequently colloquial language of *The Shoemaker's Holiday*. The spreadsheet for that play lists *Measure for Measure* in position sixty-eight.

Shakespeare doesn't seem to have engaged with the language of Dekker's canon of plays at all. There are some similarities between Dekker's *Blurt, Master Constable* and Shakespeare's comedies *Love's Labour's Lost* and *Much Ado About Nothing* (1598).[6] Dekker's title character is modelled on Dogberry, Verges, and their watch. But there is very little phraseological evidence pointing in the other direction. Looking at Shakespeare plays written after Dekker's in *Collocations and N-grams*, *All's Well that Ends Well* fares best, ranked thirty-seventh in the spreadsheet for *Blurt, Master Constable*. None of the phrases unique to these plays is particularly impressive, though.

Importantly, however, Shakespeare and Dekker collaborated on *Sir Thomas More*, their contributions offering fascinating insights into their differing styles and tempers.[7] That play survives in a manuscript kept at the British Library and appears to have been written originally by Munday and Chettle. The play was revised by Chettle, Dekker, Heywood, and Shakespeare, presumably for the Chamberlain's Men. Shakespeare's additions represent the only surviving example of his dramatic handwriting. The case for his authorship was first made in 1871 and was reinforced by a range of evidence: palaeography, orthography, and verbal and dramatic parallels.[8] Doubts have been poured over the theory of Shakespeare's hand in sections of the play in recent years: the evidence for Shakespearian spellings has been whittled down to no more than five spellings that are sufficiently rare to be worth consideration. A useful pointer to Shakespeare's quirkier habits is the spelling 'scilens' for 'silence'. Some have complained that it can also be found in a 1546 prayer book and a 1568 bible.[9] But this hardly negates the case for Shakespeare's authorship, unless we suppose the authors of these earlier works could have also been responsible for the relevant passages in *Sir Thomas More*. That the spelling doesn't feature in any other *dramatic* text is significant. Spellings aren't of primary evidential value, but they would seem to strengthen rather than weaken the case for Shakespeare's hand. The so-called '*LION* method' would also seem to point towards Shakespeare's authorship, although the 'partisanship' of this approach has been highlighted by critics.[10] But the wealth of evidence for Shakespeare's hand remains compelling. The most famous addition (delivered beautifully by Ian McKellen at various events) is the moment when Thomas More quells an anti-immigration riot:

> Grant them removed, and grant that this your noise
> Hath chid down all the majesty of England.
> Imagine that you see the wretched strangers,
> Their babies at their backs, with their poor luggage,
> Plodding to th' ports and coasts for transportation,
> And that you sit as kings in your desires,
> Authority quite silenced by your brawl,
> And you in ruff of your opinions clothed:
> What had you got? I'll tell you: you had taught
> How insolence and strong hand should prevail,

How order should be quelled. And by this pattern
Not one of you should live an agèd man,
For other ruffians, as their fancies wrought,
With selfsame hand, self reasons, and self-right,
Would shark on you, and men, like ravenous fishes,
Feed on one another. (6.82–97)

It's a speech that reaches through the ages and shakes you violently by the shoulders. This moment has a close identity with numerous passages in Shakespeare plays, including complex parallels with the Jack Cade scenes in *Henry VI Part Two*, repeated in *Julius Caesar* and *Coriolanus*.

Shakespeare's contributions reveal that he wasn't familiar with the specific names of characters in the play. This has suggested to some commentators that 'authorial revision or composition did not involve checking continuity; perhaps authors did not immerse themselves in the world of the play to which they added'.[11] Shakespeare was also unaware that his work was partly in vain because Munday had already decided to get rid of the insurrection scene. We again see Shakespeare as a man of the theatre, who not only blotted his own lines but had them deleted by collaborating authors.[12] Shakespeare also appears to have added soliloquies to the play, the first establishing 'a thematic connection' with the insurrection episode and the second joining scenes in a way that is 'more oriented to narrative', revealing the author to have been 'deeply implicated' in the revision 'process'.[13]

Although several of the contributing dramatists were associated with the Admiral's Men, it's perfectly reasonable that they would have contributed to a play put on by Shakespeare's company the Chamberlain's Men, even if it was a business rival. These playwrights were after all working on a freelance basis.[14] Heywood was an ideal reviser, having claimed to have had 'an entire hand or at least a maine finger in two hundred and twenty plays' in a career spanning the 1590s up until his death in 1641, during which he offered his services for such companies as the Admiral's Men, Derby's Men, and Worcester's Men. He appears to have been the only university-educated contributor to the play, having studied at Cambridge.

Heywood's contributions are more diverse than those of the play's other revisers. He added a substantial role for a clown to this biographical drama, new speeches to the original text, and three separate sections of the additions. Dekker's main contribution reveals his deep-rooted understanding of theatrical conditions: his conclusion to scene 8 allows more time for necessary doubling. Dekker's frequently loose, broken verse style, characterised by lines extending to twelve and even fourteen syllables, can be seen in such examples as More's speech, 'Be near allied to greatness. Observe me, sirrah' (8.28). Dekker's sprightly dialogue is consistent with his city comedies and his interest in depicting urban dwellers.[15] In *Sir Thomas More*, then, we see that the revising authors' contributions reflect their dramaturgical preferences; however, in writing collaboratively they were able to produce a work quite unlike anything either dramatist might have created unassisted. Unfortunately for them, there's no evidence the play was ever performed, let alone printed. Dealing with subject matter like immigration, with a Catholic martyr executed during the reign of Queen Elizabeth I's father taking the leading role, *Sir Thomas More* doesn't appear to have escaped the censors, whose paws are all over the surviving manuscript.

John Marston also contributed to the shift from the heavy din of revenge tragedies and history plays to the more immediate new style of city comedy. Marston was baptised on 7 October 1576 at Wardington, Oxfordshire. He was the son of a lawyer, also named John Marston, and his wife Maria.[16] Marston was admitted to the Middle Temple in 1592 and received his BA from Oxford two years later. His father urged him to continue studying law, to give up on vain fantasies of embarking on a literary career. There's no money in English literature. Why waste your time? Get a proper job. The all-too familiar clichés ball into heavy fists through time. Marston ducked the punches and published an Ovidian erotic poem and *The Scourge of Villainies* in 1598, the year in which Meres praised him as a satirist. He was also employed by Henslowe as a dramatist writing mainly for the Children of Paul's. He had a particularly difficult relationship with Jonson, which broke out in plays composed during the so-called 'War of the Theatres'. Jonson pummelled Marston with barbs in *Every Man out of His Humour* (1599), *Cynthia's Revels*, and *Poetaster*, while Marston satirised Jonson in such roles as Brabant Senior in *Jack Drum's Entertainment* (1600). Dekker followed suit by lampooning Jonson in his *Satiromastix*. These playwrights were knocking bells out of each other, child actors spitting their acidic lines on the stage. Audiences loved it. Marston couldn't help but appreciate Jonson's literary capabilities, though: he wrote a prefatory poem to Jonson's *Sejanus* and dedicated his tragedy *The Malcontent* (1603) to him. Having in 1605 married Mary Wilkes, daughter of the Reverend William Wilkes, Marston undertook a significant career change when he was ordained deacon in September 1609. What would his father have thought? Marston died in London on 24 June 1634 and was buried in Middle Temple Church, the ironical land of lawyers.

Marston was a fascinating playwright, poet, pamphleteer, and writer of aristocratic entertainments. He loved to flirt with controversy, often bought it a drink, took it home to bed. His dramatic canon consists of *Antonio and Mellida, Antonio's Revenge, Jack Drum's Entertainment*, and *What You Will* (1601), written for the Children of Paul's; *Histriomastix* (1602), presumably written for private performance at the Middle Temple by the Children of Paul's; *The Malcontent*, written for the Children of the Chapel and later revised for the King's Men; *Parasitaster* (1604), *The Dutch Courtesan* (1604), and *The Wonder of Women* (1605), written for the Children of the Chapel; and *The Insatiate Countess* (1610), which was likely written when he was associated with the Children of Paul's, although the published version was adapted by writers William Barksted and Lewis Machin, possibly for performance at Whitefriars by the Children of the King's Revels.[17] Marston co-authored with Jonson and Chapman for the Children of the Chapel *Eastward Ho* (1605), which satirised citizen mores and their literary tastes.[18] Its biting references to the Scottish rubbed King James up the wrong way, landing Chapman and Jonson in jail. Marston somehow avoided arrest. Did his legal knowledge help him out?

Marston's style is distinctly different from Shakespeare's: his verse tendencies and bent towards polysyllabic words and Latinate diction, for which Jonson mocked him in *Poetaster* by having him literally vomit pretentious words, resemble Christopher Marlowe. And yet his somewhat old-fashioned verse throngs with what one commentator calls 'exclamatory noises' like 'pah', 'whogh', and 'whop'.[19] As we are about to see, differences in Marston and Shakespeare's habits as phrasemakers are also reflected in *Collocation and N-grams*. The connections between Marston and Shakespeare that have most tantalised scholars concern *Hamlet* and the *Antonio* plays. There are especially striking narrative similarities between Shakespeare's tragedy and *Antonio's Revenge*. Marston's tragedy also takes place in a faraway setting. The ghost of the protagonist's father, the former Duke of Genoa, Andrugio, visits him and bellows for revenge. There's a revelation: he was poisoned by Antonio's father-in-law. The play culminates in Antonio murdering his target, cutting out his tongue and stabbing him repeatedly.[20] *Antonio's Revenge*, like Shakespeare's play, explodes with Senecan motifs, but it's difficult to tell whether such correspondences are down to forebears like the lost *Hamlet* play of the 1580s. Shakespeare appears to have been conscious of plays performed by the revived children's companies, as suggested by Hamlet's speech about 'little eyases, that cry out on the top of question, and are most tyrannically clapped for't' (2.2.340–2), a possible allusion to Marston's tragedy.[21] Which play came first? The direction of influence is difficult to establish. Either way the children's troupes and Shakespeare's company were breathing life into the stale genre of revenge tragedy around the same time. An editorial observation that the 'echoes of *Hamlet*' in *Antonio's Revenge* are 'precisely the kind we should expect if Marston had seen Shakespeare's play, perhaps more than once, but not been able to read it', in contrast to 'the more exact recollections of *Hamlet* in *The Malcontent*',[22] would seem to be supported by *Collocations and N-grams*. *Hamlet* is ranked a humble seventy-third in the spreadsheet for *Antonio's Revenge* and much lower at position 355 in the spreadsheet for *Antonio and Mellida*. Shakespeare's tragedy fares better in the spreadsheet for *The Malcontent*, at position fifty-six. Given the vastidity of writings on proposed links between these plays, the results are surprising. On the other hand the impact of

Marston's self-repetition is potent: in the case of *The Malcontent* the top four plays are also written by Marston.

The same can be said for *What You Will*, a play depicting a rivalry between poets Lampatho Doria and Quadratus, thinly veiled stand-ins for Jonson and Marston. The top positions are taken up by the two *Antonio* plays, *The Dutch Courtesan*, and *Histriomastix*. Marston engaged closely with Shakespeare when he wrote *What You Will*: there are doubles and shipwrecks as in *The Comedy of Errors* and, especially, *Twelfth Night*, which happens to be subtitled *What You Will*. Did Marston accidentally anticipate Shakespeare's planned title for the play we now know as *Twelfth Night*?[23] The spreadsheet for Marston's play confirms the intertextual links with Shakespeare: *Twelfth Night* appears high at position thirteen according to the number of phrases found in no other pair of plays. The results for *The Dutch Courtesan*, an experiment in city comedy revolving around the titular role of Franceschina, a charismatic sex worker, are very different. These results paint a similar picture to the relations, or lack thereof, between Shakespeare and Dekker's exploration of the genre of city comedy. If it's a famous picture, then it's surely a Jackson Pollock: frenetic, abstract, a bit drippy. The highest-ranked Shakespeare play in the spreadsheet for *The Dutch Courtesan* is *Richard III* at position thirty-two. Marston was smack bang in the middle of theatrical culture of the period, and yet, on a verbal level at least, we don't get a sense of Shakespeare paying close attention to city comedies. We can interpret these results in varying ways: maybe Shakespeare didn't have access to such plays performed by rival and children's playing companies. Shakespeare, as an actor, would have been working when plays were usually performed, so there was a higher chance that he'd be influenced by his own company's repertory than by others. But it seems likely that he spent some of his afternoons off going to other writers' theatres. Do these results reveal the development of Shakespeare's distinctive idiom at this point in his career? Can they be interpreted as something of a rejection of this popular genre on Shakespeare's part, a lack of interest in situating his plays in contemporary London? Shakespeare's closest counterpart to these comedies, as we've seen, is *The Merry Wives of Windsor*, but that play is set in a provincial town with a small population. Shakespeare was more concerned with 'the English "city commonwealth": precisely the kind of place in which Shakespeare himself was educated and grew up; and to which he subsequently returned in later life'.[24]

Dekker, Marston, and Shakespeare were all members of a community of playwrights working in London. But their stylistic feathers are of distinctly different hues. Having acted in *Every Man in His Humour* and *Sejanus*, however, Shakespeare would have found himself beautified in the feathers of a dramatist who, as the Scottish poet William Drummond reported, 'had many quarrels with Marston, beat him, and took his Pistol from him': Ben Jonson. Jonson was born in London on 11 June 1572.[25] His father, a clergyman, died beforehand, and his mother remarried a bricklayer while Jonson was a child. The family moved to Hartshorn (or Christopher) Lane, which ran from the Strand to the Thames, and Jonson attended a nearby elementary school in St Martin's Lane. He later studied at Westminster School, where he would have benefited from the tutorage of the great scholar William Camden. Having spent the years receiving vigorous rhetorical and classical training, he left the school in 1589. He planned to go to St John's College in Cambridge but he didn't have enough money. Jonson was forced to take up an apprenticeship to his stepfather as a bricklayer. We can imagine him hard at work, sweat pooling on his brow as he engaged in this ancient profession, his hands toiling in clay but his thoughts in conversation with ancient writers. Jonson was awarded an MA in 1619 from Oxford University, instigated by its Chancellor William Herbert, Third Earl of Pembroke, son of Henry Herbert, for whose playing company Jonson likely started off as an actor and dramatist.

He left his work as a bricklayer and volunteered to soldier with the English expeditionary forces of Sir Francis Vere in Flanders, where he engaged in single combat with an enemy soldier. Jonson killed the man. This violent act wouldn't be his last. The tang of combat was always bitter in his mouth. He went back to London and began a career as an actor, a profession that, unlike Shakespeare, he hurriedly abandoned when turning his hand to writing plays. On 14 November 1594 he married Anne Lewis in the church of St Magnus the Martyr, near London Bridge. Following the mysterious controversy of *The Isle of Dogs*, Jonson joined the Admiral's Men, for whom he was regularly employed as a writer by Philip Henslowe, his output including collaborative plays with dramatists such as Dekker, Chettle, and Henry Porter. Although he was praised in Meres's *Palladis Tamia* as one of the finest English tragic poets, none of his early tragedies has survived. In the same year that Meres praised his tragic abilities, Jonson's comedy *Every Man in His Humour* was performed by the Chamberlain's Men at the Curtain Theatre. It featured Richard Burbage as well as Shakespeare in leading roles. It was also in 1598 that Jonson was indicted at Shoreditch on a charge of manslaughter, following a duel with the actor Gabriel Spencer on 22 September in Hogsden Fields. Spencer's corpse had a six-inch stab wound in its side. His death similarly jagged through the playing community, making Jonson new enemies in Spencer's associates, including Henslowe, who refused to produce Jonson's next play. Jonson and Spencer had been in prison together only the previous year because of their work together on *The Isle of Dogs*. Jonson escaped the gallows and was branded on the thumb as a convicted felon. These men were producing great art, but the threat of deadly combat constantly dogged their heels. Spencer himself had once fatally stabbed the son of a goldsmith in the eye with a still-sheathed sword.

In the winter of 1599, Jonson's *Every Man out of His Humour* was performed at the Globe Theatre and again at court. *Cynthia's Revels* was performed by the Children of the Chapel at Blackfriars Theatre and at court in 1600 and 1601 and, alongside *Poetaster*, bursts with the riotous antagonism between Jonson and Dekker and Marston. His tragedy *Sejanus* was performed by the King's Men in 1603. Jonson spent much time apart from his wife, dwelling with patrons Lord Aubigny and Sir Robert Townshend. But they seem to have made up for lost time on the rare occasions they were reunited. Jonson and Anne had several children, including a daughter, Maria, who died in November 1593 at only six months of age, and a son named Benjamin who died in 1603. Jonson had had a nightmare in which his son visited him with a bloody cross on his forehead, the sign of the plague. It was an ominous dream, reminiscent of visions experienced by characters in plays by Thomas Kyd and Shakespeare. Soon afterwards Jonson learned from his wife that Benjamin had perished. The boy's death hit Jonson particularly hard: he mourned the loss of what he considered to be his best piece of poetry. Another infant named Benjamin was baptised in February 1608.

Having, alongside Dekker, contributed speeches for the royal entry of King James to the City of London on 15 March 1604, Jonson achieved royal favour on 6 January the following year with the presentation of *The Masque of Blackness* (1605) in the old Banqueting House at Whitehall. This was Jonson's first collaboration with the architect Inigo Jones. *The Masque of Blackness* must have been an awe-inspiring spectacle, costing around three thousand pounds with a cast and props list that included six blue-haired merman-like tritons; the gods Oceanus and Niger mounted on giant seahorses; and torchbearers carried by six giant sea monsters. Jonson also produced a number of plays in the ensuing years, such as *Volpone* (1606) for the King's Men; *Epicene, or The Silent Woman* (1610) for the Children of the Queen's Revels (previously known as the Children of the Chapel); *The Alchemist* (1610) and *Catiline* (1611), acted by the King's Men; *Bartholomew Fair*, performed by Lady Elizabeth's Men in 1614; and *The Devil Is an Ass* (1616) for the King's Men.

The year 1616 saw the publication of *The Works of Benjamin Jonson*, which blazed a trail for stage plays to be considered serious works of literature, as in Shakespeare's 1623 Folio and the publication in 1647 and 1679 of the Beaumont and Fletcher Folios. But Jonson's success would diminish when King James died in 1625. Like so many dramatists of the period, Jonson found himself in combat with a foe he couldn't thrust his sword at: poverty. He died in mid-August 1637 aged sixty-five, having suffered numerous health issues in the last decade of his life, including a paralytic stroke, obesity, likely caused by living above his income, and possibly Parkinson's disease. His life was a colourful one and, although their careers intersected, Shakespeare and Jonson took different routes, not only in terms of the media and genres in which they wrote and Jonson's ambitions as a classicist but also through Jonson's choice not to work continuously for a single playing company.

Much ink has been spilt on Shakespeare and Jonson's relationship.[26] Tradition holds that Shakespeare intervened when his company were about to reject *Every Man in His Humour*: 'luckily casting his eye upon it' Shakespeare convinced the acting company to 'change their minds'. From this moment onwards 'they were professed friends', though their biographer doesn't know whether Jonson 'ever made him equal return of gentleness and generosity'. Churchman and the historian Thomas Fuller recorded that Jonson, who was 'built far higher in learning', and Shakespeare, who could nevertheless rely on the 'quickness of his wit and invention', engaged in 'wit combats' in the Mermaid Tavern. It's an alluring idea: witty words flowing like ale between the men. It must have been an incredible experience for other drinkers listening in on these brilliant conversations. Jonson was one of the last people Shakespeare ever saw if the testimony of John Ward, vicar of Stratford-upon-Avon between 1662 and 1681, is to be believed. According to Ward, Shakespeare, Jonson, and Michael Drayton 'had a merry meeting and it seems drank too hard for Shakespear died of a feavour there contracted'. Did Shakespeare die of a bad hangover? He is the nation's favourite poet, and this report perhaps says something about British booze culture. In any case it's not the only account of Shakespeare being something of a hellraiser. In his salad days he supposedly travelled to Bidford-on-Avon to challenge some famous drinkers but ended up in a stupor under a crab-apple tree. Jonson contributed a heartfelt poem to Shakespeare's First Folio titled *To the Memory of My Beloved the Author, Mr. William Shakespeare*, in which he called Shakespeare a 'star of poets' (l. 77) who 'was not of an age but for all time' (l. 43).[27] Shakespeare and Jonson were close friends and deeply appreciative of each other's literary abilities. But, as in the case of Jonson's relationship with Dekker and Marston, there are indications of antagonism.

Jonson claimed in his *Timber, or Discoveries* that Shakespeare 'flowed with that facility that sometime it was necessary he should be stopped', wishing that he had blotted more of his lines and stating elsewhere that Shakespeare 'wanted art'. The irony is that, despite complaining of Shakespeare's copiousness, Jonson's writing often demands much of both readers and listeners: his tragedy *Catiline* contains a speech 'which is over 300 lines long – and which spectacularly failed to please'.[28] Part of the point of 'some of Jonson's comic writing' is 'unintelligibility', as witnessed in the conman Subtle's deluding Ananias that he is 'immensely learned' through 'scientific jargon' and 'mystifying technical terms' in Jonson's expertly plotted play *The Alchemist*.[29] Jonson also acknowledges in *Timber, or Discoveries* that he 'loved' Shakespeare 'and do honour his memory – on this side idolatry'. But here he is in *Every Man in His Humour* mocking Shakespeare's *Henry VI* plays:

> with three rusty swords,
> And help of some few foot-and-half-foot words,
> Fight over York and Lancaster's long jars,
> And in the tiring-house bring wounds to scars. (Prologue.9–12)

In the same Prologue, which was likely written around 1612 and wouldn't have formed part of the play in which Shakespeare acted, Jonson criticises some of the stage conventions seen in plays such as *Henry V*, in which the

> Chorus wafts you o'er the seas,
> Nor creaking throne comes down, the boys to please,
> Nor nimble squib is seen, to make afeard
> The gentlewomen, nor rolled bullet heard
> To say it thunders, nor tempestuous drum
> Rumbles, to tell you when the storm doth come. (Prologue.15–20)

In *Bartholomew Fair* Jonson takes aim at the character of Caliban in *The Tempest*:

> If there be never a servant-monster i'the Fair, who can help it? he says – nor a nest of antics? He is loath to make nature afraid in his plays, like those that beget *Tales*, *Tempests*, and such-like drolleries, to mix his head with other men's heels. (Induction.95–8)

In that Induction he also has a jibe at those 'that will swear *Jeronimo* or *Andronicus* are the best plays' (Induction.123–4). Jonson famously ridiculed Shakespeare's incorporation in *The Winter's Tale* of a seacoast and a desert in Bohemia. Again in *Timber, or Discoveries* he takes a swipe at a line that Shakespeare appears to have later deleted in *Julius Caesar*: 'Many times he fell into those things could not escape laughter: as when he said in the person of Caesar, one speaking to him: "Caesar thou dost me wrong"; he replied: "Caesar did never wrong, but with just cause", and such like, which were ridiculous'. He denounces *Pericles* as a 'mouldy tale' (ll. 21–2) in his *Ode to Himself* (1629).

Shakespeare and Jonson's friendship might have succeeded not because of their similarities but rather because of their complementarity. In so many respects they were opposites when it came to approaching drama. Jonson was an advocate of neoclassical dramaturgy, an emphasis on the unities of time, place, and action, largely rejected by Shakespeare with the exceptions of *The Comedy of Errors* and *The Tempest*. Jonson does break some of these unities in plays such as *Catiline* and *Volpone*. But he stuck to the Ciceronian definition of comic realism as an imitation of life. Shakespeare's plays tend to switch settings and mingle comic and tragic elements, plots and subplots, to the extent that in defining 'his theory of neoclassical comedy' Jonson uses 'Shakespeare implicitly as his opposite example', although 'Other playwrights on the public Elizabethan stage were also guilty, in Jonson's terms, of similar violations of the classical unities'.[30] One scholar notes that 'Shakespearean and Jonsonian comedy are traditionally distinguished as romantic and satiric comedy, differing in tone and in characteristic setting: "This is Illyria, lady" (*Twelfth Night*, 1.2.2) as against "Our scene in London" (Prologue, *Alchemist*, 5)'. Shakespeare explores otherworldly locations, 'green worlds' that embody 'the anarchic freedom of the imagination', while Jonson's plays 'tend to be set in confined spaces, often claustrophobic'.[31] Whereas Shakespeare's imagination often travelled abroad, Jonson's plays tend to recall London even when not set in the city (in revising *Every Man in His Humour* and *Every Man out of His Humour* he actually transferred the plays' events from Italy to London). Jonson was developing self-aware dramas representative of a sprawling metropolitan society, voices and accents now unknown carrying across the pewter surface of the Thames, trenching each and every scale of an enormous city that unfurled like a dragon.[32]

Jonson's solid dramatic verse, which, as he told William Drummond, he wrote first 'in prose, for so his master Cambden had Learned him', contrasts with Shakespeare's more effusive style. Jonson's poetic language is often considered plain but sophisticated: he avoids highly ornamented language and sticks to rules concerning metre that can be traced to his classical inheritance. Clichés about Jonson's plain style and the image of him as a classically controlled poet are sometimes deplored in writings on Jonson. Is it more accurate to see him as a poet who embodies multiple social and historical voices?[33] While it may be considered a 'crude generalisation', statistical analysis of Shakespeare and Jonson's dramatic verse reveals that Shakespeare's is 'metrically balanced, whereas Jonson's is aggressively asymmetrical'.[34] There's a severe contrast between 'Shakespeare's balances' and 'Jonson's heaps'.[35] In some respects Shakespeare's verse is more old-fashioned than Jonson's: Shakespeare plays written around the same time as Jonson's *Sejanus* feature numerous cases of words ending in *-ion* as well as a high number of redundant *do*, old-fashioned habits Shakespeare picked at throughout his career.

Shakespeare and Jonson's habits as phrasemakers are also quite different, even for plays co-existing in the King's Men repertory: in the spreadsheet for *Volpone* in *Collocations and N-grams* only one Shakespeare play features in the top sixty, *Othello* at position thirty. *Henry IV Part One* and *Hamlet* occupy positions thirty-three and thirty-four in the spreadsheet for *The Alchemist*. In the spreadsheet for *Catiline* Shakespeare's fellow Roman tragedies, *Coriolanus*, *Antony and Cleopatra* (1606), and *Julius Caesar* ascend the heights of fifth, sixth, and eleventh places respectively. Have genre and setting impacted these results? All these Shakespeare plays predate Jonson's works, giving us little indication that Shakespeare borrowed from Jonson's dramatic language. In the cases of *Every Man in His Humour* and *Sejanus*, however, we're afforded possible glimpses into Shakespeare's actor's memory. The top-ranked play in the former spreadsheet is *Twelfth Night* at thirty-nine. While this result is not quantitatively impressive, the spreadsheet containing phrases shared between *Every Man in His Humour* and all other plays of the period gives us an opportunity to trace Jonsonian speeches that seem to have embedded themselves in Shakespeare's mind when he wrote plays after 1598. Can we work out which roles Shakespeare took in Jonson's plays? Can modern technology transport us to the past, to picture Shakespeare treading the boards in his friend's dramatic efforts?

Could Shakespeare have played Matheo, anglicised in Jonson's revision as Matthew, in *Every Man in His Humour*? Matheo is a gull who writes inferior poetry: it would be a gracious part on Shakespeare's behalf if he took this role in *Every Man in His Humour*. Maybe Shakespeare took the role of the imperious parent Old Knowell? Or the jealous husband Kitely? Matching phrases between the 1601 quarto text of *Every Man in His Humour* and Shakespeare plays include Bianca's speech to her husband Thorello, 'For God's sake, sweetheart, come in **out of the air**' (1.4.182–3), to which Thorello (renamed Kitely in Jonson's revision) speaks in an aside: '**How** simple and how subtle are her answers!' (1.4.184). In *Hamlet*, Polonius asks: 'Will you walk out of the air, my lord?' (2.2.208), to which Hamlet responds: 'Into my grave' (2.2.209). Polonius says, 'Indeed, that is **out o'th' air**' (2.2.210). He then offers an aside: '**How** pregnant sometimes his replies are' (2.2.210–11). The corresponding structures and similarities in context are striking. Is this a case of Shakespeare remembering one of his cue-lines? A biographer on Jonson notes that 'Though it is not known which role Shakespeare played in *Every Man In His Humour*, one character in particular was to remain indelibly in his mind: Thorello, the obsessively jealous merchant'.[36] Shakespeare's borrowings from the role 'would not be surprising' if he had, 'as an actor, committed Thorello's part to memory'.[37] Shakespeare seems to have recalled another of Thorello's asides, 'Spite **of the devil, how** they sting my **heart**' (3.3.8), for Maria's speech in *Twelfth Night*: 'La you, an you speak ill **of the devil, how** he takes it at **heart**' (3.4.99–100). The grammatical structure is very similar and the unique word string, 'of the devil how', embraces the noun 'heart'. Are we witnessing Shakespeare's recall of lines he delivered on stage here? Shakespeare also remembered Thorello's line 'They would give out, because **my wife is fair'** (1.4.88) when he depicted Othello's destructive jealousy: "'Tis not to make me jealous / To say **my wife is fair'** (3.3.187–8). Shakespeare inverts Thorello's comic jealousy in his similarly named tragic protagonist Othello.[38] We can't be certain which role Shakespeare took in Jonson's play, but the grammatical patterning, the very cadence, and likenesses of thought in matches with Thorello suggest Shakespeare was intimately familiar with that role's lines and cues.

In *Sejanus* we have a play which Shakespeare not only acted in but possibly co-authored with Jonson. In the preface to the 1605 edition of his tragedy, Jonson writes that

> Lastly, I would inform you that this book, in all numbers, is not the same with that which was acted on the public stage, wherein a second pen had good share; in place of which I have rather chosen to put weaker (and no doubt less pleasing) of mine own, than to defraud so happy a genius of his right by my loathed usurpation. ('To the Readers', ll. 31–5)

Shakespeare was already going to be in the cast for *Sejanus*. Would that make him the logical choice to alter the text alongside Jonson for performance? George Chapman has also been proposed as Jonson's co-author.[39] Turning to *Sejanus* in *Collocations and N-grams*, we discover that Shakespeare's *Julius Caesar* is ranked third. This result is unsurprising. Jonson's tragedy, like *Julius Caesar*, draws on classical history, but, whereas Shakespeare's characteristic approach in his Roman plays is to argue *in utramque partem*, juxtaposing differing perspectives, Jonson takes a much more clear-cut approach in *Sejanus*.[40] Sejanus is an absolute tyrant, while Caesar's capacity for tyranny is up for debate. Here, despite phrases shared between these plays, we can discern different habits of mind and what John Keats referred to as Shakespeare's 'negative capability', his embracement of 'uncertainties, Mysteries, doubts, without any irritable reaching after fact & reason'.[41] Another Roman tragedy, *Coriolanus*, is ranked eighth. Again, similarities in genre and setting seem to have influenced results. When thinking about Shakespeare retaining lines he heard or delivered as an actor, it's worth bearing in mind that the weightiness of blocky speeches in *Sejanus* that he and his fellow players needed to commit to memory might have daunted them.[42] Also we know that the published text of *Sejanus* differs from the version in which Shakespeare performed. Jonson's revisions to the play were largely limited to rewriting his co-author's contributions it seems, be that co-author Shakespeare or Chapman. The fact remains that Shakespeare's borrowings from Jonson himself don't resemble those from dramatic predecessors such as Kyd, Marlowe, and Peele in terms of quantity. Several of Jonson's plays were performed by the same company during the same seasons as Shakespeare's. But as he toiled away at his desk, his fingers dyed in fresh ink, Shakespeare's mind tended to hark back to the language of earlier Elizabethan plays rather than those of contemporaries such as Dekker, Marston, and Jonson.

The matches between Jonson's tragedy and Shakespeare's later plays that leap out to the eye tend to come from Tiberius's speeches, such as '**Sprung of the noblest** ancestors' (3.1.76), which Shakespeare echoes in *Coriolanus*: 'what stock he **springs of**, / **The noble** house o'th' Martians' (2.3.237–8). Richard Burbage would have played Sejanus and Shakespeare is placed opposite Burbage in Jonson's list of the actors in that play. It would make sense that Shakespeare played Tiberius. There are interesting thematic parallels between *Sejanus* and *Othello*: manipulative servants control the plots, beguiling their social superiors, Othello and Tiberius. The vocabulary of deception rings throughout *Othello* and *Sejanus* but doesn't feature in Shakespeare's Italian source for that play.[43] *Othello* occupies the lowly position 136 in the *Sejanus* spreadsheet in *Collocations and N-grams*. Shakespeare must have had Jonson's lines in his head when he was working on *Othello*, but for some reason he chose to ignore them.

Another play sharing points of contact with Jonson's works is *The Tempest*, even though the verbal connections between Shakespeare's play and Jonson's aren't especially striking. *Bartholomew Fair*, written after Shakespeare had retired, is the top Jonson play in the spreadsheet for *The Tempest* in forty-fourth position. *Every Man in His Humour* is ranked much lower at 362. However, just as Jonson's Thorello is reworked as Othello, the names of two characters from

Every Man in His Humour, Prospero and Stephano, crop up again in *The Tempest*. It's tempting to imagine Shakespeare engaging in dialogue with Jonson's dramas in his last sole-authored play. Shakespeare, like Jonson, sticks to the unities of time, place, and action in his late Romance. But Shakespeare's approach is distinctly different from Jonson's and hardly promotes verisimilitude, the non-specific setting of *The Tempest* enhancing our sense of fleeting theatrical illusion and differing from Jonson's locales. Shakespeare was certainly conscious of courtly masques, the kind composed by Jonson, when he wrote this play, even though he never wrote a masque himself. Shakespeare, no doubt aware of the popularity of Jonson's court entertainments, incorporates masque-like elements into *The Tempest*. We get the sense that Shakespeare is parodying formal masques and their emphasis on theatrical spectacle and illusion when Prospero says:

> Our revels now are ended. These our actors,
> As I foretold you, were all spirits, and
> Are melted into air, into thin air;
> And, like the baseless fabric of this vision,
> The cloud-capped towers, the gorgeous palaces,
> The solemn temples, the great globe itself,
> Yea, all which it inherit, shall dissolve;
> And, like this insubstantial pageant faded,
> Leave not a rack behind. (4.1.148–56)

Is this moment in *The Tempest* a swipe at Jonson's artistic pretensions? Prospero's emphasis on the impermanency of the masque could be interpreted as Shakespeare expressing his scepticism of the form.[44] Prospero's instructions to Miranda at the start of the play, 'I pray thee, mark me' (1.2.67) and 'Dost thou attend me?' (1.2.78), not only break up his long narration on how they came to be stranded on the enchanted island but could be taken as something of a jibe. Shakespeare emphasises aural techniques, the power of listening, of storytelling, for upper-class Blackfriars audience members who might be accustomed to courtly masques and visual spectacle. Shakespeare creates the island through auditory techniques in Caliban's speech:

> the isle is full of noises,
> Sounds, and sweet airs, that give delight and hurt not.
> Sometimes a thousand twangling instruments
> Will hum about mine ears, and sometime voices
> That if I then had waked after long sleep,
> Will make me sleep again. (3.2.138–43)

Here Shakespeare's monster, maligned by Jonson, speaks in a far more dignified, poetic manner than many of his Italian counterparts, working on audience imaginations through evocations of instruments twanging and humming, as well as somniferous voices. For all the technological advances at Shakespeare's fingertips in his late plays, this passage reveals a playwright who operated in a theatre of the imagination. A playwright who regarded playgoing as a primarily aural experience throughout his career.

But Shakespeare's poetry wasn't a mere riposte to the gaudy spectacle of Jonsonian masques. After all, Jonson and Inigo Jones's hugely successful collaboration descended into acrimony. In his 1631 poem *An Expostulation with Inigo Jones* Jonson laments the 'mechanic age' (l. 52). Although he made admirable use of stage machinery in *The Tempest*, could Shakespeare have felt similarly? Jonson and Shakespeare's relationship was complicated. But Jonson's criticisms of Shakespeare shouldn't be seen, as his Volpone puts it, as the simple act of 'Mocking a gaping crow' (1.3.96). The two playwrights were locked in ongoing critical conversations about the very nature, the very purpose of drama. In so many respects their dramaturgical preferences and stylistic feathers differed. And yet Jonson and the man he eulogised as the swan of Stratford-upon-Avon ascended formidable poetic heights together.

8

Thomas Middleton

Shakespeare hadn't yet appeared on the scene. A decade or so would pass until he ignited his career as an actor-dramatist. But the stars were dancing for him in 1580 because it was the year when his future collaborator Thomas Middleton (1580–1627) was baptised on 18 April in St Lawrence Jewry, London.[1] Middleton was the first son of a gentleman and bricklayer named William Middleton and his wife Anne, who lived on the corner of Cateaton Street and Ironmonger Lane. After Middleton's father's death in 1586, his mother married a gentleman grocer named Thomas Harvey. It was to be an unhappy union: Harvey engaged in a long-running legal battle with Anne over Middleton and his younger sister's inheritance. In 1598 Middleton attended Queen's College, Oxford, but he didn't graduate. It's impossible to pinpoint where Middleton's literary inspiration came from. Despite their difficulties Harvey might have contributed indirectly to Middleton's future vocation. Harvey owned property near the Curtain Theatre. Did young Thomas find himself in that theatre one afternoon? Did the roars of spectators, the smell of ale and garlic, the onstage strutting and fretting stir something in him?

Middleton launched his literary career with three long poems, including a satire that was publicly burnt in June 1599. In 1600 he wrote *The Ghost of Lucrece*, an Ovidian female complaint composed in rhyme royal, influenced by Shakespeare's narrative poem. He also produced topical pamphlets, such as *The Penniless Parliament of Threadbare Poets* (1601). He had begun writing plays for the

Admiral's Men by May 1602, collaborating with dramatists such as Thomas Dekker, Michael Drayton, Anthony Munday, and John Webster, and writing a new Prologue and Epilogue for a Friar Bacon play, possibly *John of Bordeaux*, which was performed at court. As the 'War of the Theatres' raged, Middleton found himself in the line of fire. His association with Dekker drew the ire of both Ben Jonson and George Chapman, although we can't be sure whether Middleton himself engaged in this literary battle. Maybe he was an ancillary combatant.

In 1603 Middleton married Magdalen (Mary) Marbeck, the niece of Elizabeth I's chief physician, Roger Marbeck, and sister of the actor Thomas Marbeck, who was working with Middleton for the Admiral's Men and might very well have introduced the couple. They had one child, named Edward, born in 1603. The accession of King James was also fruitful for Middleton: he was commissioned to write for *The Magnificent Entertainment Given to King James*, and his earliest surviving play, *The Phoenix* (1604), a disguised duke play like *Measure for Measure*, was presented before the monarch at court. That play is 'written in a mixture of verse and prose, the one often shading into the other', fluctuating 'between morality drama, melodrama, social satire and genial comedy'.[2] Middleton continued to supply plays to the Admiral's Men (renamed Prince Henry's Men), such as *1 Honest Whore* (1604), co-written with Dekker. Between 1603 and 1606 he also wrote comedies for the Children of Paul's, such as *A Trick to Catch the Old One* (1605), *A Mad World, My Masters* (1605), and *The Puritan* (1606); a lost tragedy for the Children of Blackfriars (the renamed Children of the Chapel); as well as tragedies for the King's Men, including *A Yorkshire Tragedy*, which dramatises Walter Calverley's murder of his sons in 1605, a sensational story also taken up by the playwright George Wilkins. Another tragedy attributed to Middleton written for the King's Men is *The Revenger's Tragedy* (1606), a bitingly satirical, brilliant exploration of corruption in the Italian court. Middleton worked as a freelance writer in much the same way as his friend Dekker. Also like Dekker, he took opportunities to reflect London society, as in his comedy *Michaelmas Term* (1604), which has been described as a 'very modern morality play' depicting 'the rapacious appetite of a city economy dominated by Michaelmas term'.[3]

Following a period in which, again like Dekker, Middleton endured financial hardship, the two dramatists co-wrote more plays, such as *The Bloody Banquet* (1610) and *The Roaring Girl* (1611). In 1613 Middleton produced *A Chaste Maid in Cheapside*, arguably his comic *pièce de résistance*, for Lady Elizabeth's Men. He collaborated with William Rowley on *Wit at Several Weapons* (1613) when that company merged with Prince Charles's Men. A series of masques and pageants ensued, beginning with *The Triumphs of Truth* (1613), during which Middleton ventured into the realm of tragicomedy with *The Witch* (1616); *A Fair Quarrel* (1616), co-written with Rowley; and *An Old Law* (1619), co-authored with Rowley and Thomas Heywood. Other co-authored works include *Timon of Athens* (1607) with Shakespeare; *The World Tossed at Tennis* (1620) with Rowley, a courtly masque performed at Denmark House that later transferred to the commercial stage; *The Changeling* (1622), an accomplished blend of tragic and comic ingredients again produced with Rowley;[4] and the city comedy *Anything for a Quiet Life* (1622) with Webster. Middleton's later sole-authored plays include *Women, Beware Women* (1621) and his hugely popular, but also hugely controversial, *A Game at Chess* (1624), which offended the Spanish ambassador and the Privy Council in its depiction of a conflict between Spain and England. The play references the negotiations to wed Prince Charles to the Spanish Infanta Maria Anna, a hot topic at the time. Middleton thrust his quill firmly into the fire, transforming political figures into chess pieces: King James as the White King, his son Charles as the White Knight, and his daughter Elizabeth as the White Queen. The Spanish King became the Black King, his sister the Black Queen, and a spate of religious figures appear in such roles as the Fat Bishop. The result of this controversy: Middleton never wrote for the stage again. On 4 July 1627 he was buried in St Mary's churchyard, Newington, leaving his widow in poverty. Another tragic ending for one of Shakespeare's contemporaries.

Collocations and N-grams supports the scholar Gary Taylor's observation that 'Shakespeare influenced Middleton (and every other dramatist of his time) more than Middleton influenced Shakespeare'. While 'Middleton wrote replies to Shakespeare's *Rape of Lucrece* and *Hamlet*, alluded to *Titus Andronicus*, and was demonstrably influenced by *1 Henry IV*' there's 'no clear case of Shakespeare being influenced by Middleton'.[5] The top-ranked Shakespeare plays in the spreadsheet for *The Phoenix* were all written before Middleton's play: *Henry IV Part Two* in fifteenth position, followed by *Henry V* in forty-eighth place. On the other hand Middleton's irrepressible habit of repeating his preferred phrases has a walloping impact on results with the top eight plays including his *A Trick to Catch the Old One*; *Michaelmas Term*; *The Puritan*; *A Mad World, My Masters*; *The Revenger's Tragedy*; and the city comedy, *Your Five Gallants* (1607).

The same is true for *The Revenger's Tragedy*: *The Phoenix*, *A Mad World, My Masters*, and the Middleton collaboration with Rowley and Heywood, *An Old Law*, make up the top three plays. This is a revelation: there have been fierce arguments over the authorship of this play going back decades. Was Middleton responsible or did the English soldier and playwright Cyril Tourneur write *The Revenger's Tragedy*? The play was attributed to Tourneur by the publishers Edward Archer in 1656 and Francis Kirkman in 1661 and 1671. But it's long been noted that the play closely resembles Middleton's style.[6] Tourneur's *The Atheist's Tragedy* (1610) is in position 219 in *Collocations and N-grams*, establishing once and for all that Middleton, and not Tourneur, was indeed the author of *The Revenger's Tragedy*. How does Shakespeare fare for *The Revenger's Tragedy*? In thirty-seventh position, *All's Well that Ends Well* is the top-ranked Shakespeare play. Shakespeare's play appears to have been written before Middleton's tragedy. As we will see, however, the possibility of Middleton's revising hand might help to account for their connections.

Middleton's self-repetition also manifests itself in his collaboration with Shakespeare, *Timon of Athens*: his tragicomedy *More Dissemblers besides Women* (1621) is ranked fifth and *The Phoenix* ninth. Shakespeare's *Coriolanus* is in second place, followed by his *The Merry Wives of Windsor* in third position. *Twelfth Night* and *Antony and Cleopatra* are ranked seventh and eighth respectively.

The genetic makeup of this play suddenly becomes visible under a microscopic lens. Modern technology vindicates arguments going back decades, arguments made by academics who couldn't even dream of the discoveries now at our fingertips. *Timon of Athens*, a tale of a wealthy Athenian betrayed by his friends, was first attributed in part to Middleton in 1920. As early as the late nineteenth century it was pointed out that Shakespeare's co-author's voice sounded just like that speaking to readers of *The Revenger's Tragedy*.[7] *Timon of Athens* is a very different play from Shakespeare's unassisted tragedies: city comedy shakes hands with classical drama. The *dramatis personae* features a notable lack of personal names: the Poet, the Painter, the Jeweller, and others make up its roles. This is characteristic of Middleton's plays but unlike Shakespeare. Shakespeare and Middleton were birds of a feather when it came to ending verse lines with 'feminine' endings. But the similarities end there: Middleton employs rhymes far more often than Shakespeare does. While Shakespeare tends to use rhyme sparingly and deliberately in his speeches, Middleton has a habit of peppering his verse with moralising rhyming couplets, as in the steward Flavius's speech: 'Undone by goodness! Strange, unusual blood / When man's worst sin is, he does too much good!' (4.2.38–9). Like an erratic motorist, the verse in the play frequently swerves into prose, characteristic of 'Middleton's mixing of prose and verse in single speeches',[8] a habit that 'can be disconcerting to readers trained on Shakespeare' but 'reflects' a 'recognised trait of Middleton's writing'.[9] Take for example the Servant's speech in 3.3:

> Excellent. Your lordship's a goodly villain. The
> devil knew not what he did when he made man
> politic – he crossed himself by't, and I cannot think but
> in the end, the villainies of man will set him clear. How
> fairly this lord strives to appear foul! Takes virtuous
> copies to be wicked, like those that under hot ardent
> zeal would set whole realms on fire; of such a nature
> is his politic love.

> This was my lord's best hope. Now all are fled,
> Save only the gods. Now his friends are dead.
> Doors that were ne'er acquainted with their wards

Many a bounteous year must be employed
Now to guard sure their master;
And this is all a liberal course allows:
Who cannot keep his wealth must keep his house. (3.3.27–41)

This speech begins in prose and then shifts into erratic verse on the line, 'This was my lord's best hope'. If you turn an edition of the play sideways, Middleton's writing sometimes resembles a cardiogram on the page. Colloquialisms and contractions also help us to zone in on authors' voices: Middleton's preferences, such as "'em' for 'them', 'has' for 'hath', and his fondness for the contraction 'h'as' for 'he has', differentiate his contributions to the play from Shakespeare's.

The portfolio of evidence for Middleton as Shakespeare's co-author is fat. It gets even thicker when we look at phrases unique to *Timon of Athens* and Middleton in *Collocations and N-grams*. These phrases cluster in scenes for which he's long been the suspected author, offering us precious insights into his dramatic language. Lucius's question 'Good Servilius, will **you befriend me so** far, as to use mine own words to him?' (3.2.58–9) matches Middleton's *Women, Beware Women*: 'You see my honesty, / If **you befriend me, so**' (1.2.160–1).[10] The exact image of 'hollow bones' is unique to Timon's speech, 'Consumptions sow / In **hollow bones** of man' (4.3.151–2), and Vindice's opening soliloquy of *The Revenger's Tragedy*, 'O that marrowless age / Should stuff the **hollow bones** with damned desires' (1.1.5–6). Middleton riffs off *Hamlet* in that tragedy, his non-subtly named revenger gazing into the hollow sockets of his murdered lover's skull. Were Middleton's contributions to 4.3 of *Timon of Athens* more extensive than has been supposed?

Middleton seems to have been responsible for 1.2 and most of the third act, while 4.2 and 4.3 suggest mixed writing. Did Shakespeare and Middleton go off and work on their stints separately, or did they sometimes write in the same room?[11] Shakespeare bore responsibility for the opening of the play: a reversal of the distribution of labour in his early collaborations *Titus Andronicus* and *Edward III*. Shakespeare was the more experienced playwright, guiding his younger co-author on *Timon of Athens* while seeking to make expeditious use of the play's 'required sardonic tone and a vivid attention to the grittiness of city life'. As editors of this play have pointed out, the combination of 'tragedy and urban satire' was 'Middleton's forte'.[12] It's been suggested that Shakespeare 'took the lead, not only contributing about 65 per cent of the whole, but producing the overall plan', while Middleton took responsibility for scenes in which his 'satirical skills' might be put to best use; such as the play's 'tawdry masque and banquet scene'; the 'witty commentary' of the philosopher Apemantus; 'the scenes of attempted borrowing' and 'the debt-collecting sequences' that give a snarling commentary on gift economies; and 'most of the sections involving the faithful steward, Flavius'.[13] The result is a tragedy quite unlike any other in the Shakespeare canon, showing off the contrasting and yet complementary skillsets and stylistic feathers of two brilliant Jacobean dramatists at very different points in their careers.

Do Middleton's feathers adorn other plays in Shakespeare's dramatic canon? Middleton had gained considerable experience since collaborating directly with Shakespeare. He might have revised several Shakespeare plays, most famously *Macbeth*. The astrologer Simon Forman recorded his impressions of three Shakespeare plays he saw at the Globe: *Macbeth*, *The Winter's Tale*, and *Cymbeline*. Forman has given us the most detailed surviving accounts of attending plays during the Jacobean period. His remembrances transport us to a distant age, giving us snapshots of how Shakespeare's plays were originally staged. Having seen *Macbeth* on 20 April 1611, Forman describes, among other moments in the play, Macbeth and Banquo's encounter with the witches:

> There was to be observed first how Macbeth and Banquo, 2 noblemen of Scotland, riding through a wood, there stood before them 3 women fairies or nymphs, and saluted Macbeth, saying 3 times unto him, 'Hail Macbeth, king of Codon [thane of Cawdor], for thou shall be a king but shall beget no kings,' etc. Then said Banquo, 'What, all to Macbeth, and nothing to me?' There said the nymphs, 'Hail to thee, Banquo, thou shall beget kings, yet be no king.'

There are important differences between Forman's eyewitness account and *Macbeth* as we know it. Forman doesn't mention the

character of Hecate, the goddess of magic, the night, moon, and nec-
romancy, a curious omission given his keen interest in the occult.
He describes the witches as 'fairies or nymphs', more closely resembling the figures Shakespeare would have found in Holinshed and
totally unlike the 'midnight hags' (4.1.63) with 'skinny lips' and
'choppy' fingers (1.3.41–2) in the surviving Folio text. Forman's
account also chimes with the presentation of three sibyls before
King James in an entertainment performed at Oxford on 27 August
1605, during which the King was hailed as a royal descendant of
Banquo. Is Forman's testimony reliable in terms of detail? We can't
be sure but his account presents the possibility that the text of
Macbeth included in the First Folio might not fully represent the
version originally performed in Shakespeare's lifetime. *Macbeth* is
around 30 per cent shorter than other tragedies Shakespeare wrote at
the time like *Coriolanus*, *Antony and Cleopatra*, and *King Lear*. Was
the play abridged? *Macbeth* barrels along like a train and is often
most impactful in performance when there's a sense of claustro-
phobia, as in Trevor Nunn's 1976 production starring Ian McKellen
and Judi Dench in the tin shed that was Stratford-upon-Avon's The
Other Place, actors planted in the audience to breathe heavily as the
Macbeths plotted regicide. To read *Macbeth* is to sup full of horrors.
But the chill that reaches from the page and traces readers' spines
like a yarn mallet on the bars of a xylophone can be hard to replicate in performance. The 1980 production starring Peter O'Toole at
the Old Vic was apparently so bad that self-flagellating audiences
flocked to see it. The moment when his Macbeth descended some
stairs after murdering Duncan, drenched from head to foot in claret
and announcing, 'I have done the deed' (2.2.14), elicited uproarious
laughter every evening.

Was the action of the play sped up for audiences to make way for
alternative material? As long ago as 1869 there were suggestions
that the 'interpolator' of additional material 'was, not improbably,
Thomas Middleton; who, to please the "groundlings," expanded the
parts originally assigned by Shakespeare to the weird sisters, and
also introduced a new character, Hecate'.[14] It's been proposed that
Macbeth was adapted in the year Shakespeare died; that Middleton

was responsible for an additional 151 lines; that his writing is mixed with Shakespeare's in 72 lines; and that Middleton's contributions amount to about 11 per cent of the surviving play.[15] Theatrical exigencies likely had an impact on this process of adaptation: the 'fairies or nymphs' seen by Forman would have been played by young boys. The King's Men had more adult males at their disposal in 1616, which might have prompted the change.[16] Alongside passages featuring the character of Hecate, Middleton's hand has also been claimed in parts of the first and fourth acts.

In 3.5 the witches meet with Hecate on a heath and she scolds them for meddling in Macbeth's business without first consulting her. The cue in this scene for a song beginning 'Come away, come away' belongs to Middleton's The Witch (3.3.39–72), written around 1616. Is this proof of a much later addition to Shakespeare's play? Macbeth was likely first composed in 1606. In a series of exchanges that are superfluous to the narrative thrust of the play, Hecate speaks largely in octosyllabic couplets, lines of eight syllables, which can also be found in Hecate's dialogue in The Witch. The verse style is inconsistent with not only the rest of the play but Shakespeare's dramas in general:

HECATE
He shall spurn fate, scorn death, and bear
His hopes 'bove wisdom, grace and fear;
And you all know, security
Is mortals' chiefest enemy.
SPIRITS (singing dispersedly within)
Come away, come away.
Hecate, Hecate, come away.
HECATE
Hark, I am called! My little spirit, see,
Sits in a foggy cloud and stays for me. (3.5.30–7)

Compare the Hecate of Macbeth's speeches with Middleton's similar mix of seven-, eight-, and ten-syllable lines for Hecate in The Witch:

There take this unbaptizèd brat.
Boil it well. Preserve the fat:
You know 'tis precious to transfer
Our 'nointed flesh into the air

In moonlit nights, o'er steeple-tops,
Mountains, and pine-trees, that like pricks or stops. (1.2.15–20)

There are enough prosodic similarities here to suggest that Middleton had a revising hand in scenes involving *Macbeth*'s witches. Another cue for a song featuring in Middleton's *The Witch* (5.2.63–79) begins *'Black spirits'* and can be found in 4.1 of *Macbeth*, again following a speech delivered by Hecate:

O, well done! I commend your pains,
And everyone shall share i'th' gains.
And now about the cauldron sing
Like elves and fairies in a ring,
Enchanting all that you put in. (4.1.39–43)

In this scene Hecate appears and compliments the witches on their work before Macbeth enters and is shown a series of apparitions. The Hecate business has all the hallmarks of material inserted before a key exchange between Macbeth and the witches.

Although not all scholars agree that the additions to *Macbeth* were written by Middleton,[17] the surviving text reveals the fluidity of theatrical scripts, which were open to adaptation during the early modern period just as they are today. Hecate is often cut from modern performances, but she was certainly popular in the seventeenth and eighteenth centuries. Her scenes afford creatives opportunities for music, dance, pageantry, and dazzling spectacle, as seen in William Davenant's brilliant 1664 adaptation which featured witches zipping about on broomsticks and Hecate riding a cloud. Middleton's insertions blend the extravagance of the dramatist's Lord Mayor's shows and court masques, such as *The Triumphs of Truth* and *The Masque of Heroes* (1619), with Shakespeare's material.[18] None of Middleton's sole-authored plays cracks the top 100 in the spreadsheet for *Macbeth* in *Collocations and N-grams*, but *The Witch* isn't included among its 527 plays. Also theatrical adaptation produces 'much smaller blocks of new text than most collaborations. Smaller blocks mean less data; less data mean less evidence to support any hypothesis.'[19] Either way there are undeniable links between the surviving text of *Macbeth* and Middleton's *The Witch*. Is the version of *Macbeth* that has come down to us the product of abridgement and revision? Was Middleton the author of Hecate's scenes? If so, was he responsible for other theatrical adaptations for the King's Men playing company?

It's also been proposed that Middleton adapted *Measure for Measure*. Did the acquisition of the Blackfriars Theatre in 1608 spur the company to adapt some of Shakespeare's plays? *Measure for Measure* lacks oaths such as "slid' for 'God's lid' and "swounds' for 'God's wounds', suggesting they might have been deleted after the 1606 Act of Parliament to 'Restrain Abuses of Players', which made such profanities illegal. The play also features a song from John Fletcher's *Rollo, Duke of Normandy, or The Bloody Brother* (1617), written after Shakespeare's death. Further evidence for adaptation can be found in the duplication of the moment when Mistress Overdone (a distinctly Middletonian name) delivers news of Claudio's arrest in 1.2. Middleton's linguistic preferences, as opposed to those of other King's Men dramatists such as Fletcher, Philip Massinger, and John Webster, cluster in this proposed replacement for Shakespeare's original sequence. Some of the Provost's speeches might have been given to Lucio, an occasionally rancid gentleman who hangs out with bawds and yet has some of the most beautiful lines in the play. There are lines in 2.2 and a speech in 4.3 that provide a set-piece for a clown. Materials of this kind were often added to theatrical adaptations.[20] Did Middleton pen these lines? Middleton might also have transposed speeches delivered by the Duke in 3.1 and 4.1. Topical allusions to economic depression, European conflict, and political controversies suggest the play was adapted in late 1621 or early 1622.[21]

Collocations and N-grams doesn't offer much support for the theory of Middletonian revision when it comes to cold, hard numbers: despite their dramatic similarities, Middleton's *The Phoenix* is ranked in position 389 in the spreadsheet for *Measure for Measure*. However, Middleton's proposed revisions make up only 5 per cent of the text. Some of the longest unique phrases shared with Middleton can be found in scenes containing suspected alterations, such as 2.1, when the dim-witted constable Elbow says, '**The time is yet to come that** she was **ever** respected with man, woman, or child' (2.1.160–1).

Middleton recycles this lengthy word combination in *A Game at Chess*, '**The time is yet to come that e'er** I spoke' (5.3.147). Pompey's speech in the same scene, '**I thank your worship for your** good **counsel**' (2.1.241), matches *A Trick to Catch the Old One*: '**I thank your worship for your** hot **counsel**' (4.5.136). Though lengthy, these unremarkable phrases are unlikely to have appealed to a borrower's ear. Does their concentration suggest that Middleton was indeed responsible for revising the play? Middleton's proposed interventions are of a lighter touch than is the case with *Macbeth*, achieving 'maximum impact by minimal textual intervention'.[22]

The *New Oxford Shakespeare* team argue that Middleton added 3.2, the so-called 'fly scene', to *Titus Andronicus* at some point between 1608 and 1623.[23] The scene follows that in which Aaron tricks Titus into cutting off his hand; Marcus's bringing Lavinia on stage following her rape and mutilation; and Lucius's resolution to levy an army of Goths as revenge for his brothers' executions. Titus reacts to the series of terrible events with a manic laugh, indicative of a mental breakdown:

> TITUS
> Ha, ha, ha!
> MARCUS
> Why dost thou laugh? It fits not with this hour.
> TITUS
> Why, I have not another tear to shed. (3.1.263–5)

In 3.2 the family have a small banquet, during which Marcus kills a fly. He's rebuked by Titus until Marcus compares the fly to the villainous Aaron. Titus then praises this 'charitable deed' (3.2.70), which convinces Marcus that he's quite mad: 'Grief has so wrought on him / He takes false shadows as true substances' (3.2.78–9). The scene serves an important purpose for audience understanding of Titus's psychological disintegration. Although 3.2 isn't central to the play's plot, it is paramount in terms of character, theme, and dramatic structure. Lavinia has had her hands lopped and tongue cut out. Titus interprets her 'dumb action' (3.2.40). His resolve to 'interpret all her martyred signs' (3.2.35), her refusal to eat or drink, suggests that the later moment when Titus kills her during the play's mirror, cannibalistic banquet is also a 'charitable deed' (3.2.70), an assisted suicide rather than an act of murder. The 'fly scene' is followed by 4.1, in which Lavinia reveals that she was raped by Chiron and Demetrius by guiding a staff with her mouth and writing their names in a sandy plot.

The 1594 First Quarto of *Titus Andronicus* would seem to reflect Shakespeare and George Peele's working manuscript. The stage direction '*as many as may be*' (1.1.69.1 SD) suggests a writer who isn't sure of the size of the company he's writing for. The direction is characteristic of Peele's hand: in *Edward I* we also find the permissive phrase: '*others as many as may be*' (1.40.1 SD). The 1593 text of *Edward I* derives from the author's manuscript, or 'foul papers'. While the stage directions in the First Quarto of *Titus Andronicus* reflect the authors' intentions during the process of writing the play, those in the Folio text suggest playhouse interventions. The Folio text was set from the 1611 Third Quarto, which was based on the Second Quarto, which was in turn based on the First Quarto. The Folio text contains stage directions that have the authority of the playhouse and divides the play into five acts, reflecting the introduction of act-breaks in the Jacobean theatre. In printing 3.2 for the first time the Folio version requires a group of characters to go offstage and come straight back. This is something Shakespeare avoided like a plague outbreak. The printing of 3.2 indicates that a different copy was used than for the rest of the play, including several errors that could be due to misreadings of a manuscript copy.[24]

The *New Oxford Shakespeare* team contend that the scene must have been added to the play when the King's Men started performing at the Blackfriars Theatre, where 3.2 could have been followed by a musical interlude as candles were relit. In which case the Andronici wouldn't need to leave the stage and then immediately re-enter. However, the bibliographer W. W. Greg noted that the scene must have been added to the play *before* it was divided into acts, which could be separated by such interludes, otherwise the third act would be exceptionally short.[25] The scene isn't written in Shakespeare's post-1607 style. Does this mean that Shakespeare wasn't its author?

It's possible that the scene was written by Shakespeare in time for a revival by Sussex's Men at the Rose in 1594. But it is absent from the 1594 quarto entered in the Stationers' Register in February of that year. So this seems unlikely. If we take a model of simultaneous collaboration, or co-authorship, between Shakespeare and Peele into account, a possible explanation for the omission of 3.2 emerges. Having both worked from a single plot outline, Shakespeare would be aware that Peele bore responsibility for writing the scene in which the identities of Lavinia's harmers are revealed, but he's unlikely to have been aware of the staging details involved. Shakespeare therefore writes the 'fly scene' and, knowing that Peele will be responsible for the revelation scene, but having not read his co-author's work, he moves on to the scene labelled 4.2, which avoids breaking the Elizabethan convention of characters leaving the stage and immediately re-entering. Scene 4.2 begins with the entrance of Aaron, Chiron, and Demetrius. After Shakespeare and Peele had completed their contributions to the play, their 'foul papers' would have been brought together. But when the authors' portions are merged, a structural difficulty emerges. Peele's 4.1 is crucial to the plot of the play. It simply can't be omitted from the manuscript. So 3.2 is omitted instead: the action of 3.1, which concludes with the speech by Lucius vowing to raise an army of Goths, thus leads neatly to the entrance of Lucius's son running away from Lavinia in Peele's scene.

The 'fly scene' seems to have been copied out by a different scribe from the one who worked on the 1594 text. The scene features the modern form 'has', which doesn't appear in the quarto version of the play. It doesn't include the older form 'hath', preferred by Shakespeare. Could this suggest that, as seems to be the case with the printer's manuscript behind *The Taming of the Shrew*, the hand responsible for copying out the scene was Jacobean? Greg conjectured that 'A leaf might, of course, have been lost from the foul papers after the prompt-book had been prepared and before Q was printed from them'.[26] Others have also considered it probable that 3.2 formed part of the original play. But they've scratched their heads when it comes to the question of why Shakespeare would hold the scene back.[27] What if the scene was separated from the manuscript behind the First Quarto when Shakespeare and Peele's portions of the play were merged, because it broke an Elizabethan convention Shakespeare liked to stick to? This could explain the mystery and would also consolidate the case for simultaneous collaboration between Shakespeare and Peele, rather than revision.

The *New Oxford Shakespeare* team recognise that the 'verse' of 3.2 'does not sound like late Middleton: the proportion of feminine endings is too low, the distributions of pause patterns and of strong stresses look Elizabethan rather than Jacobean'.[28] Although, at 84 lines in length, the scene is short for analysis, it is at one with Shakespeare's other contributions to the play, its percentage of 10 for 'feminine' endings approximating the 10.7 for 4.3, a scene containing around the same number of verse lines, but sharply contrasting with Peele's 4.1, which averages only 1.5 per cent.[29] Could Middleton have 'noticed and mimicked some of the most conspicuously old-fashioned features of the verse'? Could the 'anomalous metrical features of the added scene' be the result of 'deliberate imitation of the original'?[30] It's difficult to think of any additions by a revising dramatist that are indistinguishable from the style of an original play by other authors. Even when Shakespeare rewrote 4.6 of *Henry VI Part One*, his contribution is stylistically dissimilar to the original. And why would a dramatist trying to cater to Jacobean tastes by adding to the play's action write in such an old-fashioned way? Unlike Middleton's proposed additions to *Macbeth*, the scene is woven out of the verbal fabric of Shakespeare's other contributions to the play. There are several word combinations that are rare or unique to 3.2 and Shakespeare's other scenes, but the *New Oxford Shakespeare* team dismiss them: 'Anyone commissioned to write an additional scene would be expected to integrate it into the rest of the script'.[31] But couldn't distinctive phrases shared with Shakespeare's other scenes in the play, like 'between thy teeth' (3.2.16), 'kill a fly' (3.2.76), and 'a coal black' (3.2.77), reveal the same author's working memory?

The vocabulary of the 'fly scene' resembles Shakespeare's writing during the period 1593–96,[32] hardly much later than the world's leading scholar on chronology Martin Wiggins's dating of 1592 for the play. Only one of Shakespeare's verbal parallels in 3.2 comes from the period after *Pericles*, when the King's Men started using act divisions.[33] Could this suggest that the scene was written earlier in Shakespeare's career? It's a theory that chimes with the use of 'feminine' endings. Overall the results for this scene point towards Shakespeare's authorship during the Elizabethan period, when *Titus Andronicus* was originally written. The only internal evidence against this is the claim that Middleton shares more unique phrases with the scene than Shakespeare does according to 'microattribution'. The results for Middleton are of a much lower quality than those for early Shakespeare, however. Titus's use of *polyptoton*, in the line '**unknit that** sorrow-wreathen knot' (3.2.4) closely parallels Katherina's speech in *The Taming of the Shrew*: 'Fie, fie, **unknit that** threat'ning, unkind brow' (5.2.141). Shakespeare's use of this rhetorical scheme to appeal to the audience's sympathy is characteristic of his early plays like *Richard III*. It helps to distinguish Shakespeare's portions of *Titus Andronicus* from Peele's, especially 4.1, which, though harrowing, features just two (seemingly accidental) examples of this device.[34] Titus asks his brother, 'Has sorrow **made thee dote** already?' (3.2.23), which echoes Duke Solinus's speech in *The Comedy of Errors*: 'I see thy age and dangers **make thee dote**' (5.1.331). Titus says to Lavinia: 'Wound it with sighing, girl, **kill it with groans**' (3.2.15). In *Richard II* the Queen says: 'I may strive to **kill it with** a **groan**' (5.1.100). Speech fragments shared with Middleton, such as 'in us | As] Middleton, *A Game at Chess* (including line break)'; 'or get some] or gets some (Middleton, *Microcynicon*)'; and 'art made of] Middleton, *Phoenix*',[35] pale in comparison. The 'fly scene' would seem to sit firmly within Shakespeare's Elizabethan lexicon, which is distinctly different from Middleton.

There's a more compelling argument in the *New Oxford Shakespeare* for Middleton's revision of *All's Well that Ends Well*. The play has long been noted for its stylistic and tonal discrepancies: there appear to be contrasting modes of thought mixed together and various textual layers with obvious joins.[36] In 2012 an answer was proposed for the play's supposed inconsistencies: Shakespeare co-authored it with Middleton.[37] Evidence presented for this scenario included the proportion of rhyming lines in the play, which is high for Shakespeare's Jacobean works but typical of Middleton; speech prefixes and stage directions characteristic of Middleton; and Middletonian vocabulary choices. A savage debate ensued when the attribution was rejected by academics who compared the proportion of rhyme to similar rates in *As You Like It* and *Twelfth Night* and showed that Shakespeare didn't uniformly prefer some speech prefixes.[38] The *New Oxford Shakespeare* team agree that aspects of the case for Middleton's co-authorship were faulty. However, there are clusters of stylistic markers suggesting Middleton's hand in parts of the play. The markers that Middleton used more regularly than Shakespeare, such as "em', 'e'ne', 'ha's', and 'do's', and the absence of Shakespeare markers, suggest that Middleton inserted fresh material for the gulling of Paroles in 4.3, the comic highlight of the play. These markers tend to be found in material deemed dramaturgically expendable.[39]

Middleton's hand is claimed in not only the gulling of Paroles but also the virginity dialogue between Paroles and Helena in 1.1; a speech delivered by the King of France in 2.3, possibly intended as a replacement for another speech delivered four lines later in Shakespeare's original; and in various moments of comic business. As in the cases of *Macbeth* and *Measure for Measure*, there's little numerical evidence for Middleton's hand according to *Collocations and N-grams*: *A Game at Chess* features in position 163 in the spreadsheet for *All's Well that Ends Well*, *Women, Beware Women* at 372. But so far only around 6 per cent of the play has been given to Middleton. The few unique matches with Middleton are in any case imprecise: the phrase 'breed honour', is supposedly unique to the King's speech 'In these to nature she's immediate heir, / And these breed honour' (2.3.133–4) and *A Game at Chess*. But the phrase in Middleton's play is 'diseased bedrid honour' (3.1.14), which is rather different.

Did Middleton tinker with the play for the King's Men playing company?[40] This is a new attribution theory. It'll be exciting to see how it develops. It might help to explain some textual anomalies, but the theory of revision shouldn't be treated as a means of explaining away the play's shifts in tone. *All's Well that Ends Well* is an admirably experimental play that blends fairy-tale logic with cynical realism, featuring a proactive heroine, fascinating gender role reversals with women tricking the males, and characters who are at times morally ambiguous and enigmatic.

Middleton was a significant Jacobean contemporary of Shakespeare who wrote in a variety of dramatic genres, from comedies to tragedies, history plays, masques, and pageants. He was also an important collaborator for Shakespeare on *Timon of Athens*. Middleton's writing possibly survives in Shakespeare's First Folio through processes of revision, adaptation, and abridgement. In shortening *Macbeth*, Middleton would, to quote his play *The Phoenix*, 'Take' some of Shakespeare's 'feathers down'. But his possible additions to Shakespeare plays also help to 'fetch' both dramatists 'up' (8.280), to resurrect the phoenix of their dramatic relationship.

9

John Fletcher

We hold the lives and careers of these writers like water in cupped hands. The final droplets spreading circles in our palms are especially precious as we encounter Shakespeare's last direct collaborator: John Fletcher (1579–1625).[1] Together Fletcher and Shakespeare wrote *Henry VIII*, or *All Is True* (1612), *The Two Noble Kinsmen* (1613), and the lost play *Cardenio* (1612) for the King's Men. We've seen that a song from the Fletcher collaboration *Rollo, Duke of Normandy* was interpolated, possibly by Thomas Middleton, into *Measure for Measure* after Shakespeare's death. Fletcher was the son of the cleric Richard Fletcher and Elizabeth Holland. Richard was a prodigious member of the Church of England, serving as Dean of Peterborough, Bishop of Bristol, Bishop of Worcester, and Bishop of London. He wrote his way into the history books with vehement prayers during the execution of Mary, Queen of Scots. These prayers must have been demonstrative to say the least. Richard managed to steal the attention of onlookers despite the bloody spectacle before them: a botched beheading that took several blows to cut through remaining sinews, followed by the grisly sight of Mary's small dog paddling the claret issuing from its owner's mawed neck.

Richard's son was born in Sussex around seven years before that historic event: on 20 December 1579. John Fletcher entered Corpus Christi College, Cambridge, on 15 October 1591 at the tender age of just eleven. Fletcher seems to have been destined for a clerical career, following the steep and thorny path beaten by his family members. However, having achieved an MA in 1598, he eventually turned to the stage, writing his first play, a hilarious comedy called *The Woman Hater* (1606), in which a prized fish causes mayhem in Milan, with Francis Beaumont. According to John Aubrey, Fletcher and Beaumont 'lived together on the Bankeside, not far from the Play-house', with 'one wench in the house between them, which they did so admire; the same cloathes and cloake, &c., between them', suggesting an intensely collaborative relationship, as well as a rather limited wardrobe. When Fletcher's plays first came into print, they were collectively attributed to Fletcher and Beaumont, confirming 'Beaumont's status as the regular creative partner of Fletcher (as if they were a brand name, like Rodgers and Hammerstein)'.[2] The 1647 Folio contains more writing by Philip Massinger than Beaumont, as well as the hands of authors such as Nathan Field. But the names Beaumont and Fletcher provide an irresistible combination: they 'fit well together on the page, on the tongue, and in the mind'. The 'neat symmetry of their trochaic names' and 'the way that Beaumont's French name hints at his aristocratic lineage while Fletcher's suggests a humbler background' were 'serendipitous features' and a 'gift for publishers'.[3] This tag team wrote several plays for the Children of the Queen's Revels, the company for whom Fletcher also produced his first sole-authored play *The Faithful Shepherdess* (1608), a pastoral tragicomedy. Fletcher also co-authored plays such as *The Honest Man's Fortune* (1613) for Lady Elizabeth's Men. From 1614 onwards, however, he wrote exclusively for the King's Men. Beaumont appears to have stopped writing plays around 1613, the year in which he likely married Ursula Isley, a Kentish heiress, and suffered a stroke. A year that mingled good and ill together. Three years later Beaumont was dead, his bones laid to rest in the famous Poets' Corner of Westminster Abbey.

Fletcher produced brilliant sole-authored plays, including *The Woman's Prize* (1609), a sequel to Shakespeare's *The Taming of the Shrew*. At the beginning of Fletcher's play, Katherina is dead. Petruchio has remarried another fiery woman named Maria, who has clearly been reading her Aristophanes: she refuses to consummate their marriage. Petruchio ponders how to get her into bed and decides the best route is getting her to pity him. He pretends to be sick but Maria locks him in his bedroom chamber and tells all his neighbours that he's got the plague. When Petruchio breaks out of the room he discovers his wife dressed as a sex worker, flirting with his best friends. This battle of the sexes continues and Petruchio is overwhelmed with frustration. He takes a particularly desperate step. He reckons the best way to gain Maria's sympathy is to commit pseudocide, to fake his own death. Petruchio finds himself in a coffin at his own funeral, no doubt realising that if this ruse doesn't work nothing will. He then hears Maria crying and thinks he's finally won the day. But then Maria states that she's weeping because Petruchio was so pathetic he wasted his life. In a blazing fury, Petruchio bursts out of the coffin and Maria, impressed with the lengths he's been willing to go to, agrees to a relationship of mutual respect.

The fact that Fletcher wrote a sequel to *The Taming of the Shrew* suggests audience members weren't as unquestioning of Shakespeare's depiction of gender relations as might be supposed. When the plays were performed together in 1633, the Master of the Revels recorded that Shakespeare's play was liked by the audience at St James's Palace, but that Fletcher's play was very well liked. But Fletcher evidently preferred writing in collaboration with dramatists like Philip Massinger, Nathan Field, William Rowley, and Shakespeare. Fletcher's collaborative relationship with Massinger was far more extensive than his relationship with Beaumont, leading a literary figure named Aston Cockayne to complain that the Beaumont and Fletcher Folio didn't do Massinger 'justice', or give 'each' contributing author 'his due'. Fletcher continued writing until 1625, leaving his last play, *The Noble Gentleman*, unfinished.[4] That year, the plague gripped his heart in its fatal throe. Fletcher was buried in Southwark and tradition holds that his bones were later joined by those of his longtime friend and collaborator, Massinger.

Fletcher wrote and co-wrote in a variety of genres, from comedies such as *The Scornful Lady* (1610) and *Beggars' Bush* (1616) to tragedies including *The Maid's Tragedy* (1611), as well as Roman plays such as *The False One* (1620) and *The Prophetess* (1622). Yet there can be no doubt that Fletcher and his collaborators are best known for developing English tragicomedy. The idea of mixing comedy and tragedy has classical precedents in the works of Greek and Roman writers, while Thomas Kyd imagines that 'Our scene will prove but tragicomical' (5.2.137) in his *Soliman and Perseda*. Robert Greene's plays deserve recognition as forebears of the genre. John Marston's *The Malcontent* was described in the Stationers' Register as a 'tragicomedia'. So Fletcher and his collaborators didn't exactly invent tragicomedy. But they made such profound contributions to the development of this hybrid genre that it went on to dominate the English stage.[5] Fletcher famously defined this mingled yarn of a genre in a prefatory defence of *The Faithful Shepherdess*:

> A tragi-comedie is not so called in respect of mirth and killing, but in respect it wants deaths, which is inough to make it no tragedie, yet brings some neere it, which is inough to make it no comedie.[6]

Shakespeare benefited from Fletcher and his collaborators' exploration of the tragicomic form when he wrote his late plays. *Cymbeline*, with its intricate plotlines, revelations that occasionally tax the imagination, and pastoral scenes, resembles the tragicomedies of Fletcher and his collaborators.[7] It's been suggested that Shakespeare took hints from *Philaster, or Love Lies a-Bleeding* (1609) when writing *Cymbeline*, but bardolaters have refused to believe Shakespeare could have borrowed so heavily from Beaumont and Fletcher's play.[8] In *The Tempest*, Shakespeare exploits and extends the 'dramaturgical qualities' of *The Faithful Shepherdess*, including such 'highly innovative' elements as the 'use of music, formal dance and visionary tableaux'.[9] Fletcher exerted a considerable influence on Shakespeare beyond their direct collaborations. The shift in Shakespeare's dramaturgy for his late Romance plays can be attributed in large part to Fletcher and his collaborators' influences.

Collocation and N-grams suggests that, while Shakespeare drew from the plays of fellow Jacobean dramatists for various dramaturgical qualities, he didn't imitate their language in the same way as he did for plays written by his Elizabethan predecessors. The database features spreadsheets for each of its 527 plays. These spreadsheets rank each play according to the numbers for phrases found in just one other drama of the period. In the spreadsheet for *The Winter's*

Tale, The Woman Hater is the top-ranked Fletcher play written before Shakespeare's in position thirty-seven. In the spreadsheet for *Cymbeline*, *Philaster* is ranked thirty-ninth, while *The Faithful Shepherdess* shares few verbal affinities with *The Tempest*, with Fletcher's play in position 330. Again, we get the sense that while Shakespeare was deeply conscious of dramatic ingredients that worked effectively in other plays, while he sought to take advantage of innovations in commercial drama, his poetic voice was distinctly his own as he approached the sunset of his career. Unlike the heavy borrowings from the likes of Kyd, Marlowe, and Peele, the scanty numbers for phrases shared with Fletcher tell a story of their own. A story of Shakespeare's dramatic development, the distinct hues of his later stylistic feathers.

Given that he was a particularly collaborative dramatist, it shouldn't necessarily surprise us that many of the methods developed to tell playwrights apart originated in studies of Fletcher and his co-authors. Readers have long noticed that 'feminine' endings are more numerous in Fletcher's works than those of his contemporaries, including Massinger. Fletcher has a peculiar habit of pausing at the end of lines featuring extra syllables. These extra syllables often feel unnecessary: Fletcher is so averse to regular ten-syllable lines that he can't help plopping in words like 'still', 'else', and 'too'. Massinger wasn't such a big fan of end-stopped lines: he tended to end each of his lines with words that can't be grammatically separated from the next.[10] These differences help us to work out the dramatists' shares in co-authored plays like *The Little French Lawyer*. They also help us distinguish Fletcher's portions from those of Beaumont, who was more inclined towards run-on lines and generally avoided extra syllables. Fletcher's fondness for 'feminine' endings also distinguishes his portions from Shakespeare's contributions to *All Is True* and *The Two Noble Kinsmen*. An example of Fletcher's use of an eleventh, unstressed monosyllable can be seen in 4.1 of *All Is True*: 'But 'tis so lately altered that the old name' (4.1.100). Shakespeare's scenes have a much lower incidence of 'feminine' endings formed by monosyllables. Fletcher almost doubled Shakespeare's use of 'feminine' endings in these plays, revealing the divergent styles of an experienced dramatist and his younger co-author. Whereas Shakespeare was innovative in his use of extra-metrical lines at the beginning of his career, Fletcher surpassed his rates by some distance.

As is also the case with Thomas Middleton's style, linguistic habits prove useful for telling these authors apart. Fletcher's preferences for the contracted form ''em' rather than 'them' and the pronominal form 'ye' rather than 'you' have leapt out to the eyes of generations of readers.[11] Shakespeare has much lower rates for ''em' and 'ye'. Similarly, Fletcher's hand is identifiable through his use of favoured contractions like 'i'th' instead of 'in the' and 'o'th' for 'on the'.[12] Between 1956 and 1962 the scholar Cyrus Hoy undertook a significant voyage of discovery, specifically seeking to discover who wrote which bits in Fletcher's sizeable dramatic canon.[13] Hoy combined results for verse habits, linguistic preferences, and authorial self-repetition, concluding that Fletcher was the sole or partial author of fifty-one plays and that the hands of Massinger, Beaumont, Field, Middleton, Rowley, James Shirley, Ben Jonson, John Webster, and John Ford could also be found in some of these plays. And yet many of Hoy's theories continue to present insoluble difficulties. Several plays attributed partly to Beaumont were written after that dramatist had stopped writing or even after he died in 1616! Hoy gave fourteen plays in part or wholly to Beaumont. There are eight plays we can confidently give to Fletcher and Beaumont as co-authored works: *The Woman Hater; Cupid's Revenge* (1607); *Philaster; The Coxcomb* (1609); *The Scornful Lady; A King and No King* (1611); *The Maid's Tragedy;* and *The Captain* (1612).[14] Many play portions given to Beaumont were more likely contributed by playwrights such as Field and Ford. The list of plays we can attribute to both Massinger and Fletcher is far longer: *The Honest Man's Fortune; Love's Cure, or The Martial Maid* (1615); *Beggars' Bush; The Queen of Corinth* (1617); *Rollo, Duke of Normandy; Thierry and Theodoret* (1617); *The Elder Brother* (1618); *The Knight of Malta* (1618); *Sir John van Oldenbarnevelt* (1619); *The Custom of the Country* (1619); *The Little French Lawyer; The False One; The Double Marriage* (1622); *The Prophetess; The Sea Voyage* (1622); and *The Spanish Curate* (1622). The Fletcher plays *A Very Woman*

(1623) and *The Lovers' Progress, or The Wandering Lovers* (1623) were revised by Massinger in 1634.

Fletcher was first proposed as Shakespeare's co-author on *All Is True* during the Victorian period, and no serious Shakespearian questions the overwhelming evidence today.[15] *Collocations and N-grams* offers additional support for the attribution of *All Is True* to these two dramatists, with Shakespeare contributing 1.1–2, 2.3–4, 3.2 (up to the exit of the King), and 5.1, and Fletcher writing most of the remainder. Shakespeare's *Richard III* is ranked third in the spreadsheet for *All Is True*, with the highest play containing Fletcher's hand being *Rollo, Duke of Normandy* at seventh place, a much higher position than reached for sole-authored Shakespeare plays influenced by Fletcher. The results for Fletcher's authorship are very different to those suggesting his influence. So does this mean the case is closed completely?

It's worth taking a deeper look at the case files. There are differences of opinion when it comes to the question of who wrote what bits. Cyrus Hoy saw Shakespeare as the main author of 2.1, 2.2, parts of 3.2, as well as 4.1 and 4.2. He believed that these portions contained mere touches by Fletcher, that he was just an interpolator padding Shakespeare's portions with scraps of his own writing.[16] This conclusion wasn't based on any positive evidence for Shakespeare's hand. Hoy instead pointed out the lower incidence of Fletcher's preferred form 'ye' in comparison to 'you' in these portions. But couldn't this be due to an inconsistent copyist? In any case whoever copied these portions out preserved many instances of ''em' for 'them', as favoured by Fletcher. When writing in collaboration Fletcher tended to subordinate some of the more pronounced stylistic tricks we see in his sole-authored plays. This is certainly the case when he was working with Beaumont and suggests he was conscious of accommodating his co-author.[17] Did Fletcher do the same when working with Shakespeare? We can put on our deerstalkers and try and solve this mystery. Can *Collocations and N-grams* offer us clues that evaded earlier readers? Let's focus on phrases found in these uncertain scenes of *All Is True* and just one other play in the database. Do the results suggest either author repeating his favourite word combinations?

The evidence points overwhelmingly towards Fletcher's sole authorship of 2.1, in which some gentlemen discuss the rumour that Henry is separating from Katherine. There are only a couple of matches with Shakespeare in comparison to five Fletcher links. These matches include the First Gentleman's speech, 'Many sharp reasons to **defeat the law**' (2.1.15), which echoes *Henry V*: 'Now, if these men have **defeated the law**' (4.1.165). However, his lines '**and sweetly / In all** the rest' (2.1.36–7) parallel Fletcher's *The Pilgrim* (1621): '**and sweet in all** your entertainments' (5.3.8). Buckingham's speech 'Made **my name once more** noble' (2.1.116) anticipates Fletcher's last play, *The Noble Gentleman*: 'mighty as is **my name**, / **Once more** I bid you' (4.4.82–3). Buckingham says to his captors: 'Where **you are liberal of your loves** and counsels' (2.1.127). This line looks ahead to Fletcher's *The Island Princess* (1621), the phrase 'liberal of your love' embracing the word combination 'you are': 'But since **you are** so **liberal of your love**' (4.5.24). The verbal links with Fletcher plays trump those with Shakespeare in terms of both quality and quantity. Surely Fletcher wasn't just an interpolator?

The same is true of other samples suspected of mixed authorship. In 4.1 a gentleman describes Anne's coronation with his companions. The Second Gentleman's speech in this scene, '**But I beseech you**, **what's** become of Katherine' (4.1.22), shares a phrase with Shakespeare's *Coriolanus*: '**But I beseech you**, / **What** says the other troop?' (1.1.201–2). The First Gentleman's response, 'That **I can tell you too**' (4.1.24), however, provides a unique parallel with *The Knight of Malta*: '**I could tell you too**' (3.2.124). The Queen enters and the adoring Second Gentleman exclaims: '**Heaven bless thee!** / **Thou hast** the sweetest face I ever looked on' (4.1.42–3). This speech looks forward to Fletcher's action-packed comedy *The Chances* (1617), in which a landlady, holding a child mysteriously thrust into her lodger's arms, says: '**Heaven blesse thee**, / **Thou hadst** a hasty making' (1.8.60–1). The Third Gentleman says to his companions, '**Come, gentlemen, ye shall** go **my** way' (4.1.16), which gives us a hit with Fletcher's *Love's Pilgrimage* (1616): '**Come gentlemen, you shall** /

Enter **my** roof' (4.1.239–40). The linguistic texture of this scene is clearly woven out of the language of Fletcher's plays, which almost triple the number of matches with Shakespeare. These new findings firmly establish that Fletcher was the principal author of these portions, which closely resemble the style of other scenes in the play given to him. There's little to no trace of Shakespeare here: the phrases shared with him seem largely accidental, suggesting that Fletcher wrote these scenes alone.

The dramatists selected episodes from the 1587 edition of Holinshed's *Chronicles* and John Foxe's *Acts and Monuments*, first published in 1563, to tell the story of Henry VIII's reign and the rise and fall of his chief adviser Cardinal Wolsey. A close working relationship between the dramatists, at least during the plotting phase, is suggested when Shakespeare foreshadows Queen Elizabeth's birth in 2.3 and 3.2. It was Fletcher who took responsibility for the speech praising her as 'A pattern to all princes living' (5.4.22). Shakespeare seems to have got the story under way, leaving his collaborator to tie up loose ends, in an introductory approach to plotting reminiscent of his work with Middleton on *Timon of Athens*. Fletcher and Shakespeare's collaboration differs, however, from that play: there's little evidence of mixed writing. Both playwrights placed trust in each other to bring the intertwining plots to fruition. They took joint responsibility for the relationship between Katherine, Henry VIII, and Cardinal Wolsey, which created some inconsistencies when it came to characterisation, particularly in terms of Wolsey's sudden change from pride to humility, from the malevolence of Iago to the meekness of Henry VI. Here is Wolsey as Shakespeare presents him:

> We must not stint
> Our necessary actions in the fear
> To cope malicious censurers, which ever,
> As rav'nous fishes, do a vessel follow
> That is new trimmed, but benefit no further
> Than vainly longing. What we oft do best,
> By sick interpreters, once weak ones, is
> Not ours or not allowed; what worst, as oft,
> Hitting a grosser quality, is cried up

> For our best act. If we shall stand still,
> In fear our motion will be mocked or carped at,
> We should take root here where we sit,
> Or sit state-statues only. (1.2.76–88)

This speech is characteristic of Shakespeare's late style, tortive by design, replete with caesuras that contribute to meaning-making, the crests of his semantic waves overturning, subsiding in such lines as 'For our best act. If we shall stand still'. Shakespeare's images collide, then fuse, and the opportunities for wordplay flash in his mind like windowed candlelight in early modern London as dusk sets in, the metaphor of 'rav'nous fishes' conjuring the idea of being 'carped at'. Fletcher's Wolsey has a very different melody, a rhythm of largely end-stopped lines gobbling up extra monosyllables like 'me' and 'him':

> So farewell – to the little good you bear me.
> Farewell, a long farewell, to all my greatness!
> This is the state of man. Today he puts forth
> The tender leaves of hopes; tomorrow blossoms,
> And bears his blushing honours thick upon him;
> The third day comes a frost, a killing frost,
> And, when he thinks, good easy man, full surely
> His greatness is a-ripening, nips his root,
> And then he falls, as I do. I have ventured,
> Like little wanton boys that swim on bladders,
> This many summers in a sea of glory,
> But far beyond my depth; my high-blown pride
> At length broke under me, and now has left me
> Weary, and old with service, to the mercy
> Of a rude stream, that must for ever hide me.
> Vain pomp and glory of this world, I hate ye. (3.2.351–66)

Fletcher's liking for the archaic 'ye' is clearly on show here, his metaphors sustained, such as the comparison between Wolsey and a plant's life, which gives gradual way to nautical imagery. The transitions more like melting ice than the high seas of Shakespeare's figurative language. For all the startling changes in temper and verse melodies that several characters undergo in the authors' respective contributions,[18] the collaboration succeeded in creating a play bursting with pageantry and spectacle, melding the Romance elements that Fletcher helped consolidate on the Jacobean stage with a retelling of daringly recent history.

The Two Noble Kinsmen was printed by Thomas Cotes (who also printed Shakespeare's Second Folio two years earlier) in 1634 with the quarto title page announcing Shakespeare and Fletcher as its authors. A variety of tests reveal key differences between the dramatists' verse styles and vocabularies. Fletcher contributed the Prologue, 2.2–6, 3.2–6, 4.1, 4.2, and parts of 5.1–3. Both dramatists appear to have worked from the same plotline in a similar pattern to *All Is True*. They drew from Geoffrey Chaucer's 'The Knight's Tale' and John Lydgate's 'Siege of Thebes' in *The Workes of Geffrey Chaucer* (1561) to tell a tale of jealous rivalry between the titular characters of Palamon and Arcites, a tale of disguise and unrequited love, with Shakespeare returning to Athens and the characters of Theseus and Hippolyta who had earlier appeared in his *A Midsummer Night's Dream*. Shakespeare again bore responsibility for writing the opening scenes but also, in this case, the play's conclusion. *Collocations and N-grams* validates the attribution to Fletcher and Shakespeare: the top three plays in the spreadsheet for this play are *A Midsummer Night's Dream*, *The Knight of Malta*, and Fletcher's tragicomedy *The Loyal Subject* (1618). The database also divides portions traditionally assigned to each author, with even more startling results: *The Knight of Malta* is top of the rankings for the Fletcher scenes, and *A Midsummer Night's Dream* and *Hamlet* are the top two plays for Shakespeare's portions. Again the power of authorial self-repetition emerges through the inky numbers like a flame in a dark cave. But mysteries prevail. Nobody is sure whether it was Fletcher or Shakespeare who wrote two scenes of the play. The first enigmatic scene 1.5 consists of only sixteen lines, including a rhymed song. Scene 4.3 is written in prose so we can't compare its metre to the style of either author. Can *Collocations and N-grams* help us get closer to the truth?

Let's zone in on phrases in 1.5, in which three queens mourn the deaths of their husbands. Despite the tiny size of this scene, sixteen of those phrases are found in only one other play in the database. The Third Queen's lines, 'This world's **a city full of** straying streets'

(1.5.15), matches *Coriolanus*: '**A city full**; **of** tribunes, such as you' (5.4.55). She says to the Second Queen, 'Joy seize on you again, peace sleep with **him**' (1.5.12), to which the Second Queen says to the First Queen: '**And this to** yours' (1.5.13). These lines parallel a scene in Fletcher's tragicomedy *Bonduca* (1614) featuring the similarly unnamed First and Second Daughter of Boudica, the British Celtic queen. The Second Daughter says: 'give it **him**, **and this**, / **To** see it well delivered' (2.3.125–6). These results don't give us much to go on.

The scarcity of evidence is hardly surprising given the short length of this scene. In this case it might be a good idea to turn our attention towards collocations: unique combinations of words with other words intervening. The picture alters. There are two unique hits with Fletcher, one of which can be found in a scene attributed to him in *All Is True*. On the other hand there are nine combinations that only Shakespeare among all dramatists used. Some of these are striking: the image of '**Sacred vials filled with** tears' (1.5.5) shares the association of word choices, 'sacred', 'vials', 'fill', and 'with' with Cleopatra's reaction to the news of Fulvia's death in *Antony and Cleopatra*: 'Where be the **sacred vials** thou shouldst **fill** / **With** sorrowful water?' (1.3.63–4).

Although rhyming habits can be useful for telling dramatists apart, they're largely neglected by textual sleuths. In the past this would involve poring over plays and highlighting every rhyme, a slog that few dare attempt. But we can try a different approach by putting the spreadsheet for collocations to extra use. Are any of the rhyming words in this scene found in other rhyming passages by either Fletcher or Shakespeare? The scene begins with a song:

> Urns and odours, bring away,
> Vapours, sighs, darken the day;
> Our dole more deadly looks than dying.
> Balms and gums and heavy cheers,
> Sacred vials filled with tears,
> And clamours through the wild air flying:
> Come all sad and solemn shows,
> That are quick-eyed pleasure's foes.
> We convent naught else but woes. (1.5.1–9)

This song contains the following rhymes: 'away/day'; 'cheers/tears'; and 'shows/foes/woes'. The scene also contains the couplets 'lend/ end' and 'streets/meets'. The rhyme 'foes' and 'woes' can be found in *King Lear* whereas there are no hits with Fletcher plays. On balance the evidence suggests Shakespeare's authorship of this scene, indeed the entire first act.

In 4.3 the Doctor diagnoses the Jailer's Daughter with love melancholy. She has fallen desperately for Palamon during his imprisonment. Despite being only around one hundred lines long, the scene features almost seventy phrases that are unique in the database. Five of these are found only in Shakespeare's canon and four in Fletcher's. In a state of 'profound melancholy' (4.3.46–7), the Daughter says to the Doctor, 'one would marry a leprous witch **to be rid on't**' (4.3.43–4). This speech echoes a Shakespeare scene in his collaboration with George Wilkins, *Pericles*, when Pander and the Bawd describe the 'green-sickness' (19.22) Marina has brought to their disreputable trade: 'Faith, there's no way **to be rid on't** but by the way to the pox' (19.23–4). In the surrounding text there emerges an interesting correspondence between the Daughter's image 'They shall stand in fire up to the navel and in ice up to th' heart, and there th'offending part burns and the deceiving part freezes' (4.3.39–42) and the Bawd's prose speech in which she claims Marina is 'able to freeze the god Priapus' (4.6.12–13). The Daughter's description of the pains of hell, 'Alas, 'tis a sore life they have **i'th' other place**' (4.3.28–9), resembles Hamlet's professed madness after he slays Polonius: 'seek him **i'th' other place**' (4.3.34). The Doctor says that '**I have great hope in** this' (4.3.95). That phrase echoes *Measure for Measure* and no other play: '**I have great hope in** that' (1.2.170). He resolves, '**Let us put it in** execution' (4.3.97), which shares a thought-parallel with Don Pedro's strategy to woo Hero for Claudio in *Much Ado About Nothing*: '**In** practice **let us put it** presently' (1.1.311). As for the Fletcher parallels, they're comparatively weak. The line '**as ever he may** go upon's legs' (4.3.13) resembles Fletcher's tragicomedy *The Mad Lover* (1616) in wording but not thought: '**As ever he may** find a friend' (3.1.4). Although there's not much separating the dramatists when it comes to the numbers for shared phrases, the parallels of thought accompanying identical wording, and the corresponding imagery surrounding phrases shared with Shakespeare, make it more likely that he is the scene's author. The scene also contains two examples of the archaism 'hath', which Shakespeare used often but Fletcher generally avoided.[19] Shakespeare appears to have had a prominent hand in the plotline involving the Jailer and his daughter, a plotline that he got rolling. The Jailer's Daughter has been described as 'a uniquely constructed character', who frequently appears alone on stage, with no other entrances for additional characters. Fletcher and Shakespeare had included such 'solo scenes' in *The Faithful Shepherdess* and *Cymbeline*; together in *The Two Noble Kinsmen* they make expert use of this 'unique dramaturgical tool that melds character, speech, and scene into one unit'.[20] It seems likely that the authors kept keen eyes on the dramaturgical qualities of each other's plays. They then developed these qualities further in *The Two Noble Kinsmen*, a fascinating collaboration for which Shakespeare acted as both mentor and student to his talented co-writer.

Fletcher and Shakespeare also collaborated on *The History of Cardenio*, a play attributed to both authors in a Stationers' Register entry of 1653. The first records of the play occurred long before that, on 20 May and 9 July 1613, when the King's Men were paid for separate performances of 'Cardenno', or 'Cardenna', at court. The dramatists dived into Miguel de Cervantes' 1605 novel *Don Quixote*, which features a character named Cardenio who is driven mad by Don Fernando, who steals away his lover Lucinda. Humphrey Moseley, the bookseller who registered the title, must have owned a copy of the play, and in 1719 the author Charles Gildon, enemy of such luminaries as Jonathan Swift and Alexander Pope, wrote of a 'Play written by *Beaumont and Fletcher*; and the immortal Shakespear; in the Maturity of his Judgement, a few Years before he dy'd'. Fletcher and Beaumont's names were often inextricable, so we should be wary of attaching much significance to the presence of Beaumont in this account. A song by the London composer Robert Johnson written for the King's Men, 'Woods, Rocks and Mountains', is one of just ten unattached to a specific play in a seventeenth-century manuscript.

The lyrics for this song are to be delivered by a weeping maid in a setting that matches the Sierra Morena mountains, where Cardenio and Dorothea, another victim of Don Fernando, find themselves in Cervantes' novel. The vocabulary of the song closely matches that of Thomas Shelton's 1612 translation of *Don Quixote*, which likely served as Fletcher and Shakespeare's main source. Could these song lyrics be a fragment of the lost play? Judging by their style, they were most likely written by Fletcher.[21]

But the story doesn't end there. In 1727 an author and editor of works by both Shakespeare and Fletcher, Lewis Theobald, produced a play titled *Double Falsehood, or the Distressed Lovers*. This play drew from the 'Cardenio' episode in *Don Quixote* but with changes to the names of characters. *Double Falsehood* was first performed on 13 December at the Theatre Royal, Drury Lane and was published the following year. It's uncertain whether Theobald knew of the lost *Cardenio* mentioned by Moseley.[22] Either way Theobald made the astonishing claim that his drama was an adaptation of a play by Shakespeare, which he possessed in manuscript. In fact Theobald claimed to have access to at least three manuscripts! One of these was apparently written in the hand of the prompter John Downes, who worked for Sir William Davenant's Duke's Company in the 1660s and retired in 1706. Theobald's claim was met with suspicion and often downright derision: accusations of forgery were levelled at him by the likes of Alexander Pope, who transformed his rival Shakespeare editor into the avatar of Dulness in his poem *The Dunciad*. The adaptation clearly derives from Shelton's translation. This is curious: there's no evidence that Theobald was familiar with that translation.

Theobald seems to have lost confidence in the Shakespeare attribution; he didn't include the play in his Shakespeare edition of 1733. Might this loss of confidence have been spurred by a recognition that, in large parts, the play sounded more like Fletcher than Shakespeare? Stylistic methods support the attribution of parts of the play to this duo, albeit heavily revised by Theobald. Given the association with prompter Downes, the text might have been mediated by an earlier adaptation produced by poet and playwright William Davenant, another fascinating figure in Shakespeare's story. Tradition holds that Shakespeare would stop off at an inn owned by Davenant's parents in Oxford when travelling between London and Stratford-upon-Avon. Over a glass of wine, Davenant's mouth would sometimes steal away his brain and he'd boast that he was Shakespeare's illegitimate son.

Double Falsehood differs considerably from Theobald's unaided dramatic efforts and reads like a text we would expect if he were revising an older collaboration by Fletcher and Shakespeare. The play suggests a mingling of different styles, with scenes attributed to Shakespeare featuring fewer 'feminine' endings than those that sound Fletcherian. The verse style for sections of the play suspected to have been written by Fletcher is a good match with his contributions to *All Is True* and *The Two Noble Kinsmen*. There's a contrast on show in Fletcher and Shakespeare's distinct preferences for certain forms like 'hath' and 'doth', those older forms retained by Shakespeare but seldom used by Fletcher.[23] Other approaches, including the dramatists' use of polysyllabic words at the end of verse lines, such as 'dishonourably' and 'misbecomingly', also point towards Fletcher and Shakespeare's participation. Shakespeare's hand has been traced, faintly, in the first half of the play, and Fletcher's largely in the remainder, a pattern resembling their other collaborations. Adaptors often took liberties with Shakespeare's language, whose dramatic style probably felt more old-fashioned to audiences in the late seventeenth and eighteenth centuries than that of the younger Fletcher. Thomas Otway's *The History and Fall of Caius Marius*, first performed in 1679, transfers the events of *Romeo and Juliet* from Verona to ancient Rome, the heroine of the play pondering: 'O Marius, Marius! Wherefore art thou Marius?' We might ask ourselves: 'What's in a name?' In *Double Falsehood* we have a particularly potent example of the fluidity of theatrical scripts, a palimpsest bearing traces of a lost play conceived during a fruitful period of collaboration between Fletcher and Shakespeare. Their ghostly voices in conversation, not quite drowned out by other discoursers. The story of how *Cardenio* might have come down to us in the drama *Double Falsehood* is fascinating. It's a narrative that has polarised generations of editors and scholars. As remarkable as any found in Cervantes' novel, it's a tale of loss and retrieval that speaks to us today.

We've reopened the files. It seems we've cracked some cases, cast new light on old mysteries. We now have a more precise picture of Shakespeare and Fletcher's working methods in collaboration. This is crucial: these co-authored plays were the last Shakespeare would ever write. Just a few years later he would be buried in his home town of Stratford-upon-Avon. For Fletcher it was a different story. Shakespeare's final collaborator would go on to succeed him as the King's Men's principal playwright. Maybe Fletcher had this in mind when he wrote the ending for *All Is True*: 'The bird of wonder dies – the maiden phoenix – / Her ashes new create another heir' (5.4.40–1).

Conclusion: Our other Shake-scenes

Many Shakespearians 'seem reluctant to accuse' him 'of being the borrower but prefer to assume that the other dramatist borrowed from him'.[1] So wrote the scholar Ann Thompson in 1984. There are many examples of this reluctance in the history of Shakespeare studies. Academics in the last century pointed out striking verbal parallels between Shakespeare's early works and such plays as *King Leir*, *Arden of Faversham*, and *The Troublesome Reign of King John*, nevertheless concluding that the very idea of Shakespeare 'capping in this fashion lines so freely current in the theatre will perhaps at this stage be dismissed by most readers'.[2] Many refused to believe that Shakespeare 'plundered every Kyd play he could lay his hands on' despite acknowledging that 'Passages from' *The Spanish Tragedy*, *King Leir*, and *Arden of Faversham* are 'all deftly woven into the fabric' of Shakespeare's works.[3] The reluctance to recognise that Shakespeare was, like every other dramatist of the period, a borrower persists. It can be traced in the vehemence with which *Arden of Faversham* has been welcomed into his canon. The enthusiasm for augmenting Shakespeare's canon is coupled with an assumption that Shakespeare couldn't have been the borrower, that either Shakespeare was its author or that the 'author or co-author' must have been, 'like Viola de Lesseps in the movie *Shakespeare in Love*, a devout admirer of the young Shakespeare's works, with a recall of his dialogue'.[4] Devout admirers of Shakespeare continue to detach him from the world in which he was writing. Those investigating Shakespeare's earliest collaborations, such as *Titus Andronicus*

196

and *Edward III*, have been more inclined to write of Shakespeare improving, or even salvaging, the work of more experienced dramatists, rather than learning from the process of co-authorship at the beginning of his career. There remains an unwillingness to imagine Shakespeare as a 'beginner, novice or imitator', a preference to imagine that he 'sprang, like Athena from the head of Zeus, miraculously endowed with all the artistic panoply of poet and dramatist', even though this is at 'complete variance with all that we know of the development of every great poet or artist'.[5]

To describe the world of early modern drama as a *community* of playwrights is to make an ornithological pun harking back to the attack in *Greene's Groatsworth of Wit*, which paints Shakespeare as a crow beautified in the feathers of other playwrights. But early modern drama was a veritable avian community, a magpie nest, each writer borrowing from each other, each seeking to replicate each other's commercial successes, their plays, like their dramatic personages, in conversation, sharing elements of dialogue, of theatrical vernacular. Some authors ruffled feathers more than others it seems. And yet Shakespeare was no more nor less imitative than his fellow playwrights. At the beginning of his career he was steeped in the words, the dramatic devices, of his Elizabethan contemporaries, having acted in their plays. As every schoolboy of the period would have been taught to do, Shakespeare aimed to better his sources, or at least do something different with his materials, the lines he would have buzzing in his head or lying deep in the recesses of his mind, ready to be summoned again if a play was revived and inevitably floating to the surface of his imagination during the composition of his own plays.

What if Shakespeare wasn't the target of the infamous attack in *Greene's Groatsworth of Wit* at all? An alternative candidate has been proposed: the actor Edward Alleyn.[6] Have we been getting it wrong all these years? According to this theory 'Shake-scene' isn't a glaringly obvious pun on Shakespeare's name but simply a term for a powerful performer. The paraphrase of York's line from *Henry VI Part Three*, 'O tiger's heart wrapped in a woman's hide' (1.4.138), isn't aimed at the play's author but at the actor who played the role of York. The problem is that *The True Tragedy of Richard Duke of York* (known as *Henry VI Part Three* in the First Folio) lists Pembroke's Men on its title page, a fact curiously omitted from arguments for Alleyn as Greene's target. Alleyn, who in any case could hardly be considered an 'upstart' in 1592, never worked for Pembroke's Men so far as we know. He acted for Admiral's Men and joined Strange's Men in 1591. It's possible that he played Lord Talbot in the rival 'Harey the vi' play, although the description of Talbot as a 'writhled shrimp' (2.3.22) in *Henry VI Part One* isn't an obvious fit for the very tall actor. It's been conjectured that Alleyn meddled with Greene's *A Knack to Know a Knave* (1592), which aroused Greene's anger. We can now be confident however that Greene didn't write the morality play *A Knack to Know a Knave*.[7] Alleyn is supposedly a better fit because Shakespeare wasn't known as a playwright until his name appeared on title pages in 1598. This is a fundamental and widespread problem with attempts to erode documentary evidence relating to Shakespeare. A primary source doesn't have to be contemporaneous with a specific event. We know Shakespeare was an actor. We know he was also a playwright and that the passage Greene paraphrases occurs in a play attributed to him in the First Folio. In much the same way as attempts have been made to remove Thomas Kyd as a candidate for the old *Hamlet* play, it takes a lot of interpretative gymnastics to dissociate Shakespeare from Greene's thinly veiled attack.

The idea stemming from *Greene's Groatsworth of Wit* that Shakespeare began his career patching up older plays is traceable to Edmond Malone's misplaced theory that Shakespeare was a plagiarist, that he took credit for other writers' works. There's no evidence to support this theory, but it persists in newspaper headlines detailing new discoveries concerning Shakespeare's influences and his creative output, in buzzwords like 'stole' or 'took credit'. Such headlines betray a misunderstanding of the early modern education system and commercial drama of the period. To dabble *in utramque partem*, the art of articulating two sides of a question, a staple of Shakespeare's education, these headlines cater to an eagerness to put Shakespeare down which lies at the other extreme of ways in which the playwright is spoken or written about. That eagerness is sometimes reflected in more scholarly venues, in talks delivered at conferences; in qualitative evaluations pitching Shakespeare unfavourably against other writers; in the makeup of university modules that seem designed to contend with rather than broaden knowledge of Shakespeare's works. Shakespeare has so often been detached from the community in which he wrote, so often privileged at the expense of other writers with whom he worked, that it's hardly surprising the discourse should shift towards supplanting his canonical status, to overturning the hierarchy. There have been interesting movements pushing for writers such as John Lyly to be seen as more progressive than Shakespeare or in attempts to position Thomas Middleton as 'our other Shakespeare'. But 'Attempts to decentre Shakespeare' tend to be 'self-defeating'.[8] The political agendas of individuals who have appropriated Shakespeare's works throughout history should rightly be interrogated. But Shakespeare himself isn't simply a tyrant to be toppled, nor should he be reduced to a public figure to be trolled. His works provide a conduit for the appreciation of other writers. Denigrating Shakespeare's work while privileging the output of any of his contemporaries runs the risk of eroding the appreciation of early modern drama and, most perilously in today's climate, the humanities in general, just as the opposite is true. Recognising these playwrights as members of a community is more beneficial than pitching them against each other as if they belonged in a university rankings and league table. Theatre companies and educational organisations should continue to do their bit and broaden the appreciation and understanding of plays written by authors of the period.

There has been much written about Shakespeare's place in the modern education system and trepidation concerning the removal of Shakespeare from the canon, 'cancelling' Shakespeare, or at least de-emphasising him in favour of alternative writers whose voices are regarded as more diverse and inclusive. Few readers of this book are likely to consider Shakespeare's works as exclusive or irrelevant today; it's the interpretative flexibility of Shakespeare's plays and his reticence to commit to specific ideologies that makes them ideal for study as well as reinterpretation on stage and indeed the page. We can collaborate with Shakespeare, make our own meanings, adapt him just as he adapted the works of others. While on the topic of canon construction, it might be objected that this book privileges certain writers over others. There's been much written and is still much to write about Shakespeare's relationship with playwrights such as Thomas Nashe or George Wilkins for instance. But these writers don't possess large enough surviving sole-authored dramatic canons for meaningful analysis of links between their theatrical language and Shakespeare's. Who knows, maybe advances in attribution will lead to the expansion of the canons of authors such as Nashe, or Robert Wilson, or Thomas Lodge, which could alter the picture. The spectre of that most productive of dramatists, 'Anonymous', looms in the cases of some plays from which Shakespeare drew heavily, such as *The Famous Victories of Henry V* and *The True Tragedy of Richard III* (1589). When we consider how many plays of the period are identifiably lost, as many as 744 from the London commercial theatres,[9] we can only marvel at the extent to which Shakespeare engaged with and learned from other dramatists of the period.

It might also be objected that this book has taken an author-centric approach. Might a play-centric, or genre-centric model have worked? Or a model based on different playing companies of the period? Or performance spaces? What if each chapter had instead revolved around a different Shakespeare play? No doubt we'd learn that each play could be considered a dense thicket of borrowings, that each genre is a tangle of threads. The possibilities are endless, but in shining a light on each major dramatist of the period it is to be hoped that readers have developed their understanding of the interconnected lives and works of these men, of the impact on Shakespeare that each of their plays and the genres in which they dabbled for various companies and playing spaces exerted. To appreciate Shakespeare, it is useful to grasp the ways in which he was moulded by the pens of other writers, as well as how he sometimes turned away from them. Shakespeare is to be valued: we can enhance that sense of value by situating him alongside his fellow playwrights, without whom we probably wouldn't have Shakespeare at all.

At the beginning of his career, Shakespeare exercised the rhetorical training he had received at grammar school in his capacity as an actor-dramatist. Commercial drama was abuzz with writers such as Thomas Kyd, Christopher Marlowe, Robert Greene, and George Peele who were experimenting with and conflating genres, breaking new ground when it came to dramatic language and what it was possible to do in playing spaces. Shakespeare emulated Kyd, Marlowe, and Peele, having possibly performed in some of their plays, or at least seen them during performance. And he would continue to engage with these playwrights throughout his career: imitating, parodying, and adapting their work for new audiences. At times Shakespeare's early plays read like patchworks of Kyd's, Marlowe's, and Peele's language. But even at the start of his career Shakespeare weaves threads of these authors' plays into a dramatic tapestry that is distinctly his own. Computational approaches help us to zone in on Shakespeare's verbal borrowings and recognise the ways he takes minor hints and elaborates them into major themes and character traits. New technologies offer fantastic opportunities, but they cannot replace the need to still read these plays closely, to respect them as literary and performative artefacts. Computers haven't replaced humans, or humanist scholars, and it's unlikely they ever will. There's plenty of number-crunching going on, but that hasn't stopped researchers from casting subjective slings and arrows at each other. In any case Shakespeare must have benefited greatly from co-authoring plays with fellow dramatists, whether or not we include Marlowe among that group. Did this process of imitation and adaptation, like the process of simultaneous collaboration, help service a commercial operation with a large literary turnover?

Shakespeare often seems to gaze wistfully at past dramas for inspiration. When writing plays for the Blackfriars Theatre he consulted earlier Romances written by John Lyly for that space. This discovery suggests he was deeply mindful of audience expectations but that he was also constantly exploring ways to take older work in new directions. He was evidently conscious of emerging genres as his career progressed, genres in which playwrights who differed on the conceptualisation of drama, such as Ben Jonson, had great success.

But there's little evidence, on a verbal level at least, of Shakespeare attending closely to the plays of fellow Jacobean dramatists. He was no doubt appreciative of other playwrights' dramatic capabilities during this period, collaborating frequently with John Fletcher, while Thomas Middleton would not only act as a co-author but also possibly collaborate with Shakespeare beyond the grave through revising some of his plays.

The most significant collaboration for our understanding of Shakespeare was that between John Heminges, Henry Condell, and others in producing the 1623 First Folio, or *Mr. William Shakespeare's Comedies, Histories, & Tragedies*, which contains thirty-six of Shakespeare's plays, around half of which weren't published in individual editions before the Folio's publication. The difficulty with determining the authorship of some earlier plays is that, out of twenty plays printed by 1593, seventeen don't mention the author's name on their title page, and over the following five years just 40 per cent provide an authorial ascription. Jacobean and Caroline publishers, however, seem to have recognised the selling power of an author's name. Around 70 per cent of Jacobean playbooks proclaim their authors.[10] This sometimes led to underhand dealings: the 1662 quarto attribution of William Rowley's *The Birth of Merlin* to Shakespeare is clearly wrong. Licensed as a new play in 1622, we'd have to posit that Shakespeare contributed to the play as a ghost or zombie. Similarly Philip Chetwinde's 1664 Third Folio includes seven additional plays, only one of which, *Pericles*, is partly by Shakespeare. That attempt to appeal to readers by including additional works continues today, as can be seen in plays and poems newly added to modern so-called 'Complete Works' editions.

Heminges and Condell would appear in so many respects to be the ideal editors of the First Folio and witnesses to Shakespeare's output. They were close friends of Shakespeare, partners in the King's Men acting company who'd worked closely with him since the days in which that company was known as the Lord Chamberlain's Men. Documentary evidence reveals that, alongside acting in Shakespeare's plays, Condell performed in plays by Jonson, John Webster, and Fletcher and his collaborators. Heminges also performed in the dramas of Jonson as well as John Marston and Webster's adaptation of *The Malcontent*. In 1613 a fire destroyed the Globe during a performance of Shakespeare and Fletcher's *All Is True*. Small cannons were fired and the thatch went up in smoke. Remarkably, for a theatre with a potential capacity of three thousand people, the only apparent casualty was a man's breeches, which were put out with a bottle of ale. A ballad detailing the disaster claimed that Heminges stuttered, a difficulty for an actor. Or was he simply stammering at the threat of his livelihood going up in smoke? That year Heminges acted as a trustee for Shakespeare when he purchased the Blackfriars Gatehouse in 1613 and both he and Condell were bequeathed 26 shillings and 8 pence in Shakespeare's will to buy mourning rings, an informal contract, perhaps, for overseeing the edition of Shakespeare's collected plays.[11] As the editors put it in the prefatory material to the First Folio: 'It had been a thing, we confess, worthy to have been wished that the author himself had lived to have set forth, and overseen his own writings'. But Shakespeare had been dead for several years by the time the First Folio was published.

Despite Shakespeare's absence, there was a guiding light for the editors of the First Folio: *The Works of Benjamin Jonson*. A title that gives primacy to Jonson even though he was a deeply collaborative dramatist. The *Comedies and Tragedies Written by Francis Beaumont and John Fletcher Gentlemen* would go on to privilege just two authors. Yet that edition contains the hands of numerous writers, including Philip Massinger's, which was far more extensive than Francis Beaumont's. The titular attention afforded to a single author, or a duo, suggests literary proprietorship, and Shakespeare's Folio is presented as a shrine to his genius, 'an office', as Heminges and Condell put it, 'to the dead', for they have 'procured his' works to preserve his memory. The emphasis in the prefatory material is placed on singular pronouns, 'he', 'his', the reader entreated to 'Read him, therefore, and again, and again'. The Folio 'emphatically presents' Shakespeare 'as a non-collaborating dramatist, not only by formulaic declaration on the title page' but also in 'the rhetorical strategy of the extensive preliminaries'.[12] There's no hint of other dramatists' contributions to these works: Peele goes unmentioned in the prefatory material. Kyd is mentioned only in relation to the extent to which Shakespeare transcended him in Jonson's eulogy. Nor does Nashe receive tribute, despite evidence strongly suggesting he was one of the original authors of the play printed as *Henry VI Part One*. There's no mention of Wilkins, with whom Shakespeare co-authored *Pericles*, nor of Middleton or Fletcher. In fact, *Pericles* is omitted from the edition altogether, as are Shakespeare and Fletcher's *The Two Noble Kinsmen* and *Cardenio*. Maybe *Pericles* was excluded because the surviving text is manifestly corrupt, and the editors couldn't get hold of a cleaner copy. *The Two Noble Kinsmen* and *Cardenio* might have been excluded because they were seen as belonging more to Fletcher than to Shakespeare. Although *All Is True* was also written primarily by Fletcher, it completes the Folio's history play sequence so the compilers might have been more inclined to include it.[13]

There is a great variety of potential reasons as to why several plays in which Shakespeare is believed to have had a hand weren't included. *Edward III* contains insults aimed at the Scottish; it would be risky business printing such a play during the reign of James I. *Sir Thomas More* survives only in a manuscript revealing the difficulties of writing plays in the face of political censorship; it features numerous interventions by Edmund Tilney, the Master of the Revels. Shakespeare's contributions to this play aren't substantial in any case. Nor is his writing extensive in the 1602 edition of Kyd's *The Spanish Tragedy*, even if he were solely responsible for all the additional material. There's a seemingly lost play, *Love's Labour's Won* (1598), mentioned in Francis Meres's compilation *Palladis Tamia* and in a 1603 book list belonging to the stationer Christopher Hunt. If this play were a sequel to *Love's Labour's Lost*, the reasoning behind its exclusion is unclear. The picture is inconsistent, blurry, given that around seven of the plays included in the First Folio appear to be either co-authored or contain interpolations by other dramatists. It's nevertheless notable that of the seven *omitted* plays in which Shakespeare had a hand, *Edward III*, *Love's Labour's Won*, *Sir Thomas More*, the 1602 edition of *The Spanish Tragedy*, *Pericles*, *The Two Noble Kinsmen*, and *Cardenio*, at least six were collaborative.

It's been estimated that 497 individual play texts bearing the name of a single author were printed between 1570 and 1659, in comparison to just thirty-two plays acknowledging co-authorship.[14] Although co-authorship was perfectly normal during the period, collaborative plays were evidently less likely to reach print, suggesting that publishers considered single-authored plays to be easier to market. It's also telling that Shakespeare's collaboration with Middleton, *Timon of Athens*, appears to have been an afterthought, included in the Folio only to occupy a gap while the compilers negotiated the rights to *Troilus and Cressida*. The editors of the First Folio were invested in the idea of Shakespeare as sole author, a solitary genius.[15] The irony is that Shakespeare's dramatic identity was therefore shaped in large part by his fellow company members, the people with whom he collaborated most.

It seems fair to say that Shakespeare's critical reputation has benefited from the fact that, while many contemporary playwrights were forced to work freelance, he spent much of his career, approximately 1594 to 1613, writing for a single company. In collecting most of Shakespeare's plays and publishing them posthumously in the First Folio, Heminges and Condell have afforded us a broader picture of his output than is the case with most playwrights. But Shakespeare wasn't, to invoke *Greene's Groatsworth of Wit* for a final time, 'the only Shake-scene in a countrey'. Dramatists imitated and collaborated with each other to keep the theatre companies supplied with material, each author seeking to better what had come before, to build upon the linguistic, thematic, theatrical, and narrative foundations of their predecessors and contemporaries. Shakespeare's works aren't just soliloquies: they're dialogic, firmly engaged with and dependent on communication with other playwrights, embedded in a network of affiliation and indebtedness within the early modern writing scene. We must look beyond centuries of isolative discourse that still pervades some discussions of early modern drama today. It's time to fully recognise, and indeed celebrate, the fact that in his lifetime Shakespeare was one member of a broad and brilliant community of playwrights.

Acknowledgements

It's no mean feat to pluck your own feathers. To attempt to outline each of the contributions friends and colleagues have made to my journey up to and during the composition of this book would fill far too many pages. I confine myself primarily to those who've had a direct impact on this study, and acknowledge in particular my debts to †Meghan Andrews; Charles Cathcart; Warren Chernaik; Martin Coyle; José Pérez Díez; John Drakakis; Will Green; Martin Higgins; Chris Laoutaris; Domenico Lovascio; Murat Öğütcü; John-Mark Philo; Natália Pikli; Eoin Price; Richard Proudfoot; Pervez Rizvi; Patrick Ryan; Robert Stagg; Goran Stanivukovic; Matthew Steggle; Joseph Stephenson; Marina Tarlinskaja; Gregory Thompson; Jennifer Waghorn; Michael Wagoner; James Wallace; Martin Wiggins; and Henry Woudhuysen, who have helped to shape my understanding of matters relating to Shakespeare, contemporary authors, dramatic style, and early modern chronology through correspondence and sharing helpful feedback or materials. The inspiration and knowledge I have gained from Brian Vickers over the years deserves an especial display of gratitude. It is impossible to measure the lengths in which his beams are thrown; they have so long shone in my world. It would be remiss of me not to also acknowledge the formative impact of Richard Wilson's sonorous delivery of lectures on Shakespeare's tragedies and the effervescent ways in which he introduced me to the works of Christopher Marlowe at university. I'm particularly indebted to Nick Walton, under whose warm guidance I have enjoyed teaching Shakespeare to learners all around the world,

206

for this book draws from many of the topics I have taught and my experiences lecturing for the Shakespeare Birthplace Trust. My colleagues Amy Hurst and Caroline Marchant-Wallis furnished me with volumes at the Trust's library. It's been a joy to work with Manchester University Press, especially Kim Walker, who helped this bending author to pursue the story.

Most important are the personal debts I owe to my loved ones 'twixt working on this book. After all, without my wonderful family, my mother, Georgina, my father, Wayne, and my brother, Joel, I simply couldn't have embarked on a scholarly career. I had an amazing childhood brought up in an area of Cardiff called Canton. My address was 12 Lansdowne Avenue West. Next door's house was labelled 12A, superstitious numerals. And indeed number 13 (or 12A) was apparently haunted. Visitors spoke of seeing a young woman there, fleeting, corner-of-the-eye stuff. 12A was where my best friend †Christopher Harrington lived. We grew up together. He was more like a brother to me than a next-door neighbour or friend. One evening I was staying over his and, as was my habit as a mischievous child, spent hours terrifying him with ghost stories. We eventually fell asleep, top and tailing the same bed. In the middle of the night I was woken by a scream that dismantled the dark. Christopher claimed that a woman had stood next to the bed and gazed down at him. Was this a hallucination, the inevitable result of my wild tales? Or had a real ghost visited him in the night? The years passed and Christopher and I stayed best friends. One afternoon, having given a lecture at the Shakespeare Institute, I switched on my phone to see I'd missed six calls. That day I received news that would change my life irreversibly. Christopher had been found dead. I'm still haunted by his passing. He and I shared so many unique memories; he knew things about me that nobody else did. We had faced the years together: so many of my peculiarities, my favourite expressions, certain pitches and tones in everyday conversations, can be traced to him. When Christopher left, I lost fragments of youth and adulthood. In fact, it felt like a huge chunk of who I am had been carved away. There's not a day goes by that I don't try and resurrect him, to celebrate his life. And I guess that desire to resurrect ghosts, to recall memories, has influenced my fascination with the ghosts of Shakespeare's contemporaries, how they helped him become the writer he was, how their voices can sometimes be heard in his texts if you incline your ears and eyes. I have to acknowledge Christopher as an inspiration.

I'm ridiculously lucky and eternally grateful for Emma's deep understanding and the daily sacrifices she makes to support my dreams. And I'm constantly inspired by the precious moments we get to share with our beautiful boys, Oliver and Theo, who already know their Iago from their Hamlet.

Notes

Introduction: Plucking a crow

1 Warren B. Austin, 'A Computer-Aided Technique for Stylistic Discrimination: The Authorship of *Greene's Groatsworth of Wit*', Final Report, Project No. 7-G-036, US Department of Health, Education, and Welfare (Washington, DC), April 1969.

2 Richard Westley, 'Computing Error: Reassessing Austin's Study of *Groatsworth of Wit*', *Literary and Linguistic Computing*, 21.3 (2006), 363–78.

3 For discussion on the 'Poets' War' or 'War of the Theatres' see Alfred Harbage, *Shakespeare and the Rival Traditions* (Macmillan, 1952) and James Bednarz, *Shakespeare and the Poets' War* (Columbia University Press, 2001).

4 All dates of first performances throughout this book are taken from Martin Wiggins, *British Drama 1533–1642: A Catalogue* (Oxford University Press, 2012–).

5 All references to Shakespeare's plays throughout this book are to *The Oxford Shakespeare: The Complete Works*, edited by John Jowett, William Montgomery, Gary Taylor, and Stanley Wells (Oxford University Press, 2005).

6 Goran Stanivukovic, 'The Language and Style of Early Shakespeare', in *Early Shakespeare, 1588–1594*, edited by Rory Loughnane and Andrew J. Power (Cambridge University Press, 2020), pp. 76–101 (pp. 76–7).

7 Stanley Wells, *Shakespeare & Co.* (Penguin, 2006).

8 Bart van Es, *Shakespeare in Company* (Oxford University Press, 2013).

9 Pervez Rizvi, *Collocations and N-grams* (2017), www.shakespearestext.com/can/index.htm (accessed 1 October 2022).

10 For a detailed account of scholarly endorsements and a review of the strengths and limitations of the database see Darren Freebury-Jones, 'Collocations and N-grams', *Early Modern Digital Review*, 4.4 (2021), 210–16.

11 This discovery is elaborated in Martin Mueller, 'Authors are trumps' (2011). https://literaryinformatics.wordpress.com/2011/03/31/authors-are-trumps/ (accessed 1 October 2022).

1 A player's hide

1 For further discussion on classical rhetoric in early modern education see T. W. Baldwin, *William Shakspere's Small Latine and Lesse Greeke: Volume I*, 2 vols (University of Illinois Press, 1944), pp. 581–640, and Lynn Enterline, *Shakespeare's Schoolroom: Rhetoric, Discipline, Emotion* (University of Pennsylvania Press, 2012).

2 Bart van Es, *Shakespeare in Company* (Oxford University Press, 2013), p. 36.

3 *Ibid.*, p. 34.

4 Colin Burrow writes about this method in 'Shakespeare and Humanistic Culture', in *Shakespeare and the Classics*, edited by Charles Martindale and A. B. Taylor (Cambridge University Press, 2004), pp. 9–32 (p. 13).

5 For an excellent account of Shakespeare's use of rhetorical figures see Stefan D. Keller, 'Shakespeare's Rhetorical Fingerprint: New Evidence on the Authorship of *Titus Andronicus*', *English Studies*, 84.2 (2003), 105–18.

6 Goran Stanivukovic, 'The Language and Style of Early Shakespeare', in *Early Shakespeare, 1588–1594*, edited by Rory Loughnane and Andrew J. Power (Cambridge University Press, 2020), pp. 76–101 (p. 88).

7 Greene's classical *faux pas* are discussed in Darren Freebury-Jones, *Reading Robert Greene: Recovering Shakespeare's Rival* (Routledge, 2022), pp. 40–1.

8 Philip Timberlake, *The Feminine Ending in English Blank Verse: A Study of Its Use by Early Writers in the Measure and Its Development in the Drama up to the Year 1595* (Banta, 1931).

9 The discovery of this annotation is discussed in Alan H. Nelson and Paul H. Altrocchi, 'William Shakespeare, "Our Roscius"', *Shakespeare Quarterly*, 60.4 (2009), 460–9.

10 All references to Thomas Dekker's plays throughout this book are to *The Dramatic Works of Thomas Dekker*, edited by Fredson Bowers, 4 vols (Cambridge University Press, 1953–61).

11 The evidence for Jonson as both actor and player can be found in *Henslowe's Diary, Part II*, edited by W. W. Greg, 2 vols (A. H. Bullen, 1908), p. 289 and John Aubrey, *Brief Lives: Volume II*, edited by Andrew Clark, 2 vols (Clarendon Press, 1898), p. 12.

12 Jonson also appears to have engaged with the play as a reviser. In 1601 and 1602 he was paid for 'new adicyons for Jeronymo'. *Henslowe's Diary*, edited by R. A. Foakes, 2nd edn (Cambridge University Press, 2002), p. 182, p. 203. For further discussion on the surviving additions to Kyd's play see Chapter 4.

13 All references to Ben Jonson's plays throughout this book are to *The Cambridge Edition of the Works of Ben Jonson*, edited by David Bevington, Martin Butler, and Ian Donaldson, 7 vols (Cambridge University Press, 2012).

14 All references to Thomas Kyd's plays in this book are to *The Collected Works of Thomas Kyd*, General Editor Brian Vickers, Associate Editor Darren Freebury-Jones (Boydell and Brewer, 2024).

15 For further discussion on the theory that 'Zulziman' refers to Kyd's play see Lukas Erne, *Beyond The Spanish Tragedy: A Study of the Works of Thomas Kyd* (Manchester University Press, 2001), p. 163.

16 John Southworth, *Shakespeare the Player: A Life in the Theatre* (Sutton, 2000), p. 41.

17 Readers interested in learning more about the Queen's Men should consult the invaluable study by Scott McMillin and Sally-Beth MacLean, *The Queen's Men and Their Plays* (Cambridge University Press, 1998).

18 For further information on this company in the context of its family tradition see Lawrence Manley and Sally-Beth MacLean, *Lord Strange's Men and Their Plays* (Yale University Press, 2014), pp. 12–36.

19 Andy Kesson, Lucy Munro, and Callan Davies, 'London Theatrical Culture, 1560–1590', *Oxford Research Encyclopedia of Literature* (2021), https://doi.org/10.1093/acrefore/9780190201098.013.1194 (accessed 16 October 2022).

20 For the theory that Shakespeare briefly joined Derby's Men see Martin Wiggins, *British Drama 1533–1642: A Catalogue: Volume III: 1590–1597* (Oxford University Press, 2013), p. 228.

21 These estimates are drawn from Grace Ioppolo, 'The Transmission of an English Renaissance Play-Text', in *A Companion to Renaissance Drama*, edited by Arthur F. Kinney (Blackwell, 2002), pp. 163–79 (p. 165), and Peter Thomson, 'Rogues and Rhetoricians: Acting Styles in Early Modern Drama', in *A New History of Early English Drama*, edited by John D. Cox and David Scott Kastan (Columbia University Press, 1997), pp. 320–35 (pp. 324–5). See also Tiffany Stern, *Rehearsal from Shakespeare to Sheridan* (Oxford University Press, 2000), pp. 46–80.

22 This calculation features in G. E. Bentley's *The Jacobean and Caroline Stage* (Clarendon Press, 1971), p. 199.

23 MOLA, 'The Curtain Theatre: The citizen's playhouse for high-octane drama' (2018), https://www.mola.org.uk/discoveries/news/curtain-theatre-citizens-playhouse-high-octane-drama (accessed 2 April 2023).

24 This estimate is drawn from Robert J. Fusillo, 'The Staging of Battle Scenes on the Shakespearean Stage' (Doctoral thesis: University of Birmingham, 1966), p. ii.

25 For an excellent account of diverse theatre audiences see M. J. Kidnie, 'Shakespeare's Audiences', in *Shakespeare: An Oxford Guide*, edited by Stanley Wells and Lena Cowen Orlin (Oxford University Press, 2003), pp. 32–43.

26 All references to John Lyly's plays throughout this book are to *The Complete Works of John Lyly*, edited by R. Warwick Bond, 3 vols (Clarendon Press, 1902).

27 Russ McDonald, *Shakespeare's Late Style* (Cambridge University Press, 2009), p. 33.

2 John Lyly

1 For further discussion on John Lyly's biography see G. K. Hunter, 'Lyly, John', in *Oxford Dictionary of National Biography*, edited by Henry Colin Grey Matthew and Brian Harrison (Oxford University Press, 2004).

2 For an illuminating discussion on Euphuism see Andy Kesson, *John Lyly and Early Modern Authorship* (Manchester University Press, 2011), pp. 67–102.

3 Kesson makes this argument forcibly in *John Lyly and Early Modern Authorship*, p. 70.

4 *Endymion*, edited by David Bevington (Manchester University Press, 1996), p. 48.

5 Martin Higgins casts light on distinctions between the dramatists' presentations of gods in '"Flowers of this purple dye, / Hit with Cupid's archery": Lyly, Shakespeare, and Early Modern Cupid', in *Critical Insights: A Midsummer Night's Dream*, edited by Nicolas Tredell (Grey House Publishing, 2020), pp. 118–34.

6 *Ibid.*, p. 121.

7 Andy Kesson points out resolutionary similarities in 'John Lyly and Shakespeare's Early Career', in *Early Shakespeare, 1588–1594*, edited by Rory Loughnane and Andrew J. Power (Cambridge University Press, 2020), pp. 167–79 (p. 176).

8 Discriminant analysis establishes 'variance between groups on the basis of the combined effect of multiple variables'. Martin Mueller, 'Vickers is right about Kyd' (2009), https://darrenfj.files.wordpress.com/2017/11/N-grams-and-the-Kyd-Canon-and-Vickers-is-right-about-Kyd.pdf (accessed 16 October 2022).

9 Lukas Erne points out that 'Euphuism serves Kyd to characterise the languid, effeminate Petrarchan lover' Balthazar in *The Spanish Tragedy* in *Beyond The Spanish Tragedy: A Study of the Works of Thomas Kyd* (Manchester University Press, 2001), p. 71. Balthazar's Euphuistic characterisation is closely echoed by the servant Michael in *Arden of Faversham*. For further discussion on Lyly and Kyd's relationship see Darren Freebury-Jones, 'Exploring Verbal Relations between *Arden of Faversham* and John Lyly's *Endymion*', *Renaissance and Reformation*, 41.4 (2018), 93–108.

10 This observation is made in *Cymbeline*, edited by Valerie Wayne (Bloomsbury, 2017), p. 46.

3 Christopher Marlowe

1 For further discussion on Christopher Marlowe's biography see Charles Nicholl, 'Marlowe [Marley], Christopher', in *Oxford Dictionary of National Biography*, edited by Henry Colin Grey Matthew and Brian Harrison (Oxford University Press, 2004), and Park Honan, *Christopher Marlowe: Poet and Spy* (Oxford University Press, 2005).

2 All references to Marlowe's plays in this book are to *Christopher Marlowe: The Complete Plays*, edited by Mark Thornton Burnett (Everyman, 1999).

3 The libel was most likely written by the notoriously xenophobic novelist and ballad-writer Thomas Deloney. See Matthew Dimmock, 'Tamburlaine's Curse: An Answer to a Great Marlowe Mystery', *Times Literary Supplement*, 19 November 2010, pp. 16–17.

4 For further discussion see Charles Nicholl, *The Reckoning: The Murder of Christopher Marlowe* (Vintage Books, 2002), pp. 53–4, pp. 400–1.

5 Ford K. Brown, 'Marlowe and Kyd', *Times Literary Supplement*, 2 June 1921, p. 355.

6   For more on the inquest into Marlowe's death see Leslie Hotson, *The Death of Christopher Marlowe* (Nonesuch Press, 1925).

7   David Riggs, *The World of Christopher Marlowe* (Faber and Faber, 2004), p. 261.

8   The evidence for and against Nashe's involvement is discussed by Andrew Hadfield in 'Marlowe and Nashe', *English Literary Renaissance*, 51.2 (2021), 190–216 (pp. 209–11) and in *Christopher Marlowe: Doctor Faustus, A- and B-Texts (1604, 1616)*, edited by David Bevington and Eric Rasmussen (Manchester University Press, 1993), pp. 70–2.

9   These studies are by Darren Freebury-Jones and Marcus Dahl, 'Searching for Thomas Nashe in *Dido, Queen of Carthage*', *Digital Scholarship in the Humanities*, 35.2 (2020), 296–306, and Ruth Lunney and Hugh Craig, 'Who Wrote *Dido, Queen of Carthage*?', *Journal of Marlowe Studies*, 1 (2020), 1–31.

10 Dekker's presence was proposed by David Lake in 'Three Seventeenth-Century Revisions: *Thomas of Woodstock*, *The Jew of Malta*, and *Faustus* B', *Notes and Queries*, 228 (1983), 133–43.

11 Robert Logan, *Shakespeare's Marlowe: The Influence of Christopher Marlowe on Shakespeare's Artistry* (Ashgate, 2007), p. 8.

12 James Shapiro, *Rival Playwrights: Marlowe, Jonson, Shakespeare* (Columbia University Press, 1991), p. 129.

13 Jonathan Bate, *The Genius of Shakespeare* (Oxford University Press, 1998), p. 105.

14 Richard Wilson proposes that Mercadé is Marlowe in '"The words of Mercury": Shakespeare and Marlowe', in *The Cambridge Companion to Shakespeare and Contemporary Playwrights*, edited by Ton Hoenselaars (Cambridge University Press, 2012), pp. 34–53 (p. 40).

15 For discussion on the alternative approaches taken by Marlowe and Shakespeare see *The Merchant of Venice*, edited by John Drakakis (Bloomsbury, 2011), pp. 21–3.

16 Algernon Charles Swinburne, *The Age of Shakespeare* (Chatto and Windus, 1908), p. 40.

17 T. S. Eliot, *The Sacred Wood: Essays on Poetry and Criticism* (Methuen, 1920), p. 78.

18 Bart van Es, *Shakespeare in Company* (Oxford University Press, 2013), pp. 21–2.

19 The resonances of the *Tamburlaine* plays should, of course, be considered in repertorial, not just authorial, terms. Mark Hutchings writes of 'the "*Tamburlaine* narrative"' and 'how desperate' Elizabethan playing companies such as 'the Queen's Men were to keep pace with their rivals', the Admiral's Men, who produced Marlowe's two-parter. Mark Hutchings, 'The "Turk Phenomenon" and the Repertory of the Late Elizabethan Playhouse', *Early Modern Literary Studies*, 13.2 (2007).

20 Paul Vincent notes that 'the first hundred lines of' George Peele's '*Edward I* are very nearly as Marlovian as they are Peelean' in his study of matching phrases. Paul Vincent, 'When *harey* Met Shakespeare: The Genesis of *The First Part of Henry the Sixth*' (Doctoral thesis: University of Auckland, 2005), p. 292.

21 For discussion on dramatists' differing rates for compound forms see Alfred Hart, *Shakespeare and the Homilies* (Melbourne University Press, 1934), pp. 232–9.

22 Gary Taylor and Rory Loughnane make this claim in 'The Canon and Chronology of Shakespeare's Works', in *The New Oxford Shakespeare: Authorship Companion*, edited by Gary Taylor and Gabriel Egan (Oxford University Press, 2017), pp. 417–603 (p. 498).

23 Hugh Craig, 'The Three Parts of *Henry VI*', in *Shakespeare, Computers, and the Mystery of Authorship*, edited by Hugh Craig and Arthur F. Kinney (Cambridge University Press, 2009), pp. 40–77.

24 For detailed discussion see Pervez Rizvi, 'The Interpretation of Zeta Test Results', *Digital Scholarship in the Humanities*, 34.2 (2018), 401–18.

25 Kazuaki Ota, 'Was Marlowe Shakespeare's Collaborator?: Computational Stylometry and the Authorship of The Three Parts of *Henry VI*', *Studies in Languages and Cultures*, 50 (2023), 1–17 (p. 17).

26 Rosalind Barber, 'Big Data or Not Enough? Zeta Test Reliability and the Attribution of *Henry VI*', *Digital Scholarship in the Humanities*, 36.3 (2021), 542–64 (p. 556).

27 These claims for success can be found in Hugh Craig and Arthur F. Kinney, 'Methods', in *Shakespeare, Computers, and the Mystery of Authorship*, edited by Hugh Craig and Arthur F. Kinney (Cambridge University Press, 2009), pp. 15–39 (p. 22).

28 For further discussion see Pervez Rizvi, 'Shakespeare and Principal Component Analysis', *Digital Scholarship in the Humanities*, 36.4 (2021), 1030–41, and 'The Interpretation of Zeta Test Results: A Supplement', *Digital Scholarship in the Humanities*, 37.4 (2022), 1172–8.

29 Philip Timberlake, *The Feminine Ending in English Blank Verse: A Study of Its Use by Early Writers in the Measure and Its Development in the Drama up to the Year 1595* (Banta, 1931), pp. 86–94.

30 *Ibid.*, p. 45.

31 Craig, 'The Three Parts of *Henry VI*', p. 73.

32 These figures can be found in Timberlake, *The Feminine Ending in English Blank Verse*, pp. 32–49.

33 F. P. Wilson, 'The English History Play', in *Shakespearian and Other Studies*, edited by Helen Gardner (Clarendon Press, 1969), pp. 1–53 (p. 16).

34 Douglas Bruster and Nell McKeown, 'Wordplay in Earliest Shakespeare', *Philological Quarterly*, 96.3 (2017), 293–322 (p. 299).

35 Craig, 'The Three Parts of *Henry VI*', p. 76.

36 Brian Vickers makes such observations in 'Shakespeare and Authorship Studies in the Twenty-First Century', *Shakespeare Quarterly*, 62.1 (2011), 106–42 (p. 125).

37 John V. Nance, '"We, John Cade": Shakespeare, Marlowe, and the Authorship of 4.2.33–189 2 *Henry VI*', *Shakespeare*, 13.1 (2017), 30–51.

38 Warren Chernaik poses these questions in 'Theatrical Companies and Their Plays', *Medieval and Renaissance Drama in England*, 33 (2020), 167–87 (p. 173).

39 *Ibid.*, p. 175.

40 Santiago Segarra, Mark Eisen, Gabriel Egan, and Alejandro Ribeiro, 'Attributing the Authorship of the *Henry VI* Plays by Word Adjacency', *Shakespeare Quarterly*, 67 (2016), 232–56 (p. 241).

41 As argued by Pervez Rizvi in 'Authorship Attribution for Early Modern Plays Using Function Word Adjacency Networks: A Critical View', *American Notes and Queries*, 33.4 (2020), 328–31 (p. 329).

42 The words placed in bold in this match are all included in the 'Full list of function words used in this method' in Segarra et al., 'Attributing the Authorship of the *Henry VI* Plays', p. 253.

43 Rosalind Barber, 'Function Word Adjacency Networks and Early Modern Plays', *American Notes and Queries*, 33.2 (2020), 204–13 (p. 204).

44 Pervez Rizvi offers a faithful reproduction of the WAN method in 'An Analysis of the Word Adjacency Network Method – Part 1 – The Evidence of Its Unsoundness', *Digital Scholarship in the Humanities* 38.1 (2023), 347–60.

45 For further discussion on Shakespeare's careful use of second-person pronouns see Charles Barber, '"You" and "Thou" in Shakespeare's *Richard III*', *Leeds Studies in English*, 12 (1981), 273–89.

46 David Auerbach offers a summary of potential pitfalls lying behind such methods in '"A cannon's burst discharged against a ruinated wall": A Critique of Quantitative Methods in Shakespearean Authorial Attribution', *Authorship*, 7.2 (2018), 1–16.

47 Martin Mueller, 'Vickers is right about Kyd' (2009), https://darrenfj.files. wordpress.com/2017/11/N-grams-and-the-Kyd-Canon-and-Vickers-is-right-about-Kyd.pdf (accessed 16 October 2022).

48 Albert Yang, Chung-Kang Peng, and Ary L. Goldberger, 'The Marlowe-Shakespeare Authorship Debate: Approaching an Old Problem with New Methods', *The Calvin & Rose G Hoffman Marlowe Memorial Trust Prize* (2003).

49 This approach is taken by Darren Freebury-Jones in 'Exploring Co-authorship in *2 Henry VI*', *Journal of Early Modern Studies*, 5 (2016), 201–16.

50 Bruster and McKeown, 'Wordplay in Earliest Shakespeare', pp. 309–10.

51 MacDonald P. Jackson, 'Material for an Edition of *Arden of Faversham*' (B.Litt. thesis: Oxford University, 1963), p. 149.

52 Alfred Hart, *Stolne and Surreptitious Copies: A Comparative Study of Shakespeare's Bad Quartos* (Melbourne University Press, 1942), pp. 451–4.

53 The *New Oxford Shakespeare* team also relied on analysis of the variant 'O' and 'Oh' spelling and compound forms in *Henry VI Part Two*, as well as classical allusions in Paul Vincent, 'Unsolved Mysteries in *Henry the Sixth, Part Two*', *Notes and Queries*, 246 (2001), 270–4. Brian Vickers, drawing from Pervez Rizvi's empirical evidence that compositors didn't spell 'O' or 'Oh' consistently, shows that, rather than revealing an alternating pattern in the play suggestive of different authors, their distribution is entirely random. See Brian Vickers, 'Compositors' Spelling Preferences and the Integrity of *2 Henry VI*', *The Library*, 24.2 (2023), 141–53; Pervez Rizvi, 'The Use of Spellings for Compositor Attribution in the First Folio', *Papers of the Bibliographical Society of America*, 110 (2016), 1–53 (p. 24).

Gary Taylor and Rory Loughnane agree with Vincent that errors in classical learning in the play are likely Shakespeare's, because 'the other dramatists proposed as co-authors of the play, Greene, Nashe, Peele, and Marlowe, all educated at Oxford or Cambridge, are much less likely than Shakespeare to have made such errors'. Taylor and Loughnane, 'The Canon and Chronology of Shakespeare's Works', p. 495. However, this assumption has also been challenged. See Edward Paleit, 'Shakespeare's Faulty Learning? Classical Reference in *2 Henry VI* and the Authorship Question', *Notes and Queries*, 48.4 (2018), 506–11, and Darren Freebury-Jones, *Reading Robert Greene: Recovering Shakespeare's Rival* (Routledge, 2022), pp. 40–1.

54 John V. Nance, 'Early Shakespeare and the Authorship of *The Taming of the Shrew*', in *Early Shakespeare, 1588–1594*, edited by Rory Loughnane and Andrew J. Power (Cambridge University Press, 2020), pp. 261–83.

55 Warren Chernaik, 'Review of *Early Shakespeare, 1588–1594*', *Modern Philology*, 118.3 (2021), 209–14 (p. 214).

56 These figures can be found in Nance, 'Early Shakespeare and the Authorship of *The Taming of the Shrew*', p. 269.

57 *Ibid.*, Appendix B, pp. 307–9.

58 As observed by John P. A. Ioannidis in 'Why Most Published Research Findings Are False', *PLoS Medicine*, 2.8 (2005), https://doi.org/10.1371/journal.pmed.0020124 (accessed 29 October 2022).

59 For further discussion see Darren Freebury-Jones, 'New Perspectives on Thomas Kyd's Restored Canon', *Notes and Queries*, 69.1 (2022), 15–17.

60 Taylor and Loughnane, 'The Canon and Chronology of Shakespeare's Works', p. 502.

61 *Ibid.*, p. 503. See also Marina Tarlinskaja, *Shakespeare and the Versification of Elizabethan Drama 1561–1642* (Ashgate, 2014), Tables B.4, B.5.

62 E. K. Chambers, *William Shakespeare a Study of Facts and Problems: Volume I*, 2 vols (Oxford University Press, 1930), pp. 322–8.

63 *Ibid.*, p. 324.

64 This fact is revealed in Timberlake's *The Feminine Ending in English Blank Verse*, p. 84.

65 Karl Wentersdorf, 'The Authenticity of *The Taming of the Shrew*', *Shakespeare Quarterly*, 5 (1954), 11–32 (p. 12).

66 For a fascinating account of Shakespeare's gendered rhymes see Robert Stagg, 'Rhyme's Voices: Hearing Gender in *The Taming of the Shrew*', *Studies in Philology*, 119.2 (2021), 323–46.

67 Lukas Erne, 'Disintegrating Marlowe', *Studies in Philology*, 119.2 (2021), 272–97 (p. 297).

68 *Ibid.*, p. 286.

69 Hart, *Stolne and Surreptitious Copies*, p. 388.

70 Email correspondence with Martin Wiggins (1 November 2022). Wiggins also notes that 'the text' of *The Taming of the Shrew* 'seems to contain two conceptual layers in the organisation of the Bianca plot, with Hortensio as the crunch point where they fail to mesh together perfectly'. He considers it unlikely that Shakespeare would have got 'into the significant difficulties he did over Hortensio if there had been a second author working with him',

because co-authorship 'necessarily means that the whole exercise is subject to much more planning and discussion beforehand'. He therefore observes that the underlying manuscript appears to be Shakespeare's alone.

71 For further discussion on Marlowe's escapades in the Netherlands see E. B. Wernham, 'Christopher Marlowe at Flushing in 1592', *English Historical Review*, 91 (1976), 344–5.

4 Thomas Kyd

1 For further discussion on Thomas Kyd's biography see J. R. Mulryne, 'Kyd, Thomas', in *Oxford Dictionary of National Biography*, edited by Henry Colin Grey Matthew and Brian Harrison (Oxford University Press, 2004).

2 *The Works of Thomas Kyd*, edited by Frederick S. Boas (Clarendon Press, 1901), p. lxxxi.

3 Lukas Erne makes this observation in *Beyond The Spanish Tragedy: A Study of the Works of Thomas Kyd* (Manchester University Press, 2001), p. 163.

4 The proposal that the old *Hamlet* play belonged to Pembroke's Men can be found in *Henslowe's Diary, Part II*, edited by W. W. Greg, 2 vols (A. H. Bullen, 1908), p. 105.

5 T. S. Eliot makes this argument in the Introduction to *Seneca, His Tenne Tragedies* (Constable, 1927), p. v.

6 As noted by Erne in *Beyond The Spanish Tragedy*, p. 81. For further discussion on Senecan influences see Gordon Braden, *Renaissance Tragedy and the Senecan Tradition: Anger's Privilege* (Yale University Press, 1985), and Curtis Perry, *Shakespeare and Senecan Tragedy* (Cambridge University Press, 2020).

7 Jordi Coral, 'Seneca, what Seneca? The Chorus in *The Spanish Tragedy*', *The Spanish and Portuguese Society for English Renaissance Studies*, 17 (2007), 5–26 (p. 16).

8 Miles Drawdy gives a brilliant account of Kyd and the *theatrum mundi* in '"See here my show": Providence and The Theatrum Mundi in Thomas Kyd's *The Spanish Tragedy*' (Honors thesis: College of William and Mary, Virginia, 2014), p. 6.

9 For further discussion on Senecan choruses intervening in the action of plays see Coral, 'Seneca, what Seneca?', p. 18.

10 These similarities are observed by Ann Thompson in '*The Taming of the Shrew* and *The Spanish Tragedy*', *Notes and Queries*, 31 (1984), 182–4 (p. 182).

11 For further discussion see Marjorie Garber, *Dream in Shakespeare: From Metaphor to Metamorphosis* (Yale University Press, 1974), p. 28.

12 Erne, *Beyond The Spanish Tragedy*, p. 85.

13 As shown by Thompson in '*The Taming of the Shrew* and *The Spanish Tragedy*', p. 183.

14 T. S. Eliot, *The Sacred Wood: Essays on Poetry and Criticism* (Methuen, 1920), pp. 88–9. Stanley Wells writes that the 'style' of *The Spanish Tragedy* is 'rhetorical rather than poetical, powerful if self-conscious in its patterning'

and that it is 'easy to find parallels to this kind of writing in Shakespeare's early history plays' in *Shakespeare & Co.* (Penguin, 2006), p. 74.

15 Samuel Taylor Coleridge, *The Collected Works of Samuel Taylor Coleridge: Volume XIV*, edited by Carl Woodring, 14 vols (Princeton University Press, 1990), p. 355. For further discussion see Brian Vickers, 'Identifying Shakespeare's Additions to *The Spanish Tragedy* (1602): A New(er) Approach', *Shakespeare*, 8 (2012), 13–43.

16 Thomas Bancroft recorded that on the stage Richard Burbage would sometimes 'Grow big with wrath, and make his buttons fly' in *Time's Out of Tune* (W. Godbid, 1658), p. 44.

17 Kyd's authorship of this play is discussed in *The Plays and Poems of William Shakespeare: Volume II*, edited by James Boswell, 21 vols (F. C. and J. Rivington, 1821), p. 372, and Erne, *Beyond The Spanish Tragedy*, p. 147.

18 Arthur Freeman makes this point in his valuable biography, *Thomas Kyd: A Study of Facts and Problems* (Clarendon Press, 1967), p. 41.

19 Gary Taylor, 'Shakespeare's Early Gothic *Hamlet*', in *Shakespeare & the First Hamlet*, edited by Terri Bourus (Berghahn Books, 2022), pp. 7–34 (p. 14).

20 For a wonderful discussion on the evolution of the ghost in English Renaissance drama see Pierre Kapitaniak, 'Bending One's Eye on Vacancy? Stage Ghosts, Shakespeare and the Question of Visibility in English Drama', *Arrêt sur scène / Scene Focus*, 11 (2022), 1–26.

21 An enlightening discussion of Shakespeare both borrowing and turning away from older 'Turk plays' can be found in Daniel Vitkus's *Turning Turk: English Theater and the Multicultural Mediterranean, 1570–1630* (Macmillan, 2003), p. 2.

22 These figures can be found in Philip Timberlake, *The Feminine Ending in English Blank Verse: A Study of Its Use by Early Writers in the Measure and Its Development in the Drama up to the Year 1595* (Banta, 1931), p. 46.

23 William Wells, 'Thomas Kyd and the Chronicle-History', *Notes and Queries*, 30 (1940), 218–24, 238–43 (p. 243).

24 As pointed out by Erne in *Beyond The Spanish Tragedy*, p. 96.

25 Alfred Harbage, 'Intrigue in Elizabethan Tragedy', in *Essays on Shakespeare and Elizabethan Drama in Honor of Hardin Craig*, edited by Richard Hosley (University of Missouri Press, 1962), pp. 37–44 (p. 37).

26 See W. H. Auden, *The Dyer's Hand and Other Essays* (Faber and Faber, 1948), pp. 246–72.

27 Andrew Hadfield, 'A More Brilliant Bird: Compiling the Canon of Shakespeare's First Critic and Rival', *Times Literary Supplement*, 7 October 2022, pp. 20–1 (p. 20). The 'extended' Kyd canon was first proposed by Brian Vickers in 'Thomas Kyd, Secret Sharer', *Times Literary Supplement*, 18 April 2008, pp. 13–15.

28 Striking similarities between Nashe's and Greene's attacks are pointed out by Darren Freebury-Jones in 'Possible Light on the Authorship of *Fair Em*', *Notes and Queries*, 64.2 (2017), 252–4.

29 For full discussion of the evidence for expanding Kyd's canon see Darren Freebury-Jones, *Shakespeare's Tutor: The Influence of Thomas Kyd* (Manchester University Press, 2022). See also *The Collected Works*

of Thomas Kyd, General Editor Brian Vickers, Associate Editor Darren Freebury-Jones (Boydell and Brewer, 2024).

30 W. W. Greg makes this observation in 'The Date of *King Lear* and Shakespeare's Use of Earlier Versions of the Story', *The Library*, 20 (1940), 377–400 (p. 381).

31 *Soliman and Perseda [1592/93]*, edited by Lukas Erne (Malone Society Reprints, 2014), p. xvi.

32 Earlier scholars who gave *Arden of Faversham* solely to Kyd include F. G. Fleay, *A Biographical Chronicle of the English Drama: Volume II*, 2 vols (Reeves and Turner, 1891), p. 26; Charles Crawford, *Collectanea: First Series* (Shakespeare Head Press, 1906); Walter Miksch, *Die Verfasserschaft des Arden of Feversham* (Breslau, 1907); H. Dugdale Sykes, *Sidelights on Shakespeare* (Shakespeare Head Press, 1919), pp. 48–9; Eliot, *The Sacred Wood*, pp. 87–94 (pp. 88–9); Timberlake, *The Feminine Ending in English Blank Verse*, pp. 52–3; Paul V. Rubow, *Shakespeare og hans samtidige* (Gyldendubidal, 1948), pp. 145–55; *Arden de Faversham: Etude Critique, Traduction et Notes*, edited by Félix Carrère (Montaigne, 1950), pp. 21–85.

33 For further discussion on biographical links to Kyd see Darren Freebury-Jones, 'Elevating Thomas Watson: An Investigation into New Authorship Claims', *Early Modern Literary Studies*, 22.1 (2021), 1–19.

34 MacDonald P. Jackson, 'Material for an Edition of *Arden of Faversham*' (B.Litt. thesis: Oxford University, 1963), pp. 101–4.

35 MacDonald P. Jackson, 'Parallels and Poetry: Shakespeare, Kyd, and *Arden of Faversham*', *Medieval and Renaissance Drama in England*, 23 (2010), 17–33 (p. 28).

36 As contended by MacDonald P. Jackson in his *Determining the Shakespeare Canon: Arden of Faversham and A Lover's Complaint* (Oxford University Press, 2014), p. 76.

37 Christa Jansohn points out scenic similarities in '*Arden of Faversham*', in *Studying English Literature in Context: Critical Readings*, edited by Paul Poplawski (Cambridge University Press, 2022), pp. 101–16 (p. 106).

38 The results can be found in Jackson's *Determining the Shakespeare Canon*, pp. 219–32.

39 *Ibid.*, p. 225 n. 11.

40 Many more examples can be given. See Darren Freebury-Jones, '*Arden of Faversham*: Authorship Commentary', in *The Collected Works of Thomas Kyd*, General Editor Brian Vickers, Associate Editor Darren Freebury-Jones.

41 The comparison is also found in the works of Shakespeare and Thomas Dekker. For further discussion on Shakespeare's phrasal and imagistic borrowings from *Arden* and key differences in usage, see Freebury-Jones, *Shakespeare's Tutor*, pp. 91–2.

42 For further discussion see Rebekah Owens, 'The Reception History of Frederick Samuel Boas' *Works of Thomas Kyd*' (Doctoral thesis: Anglia Ruskin University, 2020).

43 *The Works of Thomas Kyd*, edited by Frederick S. Boas, p. xc.

44 Arthur F. Kinney, 'Authoring *Arden of Faversham*', in *Shakespeare, Computers, and the Mystery of Authorship*, edited by Hugh Craig and Arthur F. Kinney (Cambridge University Press, 2009), pp. 78–99 (p. 93).

45 For alternative stylometric studies that give the play wholly to Kyd and sharply distinguish it from Shakespeare see Lene B. Petersen, *Shakespeare's Errant Texts: Textual Form and Linguistic Style in Shakespearean 'Bad' Quartos and Co-authored Plays* (Cambridge University Press, 2010), pp. 213–14, and Albert Yang, 'Validating the Enlarged Kyd Canon: A New Approach', *American Notes and Queries*, 33.2 (2020), 189–97. Ward Elliott's analysis reveals that although scene 8 is the one that MacDonald P. Jackson 'originally thought looked most like Shakespeare', it has eighteen rejections by his method '(our cutoff is two). With that much Shakespeare discrepancy, Scene 8 looks improbable to us.' He concludes that *Arden of Faversham* as a whole 'has ten Shakespeare rejections and is wildly improbable as a solo Shakespeare work' in 'Notes from the Claremont Shakespeare Clinic', *The Shakespeare Newsletter* (2011), pp. 105–12 (p. 110).

46 Brett Greatley-Hirsch and Jack Elliott, '*Arden of Faversham*, Shakespearian Authorship, and "The Print of Many"', in *The New Oxford Shakespeare: Authorship Companion*, edited by Gary Taylor and Gabriel Egan (Oxford University Press, 2017), pp. 139–81 (p. 181).

47 For critiques of this method and the interpretations of its results see Joseph F. Stephenson, 'Review of *The New Oxford Shakespeare: Authorship Companion*', *Sixteenth Century Journal*, 49.4 (2018), 1314–17 (p. 1316); Pervez Rizvi, 'The Interpretation of Zeta Test Results', *Digital Scholarship in the Humanities*, 34.2 (2018), 401–18; David Auerbach, 'Statistical Infelicities in *The New Oxford Shakespeare Authorship Companion*', *American Notes and Queries*, 33.1 (2020), 28–31; '"A cannon's burst discharged against a ruinated wall": A Critique of Quantitative Methods in Shakespearean Authorial Attribution', *Authorship*, 7.2 (2018), 1–16; 'Review of *The New Oxford Shakespeare: Authorship Companion*', *American Notes and Queries*, 33.2 (2020), 236–41.

48 Timberlake, *The Feminine Ending in English Blank Verse*, p. 52.

49 See Marina Tarlinskaja, *Shakespeare and the Versification of Elizabethan Drama 1561–1642* (Ashgate, 2014), p. 110 and Appendix B: Table B.3.

50 Douglas Bruster makes this argument in *Seeing Shakespeare's Style* (Routledge, 2022), pp. 224–47.

51 Kyd's distinct use of dispersed rhyme was noted over a century ago by James E. Routh Jr in 'Thomas Kyd's Rime Schemes and the Authorship of *Soliman and Perseda* and of *The First Part of Jeronimo*', *Modern Language Notes*, 20.2 (1905), 49–51.

52 These 'rhymes' are presented as evidence for Shakespeare's authorship by Bruster in *Seeing Shakespeare's Style*, pp. 224–47.

53 There are eight instances of the *aca* scheme in *The Taming of the Shrew*: 'free/you/she'; 'you/daughter/two'; 'day/gone/stay' (these examples are dispersed between speakers and are therefore quite different from Kyd's incorporation of this scheme in blank verse speeches we saw in *Arden of Faversham* and *Soliman and Perseda*); 'dower/love/her'; 'accord/passion/lord'; 'company/monument/prodigy'; 'today/myself/way'; 'esteem/birth/beseem'. Although Douglas Bruster considers such dispersed rhymes to be more frequent in

Arden of Faversham than in other works no matter who the author, the total for patterns in *Arden of Faversham* found elsewhere in Kyd's plays is twenty, lower than the totals of twenty-three in *The Spanish Tragedy* and thirty examples in *Cornelia*. See Freebury-Jones, *Shakespeare's Tutor*, p. 150.

54 As pointed out by Scott McMillin and Sally-Beth MacLean in *The Queen's Men and Their Plays* (Cambridge University Press, 1998), p. 146.

55 *The First Part of King Henry VI*, edited by John Dover Wilson (Cambridge University Press, 1952), p. xlvi.

56 For discussion of the evidence amassed by scholars in support of Nashe since the early twentieth century see Freebury-Jones, *Shakespeare's Tutor*, pp. 111–13.

57 These observations were made by Paul Vincent in 'When *harey* Met Shakespeare: The Genesis of *The First Part of Henry the Sixth*' (Doctoral thesis: University of Auckland, 2005), p. 190. Vincent was unable to work out who wrote the bulk of the play but didn't compare these stylistic markers to Kyd.

58 This claim is made in *The New Oxford Shakespeare: Modern Critical Edition*, edited by Gary Taylor, John Jowett, Terri Bourus, and Gabriel Egan (Oxford University Press, 2016), p. 926.

59 Margaret steps into a role that continues Joan's as a prophetess mistreated by her English counterparts. See Harold F. Brooks, '*Richard III*, Unhistorical Amplifications: The Women's Scenes and Seneca', *Modern Language Review*, 75.4 (1980), 721–37.

60 For an illuminating account of Shakespeare's creation of this scene see Vincent, 'When *harey* Met Shakespeare', p. 115.

61 For further discussion on Shakespeare's rhyming habits see Brian Vickers, 'Incomplete Shakespeare: Or, Denying Coauthorship in *1 Henry VI*', *Shakespeare Quarterly*, 58.3 (2007), 311–52 (pp. 342–3), and F. W. Ness, *The Use of Rhyme in Shakespeare's Plays* (Yale University Press, 1941), pp. 95–105.

62 The speech is deemed characteristic of Shakespeare on this basis by Gary Taylor in 'Shakespeare and Others: The Authorship of *Henry the Sixth Part One*', *Medieval and Renaissance Drama*, 7 (1995), 145–205 (p. 167), and Vincent in 'When *harey* Met Shakespeare', p. 199.

63 Vincent offers this interpretation in 'When *harey* Met Shakespeare', p. 249.

64 *Ibid.*, p. 197.

65 For further discussion see Jackson, *Determining the Shakespeare Canon*, p. 108; Freebury-Jones, *Shakespeare's Tutor*, pp. 117–18.

66 The craftsmanship of these scenes is discussed by Alan Dessen in *Elizabethan Stage Conventions and Modern Interpreters* (Cambridge University Press, 1984), p. 94.

67 Erne, *Beyond The Spanish Tragedy*, pp. 191–2.

68 *First King Henry VI*, edited by John Dover Wilson, p. xiii.

69 John Semple Smart, *Shakespeare: Truth and Tradition* (E. Arnold, 1928), p. 17.

70 Edward Capell, *Prolusions; or select pieces of antient Poetry* (J. and R. Tonson, 1760), p. ix.

71 An 'Ur-Countess' episode is conjectured in *Edward III: The New Cambridge Shakespeare*, edited by Giorgio Melchiori (Cambridge University Press, 1998), pp. 37–8.

72 R. M. Smith, '*Edward III* A Study of the Authorship of the Drama in the Light of a New Source', *Journal of English and German Philology*, 10 (1911), 90–104 (p. 101).

73 The theory of revision is revived in *King Edward III*, edited by Richard Proudfoot and Nicola Bennett (Bloomsbury, 2017), p. 64.

74 E. K. Chambers, *William Shakespeare a Study of Facts and Problems: Volume I*, 2 vols (Oxford University Press, 1930), p. 516; *The Oxford Shakespeare: The Complete Works*, edited by John Jowett, William Montgomery, Gary Taylor, and Stanley Wells (Oxford University Press, 2005), p. 257.

75 Timberlake pointed out notable differences in verse structure in *The Feminine Ending in English Blank Verse*, p. 79.

76 As first highlighted by Gregor Sarrazin in *Thomas Kyd und sein Kreis: Eine Litterarhistorische Untersuchung* (E. Felber, 1892), p. 124. For a detailed attribution history of the play to Shakespeare and Kyd see Freebury-Jones, *Shakespeare's Tutor*, pp. 143–5, pp. 147–9.

77 Will Sharpe, 'Authorship and Attribution', in *William Shakespeare & Others: Collaborative Plays*, edited by Jonathan Bate and Eric Rasmussen (Macmillan, 2013), pp. 641–730 (p. 666).

5 Robert Greene

1 For further discussion on Robert Greene's biography see Lori Humphrey Newcomb, 'Greene, Robert', in *Oxford Dictionary of National Biography*, edited by Henry Colin Grey Matthew and Brian Harrison (Oxford University Press, 2004). See also *The Plays & Poems of Robert Greene*, edited by John Churton Collins, 2 vols (Oxford University Press, 1905), and Brenda Richardson, 'Robert Greene's Yorkshire Connexions: A New Hypothesis', *Yearbook of English Studies*, 10 (1980), 160–80.

2 Stanley Wells, *Shakespeare & Co.* (Penguin, 2006), p. 66.

3 These proposed ripostes to Greene are detailed in Stephen Greenblatt, *Will in the World: How Shakespeare Became Shakespeare* (The Bodley Head, 2004), p. 219; Maureen Godman, '"Plucking a Crow" in *The Comedy of Errors*', *Early Theatre*, 8.1 (2005), 53–68; and Robert Stagg, 'Shakespeare's Bombastic Blanks', *Review of English Studies*, 72.307 (2021), 882–99.

4 Wolfgang Clemen, *English Tragedy before Shakespeare: The Development of Dramatic Speech* (Methuen, 1961), p. 182.

5 *Robert Greene*, edited by Thomas H. Dickinson (T. Fisher Unwin, 1909), p. xxxi.

6 All references to Robert Greene's traditionally accepted plays throughout this book are to *Robert Greene*, edited by Thomas H. Dickinson (T. Fisher Unwin, 1909). A new critical edition of his collected plays, the first in over a century, is being prepared: *The Collected Plays of Robert Greene*, General Editor Darren Freebury-Jones (Edinburgh University Press, 2028).

7 Alan Dessen suggests that Greene sometimes sought 'a more spectacular effect than may indeed be possible' in *Elizabethan Stage Conventions and Modern Interpreters* (Cambridge University Press, 1984), p. 26.

8 Wells, *Shakespeare & Co.*, p. 68.

9 William Empson credits Greene with the invention of the double plot in *Some Versions of Pastoral* (Chatto and Windus, 1935), p. 33. Charles W. Hieatt makes a case for multiple plotlines in 'Multiple Plotting in *Friar Bacon and Friar Bungay*', *Renaissance Drama*, 16 (1985), 17–34.

10 For further discussion on the divisions of authorship in this play see Darren Freebury-Jones, *Reading Robert Greene: Recovering Shakespeare's Rival* (Routledge, 2022), pp. 82–92.

11 Edward Meyer, *Machiavelli and the Elizabethan Drama* (Felber, 1897), pp. 63–4.

12 For full discussion see Freebury-Jones, *Reading Robert Greene*, pp. 105–42.

13 Lawrence Manley and Sally-Beth MacLean argue that, because Lodge was 'closely connected with the Stanley household since his youth', it's likely that *A Looking-Glass for London and England* 'belonged in the first instance to Lord Strange's Men'. *Lord Strange's Men and Their Plays* (Yale University Press, 2014), p. 102.

14 As the great bibliographer W. W. Greg put it: 'no one has ever denied that a strong case can be made out for Greene's authorship of *Locrine*'. 'Review of *The Plays & Poems of Robert Greene*; J. Churton Collins', *Modern Language Review*, 1.3 (1906), 238–51 (p. 243).

15 The dubious case for *Locrine* as a revision of a lost *Estrild* play is discussed by Roslyn Knutson in 'Ur-Plays and Other Exercises in Making Stuff Up', in *Lost Plays in Shakespeare's England*, edited by David McInnis and Matthew Steggle (Palgrave, 2014), pp. 31–54, and MacDonald P. Jackson in '*Locrine* and Robert Greene's Dramatic Canon', *Notes and Queries*, 70.3 (2023), 154–9.

16 These preliminary findings were publicised in Darren Freebury-Jones, 'Determining Robert Greene's Dramatic Canon', *Style*, 54.4 (2020), 377–98, and Dalya Alberge, 'Poetic justice as Shakespeare rival Robert Greene takes play credit', *The Telegraph*, 28 November 2020, p. 3.

17 Roslyn Knutson points out that *Locrine* is a strong 'candidate' for a play in 'the career of the Queen's Men' in 'The Start of Something Big', in *Locating the Queen's Men, 1583–1603: Material Practices and Conditions of Playing*, edited by Helen Ostovich, Holger Schott Syme, and Andrew Griffin (Routledge, 2009), pp. 99–108 (p. 103).

18 Roslyn Knutson, *The Repertory of Shakespeare's Company 1594–1613* (University of Arkansas Press, 1991), p. 70. For further discussion on Greene's influence on these plays see Freebury-Jones, *Reading Robert Greene*, pp. 92–101.

19 *The Tragical Reign of Selimus, Sometime Emperor of the Turks*, edited by A. B. Grosart (J. M. Dent and Co., 1898), pp. vi.

20 *Ibid.*, p. ix.

21 See for example Meredith Skura's discussion in 'What Shakespeare Did with the Queen's Men's *King Leir* and When', *Shakespeare Survey*, 63 (2010), 316–25.

6 George Peele

1 For further discussion on George Peele's biography see Reid Barbour, 'Peele, George', in *Oxford Dictionary of National Biography*, edited by Henry Colin Grey Matthew and Brian Harrison (Oxford University Press, 2004).

2 David Horne challenges such slurs on Peele's character in *The Life and Minor Works of George Peele* (Yale University Press, 1952).

3 For the full range of evidence for Peele's authorship of this play see Brian Vickers, '*The Troublesome Reign*, George Peele, and the Date of *King John*', in *Words that Count: Essays on Early Modern Authorship in Honor of MacDonald P. Jackson*, edited by Brian Boyd (Associated University Presses, 2004), pp. 76–118, and *The Troublesome Reign of John, King of England*, edited by Charles R. Forker (Manchester University Press, 2011).

4 *Renaissance Drama: An Anthology of Plays and Entertainments*, edited by Arthur F. Kinney and David A. Katz, 3rd edn (Wiley, 2022), p. 377.

5 Peele's and Shakespeare's approaches towards parody are discussed by Tom Rutter in *Shakespeare and the Admiral's Men: Reading across Repertoires on the London Stage, 1594–1600* (Cambridge University Press, 2017), pp. 111–15.

6 All references to George Peele's plays in this book are to *The Life and Works of George Peele*, edited by C. T. Prouty, 3 vols (Yale University Press, 1952–70), except for references to *The Troublesome Reign of John*, edited by Charles R. Forker.

7 Stanley Wells, *Shakespeare & Co.* (Penguin, 2006), p. 70.

8 *Renaissance Drama*, edited by Arthur F. Kinney and David A. Katz, p. 377.

9 Scott McMillin and Sally-Beth MacLean offer a great account of Peele's craftsmanship in *The Queen's Men and Their Plays* (Cambridge University Press, 1998), p. 138.

10 Several scholars have traced the influence of *The Troublesome Reign of King John* on Shakespeare before he came to adapt it. See E. A. J. Honigmann, *Shakespeare's Impact on his Contemporaries* (Macmillan, 1982), p. 80, and Charles R. Forker, '*The Troublesome Reign, Richard II*, and the Date of *King John*: A Study in Intertextuality', *Shakespeare Survey*, 63 (2010), 127–48.

11 George Wilkins's hand in *Pericles* is discussed in significant detail by Brian Vickers in *Shakespeare, Co-author: A Historical Study of Five Collaborative Plays* (Oxford University Press, 2002), pp. 291–332, and by MacDonald P. Jackson in *Defining Shakespeare: Pericles as Test Case* (Oxford University Press, 2003).

12 Studies revealing Peele's authorship of parts of *Titus Andronicus* are most usefully summarised and extended by Vickers in *Shakespeare, Co-author*, pp. 148–243.

13 Philip Timberlake, *The Feminine Ending in English Blank Verse: A Study of Its Use by Early Writers in the Measure and Its Development in the Drama up to the Year 1595* (Banta, 1931), p. 24.

14 For discussion on Peele's rhetoric see Brian B. Ritchie, *The Plays of Christopher Marlowe and George Peele: Rhetoric and Renaissance Sensibility* (Universal Publishers, 1999), and Stefan D. Keller, 'Shakespeare's Rhetorical

Fingerprint: New Evidence on the Authorship of *Titus Andronicus*', *English Studies*, 84.2 (2003), 105–18.

15 William Weber attributes 4.1 to Shakespeare in 'Shakespeare After All? The Authorship of *Titus Andronicus* 4.1 Reconsidered', *Shakespeare Survey*, 67 (2014), 69–84.

16 MacDonald P. Jackson first introduced the '*LION* method' in 'Determining Authorship: A New Technique', *Research Opportunities in Renaissance Drama*, 41 (2002), 1–14.

17 Jackson's method was used by Weber in 'Shakespeare After All?' and Anna Pruitt in 'Refining the *LION* Collocation Test: A Comparative Study of Authorship Test Results for *Titus Andronicus* Scene 6 (= 4.1)', in *The New Oxford Shakespeare: Authorship Companion*, edited by Gary Taylor and Gabriel Egan (Oxford University Press, 2017), pp. 92–106. Issues were highlighted by Mark Hulse in 'The Case for Peele's Authorship of *Titus Andronicus* 4.1: Cross-Examining Attribution Methods in a Disputed Scene', *Review of English Studies*, 72 (2021), 860–81 and 'Review of "Determining Authorship: A New Technique"', *Renaissance and Reformation*, 4.4 (2021), 204–10. Brian Vickers also offers a critique in 'Is EEBO-TCP / LION Suitable for Attribution Studies?', *Early Modern Literary Studies*, 22.1 (2019), 1–34.

18 *Titus Andronicus: Revised Edition*, edited by Jonathan Bate (Bloomsbury, 2018), pp. 129–35.

19 The theory that *Titus Andronicus* represents a revision of a lost Strange's Men play titled *Titus and Vespasian* (1592), which likely dramatised the siege of Jerusalem, has been countered by Martin Wiggins in *British Drama 1533–1642: A Catalogue: Volume III: 1590–1597* (Oxford University Press, 2013), pp. 172–3.

20 In his earlier edition of the play Bate contended that the 'play's tight structural unity suggests a single authorial hand'. *Titus Andronicus*, edited by Jonathan Bate (Routledge, 1995), p. 81.

21 *The RSC Complete Works of Shakespeare*, edited by Jonathan Bate and Eric Rasmussen (Macmillan, 2007), p. xviii.

22 For further discussion on the sparse links between portions given to Shakespeare and Peele see Darren Freebury-Jones, 'Exploring Co-authorship in *2 Henry VI*', *Journal of Early Modern Studies*, 5 (2016), 201–16. Rory Loughnane proposes that Shakespeare lightly revised Peele's opening act, which is possible. However, it's debatable whether the use of an 'aloft' space, which apparently 'has a distinct Shakespearean flavour', is a compelling authorship marker. Could these changes have been made by a playhouse scribe? Rory Loughnane, 'Re-editing Non-Shakespeare for the Modern Reader: The Murder of Mutius in *Titus Andronicus*', *Review of English Studies*, 68.284 (2017), 268–95 (p. 289).

23 Martin Wiggins's position is that 'Peele plotted the play'. Email correspondence (29 January 2023).

24 A. H. Thorndike, 'The Relations of *Hamlet* to Contemporary Revenge Plays', *Modern Language Association*, 17.2 (1902), 125–220 (p. 125).

25 Stanley Wells and Gary Taylor point out the 'remarkable difference in dramatic power and stylistic control' between *Henry VI Part Three* and *Richard*

III in *William Shakespeare: A Textual Companion* (Clarendon Press, 1987), p. 115.

26 Insightful accounts of Shakespeare's process of adapting Peele's play are provided by Forker in his essay *'The Troublesome Reign'* and his edition of *The Troublesome Reign of King John*, as well as by Vickers in *'The Troublesome Reign, George Peele, and the Date of King John'*. Readers interested in Shakespeare's duplication of stage directions might also consult Sidney Thomas's *'"Enter a Sheriff"*: Shakespeare's *King John* and *The Troublesome Raigne'*, *Shakespeare Quarterly*, 37 (1986), 98–100.

27 These inconsistencies in *King John* are itemised in Stuart Gillespie's edition for *The Complete Works of William Shakespeare: The Alexander Text* (HarperCollins, 2006), p. 445.

7 Thomas Dekker, John Marston, and Ben Jonson

1 For further discussion on Thomas Dekker's biography see John Twyning, 'Dekker, Thomas', in *Oxford Dictionary of National Biography*, edited by Henry Colin Grey Matthew and Brian Harrison (Oxford University Press, 2004).

2 Darryll Grantley, 'Thomas Dekker and the Emergence of City Comedy', in *The Cambridge Companion to Shakespeare and Contemporary Playwrights*, edited by Ton Hoenselaars (Cambridge University Press, 2012), pp. 83–96 (p. 85).

3 For discussion on Dekker's authorship of *Blurt, Master Constable* see MacDonald P. Jackson and Gary Taylor, 'Works Excluded from this Edition', in *Thomas Middleton and Early Modern Textual Culture: A Companion to the Collected Works*, edited by Gary Taylor and John Lavagnino (Oxford University Press, 2007), pp. 444–8.

4 Stanley Wells, *Shakespeare & Co.* (Penguin, 2006), p. 111.

5 E. E. Stoll makes this point in *John Webster: The Periods of His Work as Determined by His Relations to the Drama of His Day* (Alfred Mudge, 1905), pp. 76–8. For further discussion on city comedy, or citizen comedy, see Alexander Leggatt, *Citizen Comedy in the Age of Shakespeare* (University of Toronto Press, 1974), and Brian Gibbons, *Jacobean City Comedy* (Methuen, 1980). Jean E. Howard gives a fascinating account of Shakespeare's engagement with the genre in *Theater of a City: The Places of London Comedy, 1598–1642* (University of Pennsylvania Press, 2011), p. 215.

6 Natália Pikli points out links between these plays in *'"As for that light hobby-horse, my sister"*: Shakespearean Influences and Popular Discourses in *Blurt Master Constable'*, *Shakespeare Survey*, 70 (2017), 259–71.

7 Although there are few similarities between Dekker's and Shakespeare's language, academics have had some difficulty distinguishing their authorship in the case of 'To the Queen', an Epilogue or prayer delivered in 1599 for a play performed at Richmond Palace. Michael Hattaway and Helen Hackett have argued for Dekker's authorship in 'Dating *As You Like It*, Epilogues and Prayers, and the Problems of "As the Dial Hand Tells O'er"', *Shakespeare Quarterly*, 60 (2009), 154–67, and *'"As the Diall Hand tells*

Ore": The Case for Dekker, Not Shakespeare, as Author', *Review of English Studies*, 63 (2011), 34–57 respectively. John V. Nance has contended for Shakespeare's authorship in 'From Shakespeare "To ye Q."', *Shakespeare Quarterly*, 67 (2016), 204–31. Nance's attribution method and conclusions have been challenged by Brian Vickers, who revives the case for Dekker and concludes that Nance's 'claim to have found "Shakespeare's six unique parallels" proves, on closer examination, to be groundless. When the phrasal matches identified by the search engines' of databases 'are restored to their context in Shakespeare's plays they turn out to have completely different meanings or referents'. '"The Dial Hand" Epilogue: by Shakespeare, or Dekker?', *Authorship*, 7.2 (2018), 1–18 (p. 18).

8 Richard Simpson detected Shakespeare's hand in *Sir Thomas More* in 'Are There Any Extant MSS. in Shakespere's Handwriting?', *Notes and Queries*, 183 (1871), 1–3. For useful surveys of the evidence see Brian Vickers, *Shakespeare, Co-author: A Historical Study of Five Collaborative Plays* (Oxford University Press, 2002), pp. 34–43, and Gary Taylor and Rory Loughnane, 'The Canon and Chronology of Shakespeare's Works', in *The New Oxford Shakespeare: Authorship Companion*, edited by Gary Taylor and Gabriel Egan (Oxford University Press, 2017), pp. 417–603 (pp. 548–53).

9 Cathy L. Shrank and Paul Werstine question the evidence for Shakespeare's penmanship in 'The Shakespeare Manuscripts', in *The Arden Research Handbook of Shakespeare and Textual Studies*, edited by Lukas Erne (Bloomsbury, 2021), pp. 53–70.

10 *Ibid.*, p. 57. MacDonald P. Jackson applied the '*LION* method' on passages of *Sir Thomas More* in "The Date and Authorship of Hand D's Contribution to *Sir Thomas More*: Evidence from "Literature Online"', *Shakespeare Survey*, 59 (2006), 69–78.

11 Ian H. De Jong and Eric Rasmussen, 'Non-English Words in *The Spanish Tragedy*', *American Notes and Queries*, 33.2 (2020), 133–42 (p. 139).

12 Ton Hoenselaars provides a fascinating discussion of Shakespeare's collaborative process for *Sir Thomas More* in 'Shakespeare: Colleagues, Collaborators, Co-authors', in *The Cambridge Companion to Shakespeare and Contemporary Playwrights*, edited by Ton Hoenselaars (Cambridge University Press, 2012), pp. 97–119 (p. 110).

13 *Sir Thomas More*, edited by John Jowett (Arden Shakespeare, 2011), p. 22.

14 Martin Wiggins discusses the plausibility of these dramatists contributing to the play for the Chamberlain's Men in *British Drama 1533–1642: A Catalogue: Volume IV: 1598–1602* (Oxford University Press, 2014), p. 280.

15 For a detailed account of Dekker and Heywood's contributions see *Sir Thomas More*, edited by John Jowett, pp. 23–5. Readers might also consult Scott McMillin's *The Elizabethan Theatre and The Book of Sir Thomas More* (Cornell University Press, 1987), pp. 80–1.

16 For further discussion on John Marston's biography see James Knowles, 'Marston, John', in *Oxford Dictionary of National Biography*, edited by Henry Colin Grey Matthew and Brian Harrison (Oxford University Press, 2004).

17 Charles Cathcart makes this argument in *Marston, Rivalry, Rapprochement, and Jonson* (Ashgate, 2008), pp. 59–60. Michael Scott has also argued for an earlier date for the original play in 'Marston's Early Contribution to *The Insatiate Countess*', *Notes and Queries*, 222 (1977), 116–17.

18 For an account of the scope of Marston's dramatic canon see Darren Freebury-Jones, Marina Tarlinskaja, and Marcus Dahl, 'Attributing John Marston's Marginal Plays', *Studia Metrica et Poetica*, 5.1 (2018), 28–51. Marston's distinctive style is also discussed by Darren Freebury-Jones, Marina Tarlinskaja, and Marcus Dahl in 'The Boundaries of John Marston's Dramatic Canon', *Medieval and Renaissance Drama in England*, 31 (2018), 43–77.

19 *Antonio and Mellida*, edited by G. K. Hunter (University of Nebraska Press, 1965), p. xix.

20 For further discussion on connections between *Hamlet* and Marston's plays, see Charles Cathcart, '*Hamlet*: Date and Early Afterlife', *Review of English Studies*, 52.207 (2001), 341–59.

21 See Janet Clare, *Shakespeare's Stage Traffic: Imitation, Borrowing and Competition in Renaissance Theatre* (Cambridge University Press, 2014), p. 193. For discussion on the company identity of the 'eyases' see Roslyn Knutson, 'Falconer to the Little Eyases: A New Date and Commercial Agenda for the "Little Eyases" Passage in *Hamlet*', *Shakespeare Quarterly*, 46.1 (1995), 1–31.

22 *The Selected Plays of John Marston*, edited by MacDonald P. Jackson and Michael Neill (Cambridge University Press, 1986), p. 96.

23 Matthew Steggle poses this question in 'Urbane John Marston: Obscenity, Playfulness, Co-operation', in *The Cambridge Companion to Shakespeare and Contemporary Playwrights*, edited by Ton Hoenselaars (Cambridge University Press, 2012), pp. 70–82 (p. 74). Links between *Twelfth Night* and Marston are also explored by Meghan C. Andrews in 'Shakespeare the Formalist: Reading and Rewriting John Marston in the Poets' War', *Texas Studies in Literature and Language*, 63.1 (2021), 1–27.

24 Phil Withington interprets *The Merry Wives of Windsor* as a perverse response to the genre of city comedy. See 'Putting the City into Shakespeare's City Comedy', in *Shakespeare and Early Modern Political Thought*, edited by David Armitage, Conal Condren, and Andrew Fitzmaurice (Cambridge University Press, 2009), pp. 197–216.

25 For further discussion on Ben Jonson's biography see Ian Donaldson, 'Jonson, Benjamin [Ben]', in *Oxford Dictionary of National Biography*, edited by Henry Colin Grey Matthew and Brian Harrison (Oxford University Press, 2004); *Ben Jonson: A Life* (Oxford University Press, 2012).

26 For a useful survey of criticism on parallels between Shakespeare and Jonson's dramatic works see John-Mark Philo, 'Ben Jonson's *Sejanus* and Shakespeare's *Othello*: Two Plays Performed by the King's Men in 1603', *Shakespeare Survey*, 75 (2022), 122–36.

27 In 'Jonson and Shakespeare: A Spirited Friendship', *Ben Jonson Journal*, 23.1 (2016), 1–23 (p. 20), the great Shakespeare scholar and editor David Bevington rightly points out that biographer Nicholas Rowe 'was not quite fair to wonder whether Jonson ever made Shakespeare an "equal return of

gentleness and generosity"' because Jonson's tributes to Shakespeare 'are both gentle and generous, all the more remarkably so from a man who was notoriously prickly'.

28 Wells, *Shakespeare & Co.*, p. 155.

29 *Ibid.*, p. 152.

30 Bevington, 'Jonson and Shakespeare', p. 3.

31 Warren Chernaik, 'The Dyer's Hand: Shakespeare and Jonson', in *The Cambridge Companion to Shakespeare and Contemporary Playwrights*, edited by Ton Hoenselaars (Cambridge University Press, 2012), p. 60.

32 Martin Butler casts light on Jonson's representations of city life in 'Jonson's London and Its Theatres', in *The Cambridge Companion to Ben Jonson*, edited by Richard Harp and Stanley Stewart (Cambridge University Press, 2000), pp. 15–29.

33 Colin Burrow points out generalisations about Jonson's style in 'Ben Jonson', in *The Cambridge Companion to English Poets*, edited by Claude Rawson (Cambridge University Press, 2011), pp. 122–38. See also José María Pérez Fernández, 'Stoicism and Plain Style in Ben Jonson: An Analysis of Some of His Verse Epistles', *Atlantis*, 18.1 (1996), 337–47 (p. 341), and Wesley Trimpi, *Ben Jonson's Poems: A Study in the Plain Style* (Stanford University Press, 1962).

34 Russ McDonald, 'Jonson and Shakespeare and the Rhythm of Verse', in *The Cambridge Companion to Ben Jonson*, edited by Richard Harp and Stanley Stewart (Cambridge University Press, 2000), pp. 103–18 (p. 109).

35 *Ibid.*, pp. 117–18. Jonas Barish also points out the irregularity of Jonson's verse when compared to Shakespeare's in *Ben Jonson and the Language of Prose Comedy* (Harvard University Press, 1960). See too Michael Warren's *The Verse Style of Ben Jonson's Roman Plays* (Doctoral thesis: University of California, 1968), while Marina Tarlinskaja highlights stylistic differences between Shakespeare and Jonson in *Shakespeare and the Versification of Elizabethan Drama 1561–1642* (Ashgate, 2014), p. 175.

36 Donaldson, *Ben Jonson: A Life*, p. 131.

37 Ian Donaldson, 'Looking Sideways: Jonson, Shakespeare and the Myths of Envy', in *Shakespeare, Jonson, Marlowe: New Directions in Biography*, edited by Takashi Kozuka and J. R. Mulryne (Ashgate, 2006), pp. 241–58 (p. 252).

38 Russ McDonald provides an enlightening discussion in 'Othello, Thorello, and the Problem of the Foolish Hero', *Shakespeare Quarterly*, 30 (1979), 51–67, and John Drakakis explores the ways in which the role of Thorello was diffused throughout Shakespeare's oeuvre in *Shakespeare's Resources* (Manchester University Press, 2021), pp. 289–317.

39 Anne Barton proposes Shakespeare as Jonson's collaborator in *Ben Jonson, Dramatist* (Cambridge University Press, 1984), p. 94. Scholars who have plumped for Chapman include F. G. Fleay in *A Biographical Chronicle of the English Drama: Volume I*, 2 vols (Reeves and Turner, 1891), p. 372, and R. P. Corballis, 'The "second Pen" in the Stage Version of "Sejanus"', *Modern Philology*, 76 (1979), 273–7. Gary Taylor and Rory Loughnane acknowledge that 'It is of course impossible to prove that Shakespeare wrote passages in *Sejanus* that have not survived; we cannot test lost writing for

internal evidence of authorship or date'. They nevertheless conclude that 'the external evidence makes Shakespeare the most plausible candidate' in 'The Canon and Chronology of Shakespeare's Works', p. 541.

40 Chernaik points out the dramatists' different approaches to Roman history in 'The Dyer's Hand', pp. 64–5.

41 *The Letters of John Keats: Volume I*, edited by H. E. Rollins, 2 vols (Cambridge University Press, 1958), pp. 193–4.

42 Wells makes this point in *Shakespeare & Co.*, p. 142.

43 Philo explores parallels between these plays in 'Ben Jonson's *Sejanus* and Shakespeare's *Othello*'. David Farley-Hills notes that 'Jonson's lines must certainly have been running in Shakespeare's head at the time, but in spite of this it is remarkable that we can detect little verbal influence of *Sejanus* on *Othello*' in *Shakespeare and the Rival Playwrights, 1600–1606* (Routledge, 1990), p. 128.

44 Martin Butler points out that Jonson's '*Hymenaei* (1606) and *The Haddington Masque* (1608)' supplied 'several of *The Tempest*'s props and some of the imagery for Prospero's farewell to the revels' in '*The Tempest* and the Jonsonian Masque', in *Performances at Court in the Age of Shakespeare*, edited by S. Chiari and J. Mucciolo (Cambridge University Press, 2019), pp. 150–61 (p. 154).

8 Thomas Middleton

1 For further discussion on Thomas Middleton's biography see Gary Taylor, 'Middleton, Thomas', in *Oxford Dictionary of National Biography*, edited by Henry Colin Grey Matthew and Brian Harrison (Oxford University Press, 2004).

2 Stanley Wells, *Shakespeare & Co.* (Penguin, 2006), p. 172.

3 Michelle O'Callaghan, 'Thomas Middleton and the Early Modern Theatre', in *The Cambridge Companion to Shakespeare and Contemporary Playwrights*, edited by Ton Hoenselaars (Cambridge University Press, 2012), pp. 165–80 (pp. 166–7).

4 For a superb exploration of Middleton and Rowley's collaborations see David Nicol, *Middleton and Rowley: Forms of Collaboration in the Jacobean Playhouse* (University of Toronto Press, 2012).

5 Gary Taylor, 'Empirical Middleton: *Macbeth*, Adaptation, and Micro-authorship', *Shakespeare Quarterly*, 65 (2014), 239–72 (p. 251). For further discussion on Shakespeare's influence on Middleton see Roger Holdsworth, 'Shakespeare and Middleton: A Chronology for 1605–6', in *The New Oxford Shakespeare: Authorship Companion*, edited by Gary Taylor and Gabriel Egan (Oxford University Press, 2017), pp. 366–84.

6 The evidence for Middleton's authorship of this play is discussed by David Lake in *The Canon of Thomas Middleton's Plays* (Cambridge University Press, 1975), pp. 136–49, and by Gary Taylor in 'Works Included in this Edition', in *Thomas Middleton and Early Modern Textual Culture: A Companion to the Collected Works*, edited by Gary Taylor and John Lavagnino (Oxford University Press, 2007), pp. 335–444 (pp. 360–3).

7 William Wells attributed parts of the play to Middleton in '*Timon of Athens*', *Notes and Queries*, 12.6 (1920), 266–9. F. G. Fleay pointed out similarities with *The Revenger's Tragedy* in his essay 'On the Authorship of *Timon of Athens*', *Transactions of the New Shakspere Society*, 1 (1874), 130–51. For a magisterial survey of the attribution history of *Timon of Athens* see Brian Vickers, *Shakespeare, Co-author: A Historical Study of Five Collaborative Plays* (Oxford University Press, 2002), pp. 244–90.

8 *The Oxford Shakespeare: Timon of Athens*, edited by John Jowett (Oxford University Press, 2004), p. 130.

9 *Ibid.*, p. 139.

10 All references to Thomas Middleton's plays in this book are to *Thomas Middleton: The Collected Works*, edited by Gary Taylor and John Lavagnino (Oxford University Press, 2007).

11 Eilidh Kane notes that a 'process of co-writing which combined simultaneous and consecutive stints' would help to 'explain' the play's 'mixture of Shakespeare-only, Middleton-only, and Shakespeare-Middleton scenes' in 'Shakespeare and Middleton's Co-Authorship of *Timon of Athens*', *Journal of Early Modern Studies*, 5 (2016), 217–35 (p. 232).

12 *Timon of Athens*, edited by Anthony B. Dawson and Gretchen E. Minton (Arden Shakespeare, 2008), p. 3.

13 *Ibid.*, pp. 4–5.

14 *Macbeth*, edited by W. G. Clark and William Aldis Wright (Clarendon Press, 1869), p. xii.

15 Gary Taylor discusses the proposed divisions of authorship in *Macbeth* in 'Works Included in this Edition', p. 397.

16 Gary Taylor and Rory Loughnane offer this theory for Middleton's change of 'nymphs' to witches in 'The Canon and Chronology of Shakespeare's Works', in *The New Oxford Shakespeare: Authorship Companion*, edited by Gary Taylor and Gabriel Egan (Oxford University Press, 2017), p. 567.

17 Scholars who disagree with claims for Middleton's hand in *Macbeth* include J. M. Nosworthy in *Shakespeare's Occasional Plays: Their Origin and Transmission* (Edward Arnold, 1965), pp. 8–53, and Brian Vickers in 'Disintegrated: Did Thomas Middleton Really Adapt *Macbeth*?', *Times Literary Supplement*, 28 May 2010, pp. 14–15.

18 Caroline Baird points out that Middleton frequently appropriated masques for commercial plays and that 'up to 1611' he was in fact 'the only dramatist to take the device outside the repertoire of the children's troupes' in 'From Court to Playhouse and Back: Middleton's Appropriation of the Masque', *Early Theatre*, 18.2 (2015), 57–85 (p. 58).

19 Taylor, 'Empirical Middleton', p. 242.

20 John Jowett offers a detailed case for adaptation in '*Measure for Measure*: A Genetic Text', in *Thomas Middleton: The Collected Works*, edited by Gary Taylor and John Lavagnino (Oxford University Press, 2007), pp. 1542–3.

21 For further discussion see Gary Taylor and John Jowett, *Shakespeare Reshaped, 1606–1623* (Clarendon Press, 1993).

22 Taylor and Loughnane, 'The Canon and Chronology of Shakespeare's Works', p. 557.

23 Gary Taylor and Doug Duhaime, 'Who Wrote the Fly Scene (3.2) in *Titus Andronicus*?: Automated Searches and Deep Reading', in *The New Oxford Shakespeare: Authorship Companion*, edited by Gary Taylor and Gabriel Egan (Oxford University Press, 2017), pp. 67–91.

24 Jonathan Bate subjects the play to this textual analysis in *Titus Andronicus: Revised Edition* (Bloomsbury, 2018), pp. 96–116.

25 W. W. Greg, *The Shakespeare First Folio: Its Bibliographical and Textual History* (Clarendon Press, 1955), pp. 204–5.

26 *Ibid.*, p. 205.

27 Hereward T. Price, 'Mirror-Scenes in Shakespeare', in *Joseph Quincy Adams Memorial Studies*, edited by James G. McManaway, Giles E. Dawson, and Edwin E. Willoughby (Folger Shakespeare Library, 1948), pp. 101–13.

28 Taylor and Duhaime, 'Who Wrote the Fly Scene (3.2)', p. 84.

29 Philip Timberlake, *The Feminine Ending in English Blank Verse: A Study of Its Use by Early Writers in the Measure and Its Development in the Drama up to the Year 1595* (Banta, 1931), p. 114.

30 Taylor and Duhaime, 'Who Wrote the Fly Scene (3.2)', p. 91.

31 *Ibid.*, p. 75.

32 See Gary Taylor, 'Rare Vocabulary in the Two Texts of *King Lear*', in *The Division of the Kingdoms: Shakespeare's Two Versions of King Lear*, edited by Gary Taylor and Michael Warren (Clarendon Press, 1983), pp. 462–4.

33 Taylor and Duhaime, 'Who Wrote the Fly Scene (3.2)', p. 77.

34 See Stefan D. Keller's superb analysis of Shakespeare and Peele's rhetoric in 'Shakespeare's Rhetorical Fingerprint. New Evidence on the Authorship of *Titus Andronicus*', *English Studies*, 84.2 (2003), 105–18 (p. 117).

35 Gary Taylor and Doug Duhaime, 'Dataset 1.2', in *The New Oxford Shakespeare: Authorship Companion*, edited by Gary Taylor and Gabriel Egan (Oxford University Press, 2017), pp. 605–7.

36 See the observations in *Shakespeare's Plays; with his Life: Volume II*, edited by G. C. Verplanck, 3 vols (Harper and Brothers, 1847), p. 6, and *All's Well that Ends Well*, edited by John Dover Wilson (Cambridge University Press, 1929), p. 104.

37 Laurie Maguire and Emma Smith attributed parts of the play to Middleton in 'Many Hands: A New Shakespeare Collaboration?', *Times Literary Supplement*, 20 April 2012, pp. 13–15.

38 Brian Vickers and Marcus Dahl rejected the attribution in '"What is infirm …" *All's Well That Ends Well*: An Attribution Rejected', *Times Literary Supplement*, 11 May 2012, pp. 14–15. Dahl, writing of Middletonian preferences, such as 'h'as' for 'he has', points out that 'In actual fact, of the abbreviations listed by Maguire and Smith, there are "Shakespearean" equivalents, equal or greater counts, by scene, act, or full play to all of the perceived "irregular" counts in *All's Well That Ends Well*'. Marcus Dahl, 'Authors of the Mind', *Journal of Early Modern Studies*, 5 (2016), 157–73 (p. 161).

39 For full discussion of the stylistic evidence for Middleton's adaptation see Rory Loughnane, 'Thomas Middleton in *All's Well that Ends Well*? Part

One', in *The New Oxford Shakespeare: Authorship Companion*, edited by Gary Taylor and Gabriel Egan (Oxford University Press, 2017), pp. 278–302, and 'Thomas Middleton in *All's Well that Ends Well*? Part Two', in *The New Oxford Shakespeare: Authorship Companion*, pp. 307–20. The expendable material is identified by Terri Bourus and Farah Karim-Cooper in '*All's Well that Ends Well* 4.3: Dramaturgy', in *The New Oxford Shakespeare: Authorship Companion*, pp. 303–6.

40 If Middleton did adapt the play, he most likely did so in 1622, during the Thirty Years War that took place between 1618 and 1648. William Green points out that the Thirty Years War 'inspired numerous responses by Middleton in his works of the early 1620s' in 'Thomas Middleton and the Adaptation of Shakespeare: Late Jacobean Politics in Print and Performance, 1616–1623' (Doctoral thesis: University of Birmingham, 2021), p. 14. See also Gary Taylor, '*All's Well that Ends Well*: Text, Date, and Adaptation', in *The New Oxford Shakespeare: Authorship Companion*, edited by Gary Taylor and Gabriel Egan (Oxford University Press, 2017), pp. 337–65.

9   John Fletcher

1 For further discussion on John Fletcher's biography see Gordon McMullan, 'Fletcher, John', in *Oxford Dictionary of National Biography*, edited by Henry Colin Grey Matthew and Brian Harrison (Oxford University Press, 2004).

2 *The Collected Works of John Ford: Volume II*, edited by Brian Vickers, 5 vols (Oxford University Press, 2017), p. 13.

3 Eoin Price, 'The Dearth of the Author: Philip Massinger and the Beaumont and Fletcher Folio', *Review of English Studies*, 74.313 (2023), 78–94 (p. 85).

4 For further discussion see Darren Freebury-Jones, 'John Fletcher's Collaborator on *The Noble Gentleman*', *Studia Metrica et Poetica*, 7.2 (2020), 43–60.

5 Catherine Henze provides a useful account of the genre in 'Francis Beaumont and John Fletcher's Tragicomedy as Musical Melodrama', in *The Cambridge Companion to Shakespeare and Contemporary Playwrights*, edited by Ton Hoenselaars (Cambridge University Press, 2012), pp. 149–64 (p. 149).

6 *The Dramatic Works in the Beaumont and Fletcher Canon: Volume III*, edited by Fredson Bowers, 10 vols (Cambridge University Press, 1976), p. 497. All references to Fletcher's works throughout this book are to the Bowers edition (1966–96).

7 Valerie Wayne itemises striking connections with Fletcher and his collaborators in her edition of *Cymbeline* (Bloomsbury, 2017), p. 25.

8 Suzanne Gossett rectifies the 'atmosphere of bardolatry' that led scholars to 'disparage' proposals that Shakespeare 'took hints for the writing of *Cymbeline*' from *Philaster*. See *Philaster*, edited by Suzanne Gossett (Arden Shakespeare, 2009), pp. 4–5, and A. H. Thorndike, *The Influence of Beaumont and Fletcher on Shakespeare* (O. B. Wood, 1901), pp. 149–50.

9 Bart van Es, 'Reviving the Legacy of Indoor Performance', in *Moving Shakespeare Indoors: Performance and Repertoire in the Jacobean Playhouse*, edited by Andrew Gurr and Farah Karim-Cooper (Cambridge University Press, 2014), pp. 237–50 (p. 247). Elsewhere Bart van Es argues that Shakespeare's 'supposed phase of introspective maturity' looks 'much more like a return to the literary mainstream' when Shakespeare's work is placed next to contemporaries such as Fletcher. *Shakespeare in Company* (Oxford University Press, 2013), p. 276.

10 For further discussion see F. G. Fleay, 'On Metrical Tests as Applied to Dramatic Poetry. Part II. Fletcher, Beaumont, Massinger', *Transactions of the New Shakspere Society*, 1 (1874), 51–72; E. H. C. Oliphant, *The Plays of Beaumont and Fletcher: An Attempt to Determine Their Respective Shares and the Shares of Others* (Yale University Press, 1927); and Ants Oras, '"Extra Monosyllables" in *Henry VIII* and the Problem of Authorship', *Journal of English and Germanic Philology*, 52 (1953), 198–213.

11 Thorndike noticed Fletcher's preference for "em' over 'them' in *The Influence of Beaumont and Fletcher on Shakespeare*, p. 24. Fletcher's preferred pronouns were first pointed out in W. W. Greg's edition of *The Elder Brother*, in *The Works of Francis Beaumont and John Fletcher: Volume II*, edited by A. H. Bullen, 4 vols (G. Bell and Sons, 1905), p. 4, and R. B. McKerrow's edition of *The Spanish Curate*, in *The Works of Francis Beaumont and John Fletcher: Volume II*, p. 104.

12 For early discussions on Fletcher's favoured contractions in comparison to Shakespeare's see Willard Farnham, 'Colloquial Contractions in Beaumont, Fletcher, Massinger, and Shakespeare as a Test of Authorship', *Publications of the Modern Language Association of America*, 31.2 (1916), 326–58, and A. C. Partridge, *The Problem of Henry VIII Reopened* (Cambridge University Press, 1949).

13 Cyrus Hoy, 'The Shares of Fletcher and His Collaborators in the Beaumont and Fletcher Canon', *Studies in Bibliography*, 8–15 (1956–62).

14 As Martin Wiggins puts it: 'Differentiating the "*shadow Beaumont*" from the real one would be a useful task for future authorship research'. *British Drama 1533–1642: A Catalogue: Volume VI: 1606–1619* (Oxford University Press, 2015), p. 518.

15 James Spedding first proposed Fletcher as Shakespeare's collaborator in 'Who Wrote *Henry VIII?*', *Gentleman's Magazine*, 34 (August 1850), 115–23. The wide range of evidence is most usefully summarised by Brian Vickers in *Shakespeare, Co-author: A Historical Study of Five Collaborative Plays* (Oxford University Press, 2002), pp. 333–432.

16 Cyrus Hoy, 'The Shares of Fletcher and His Collaborators in the Beaumont and Fletcher Canon (VII)', *Studies in Bibliography*, 15 (1962), 76–85, 90.

17 Marco Mincoff pointed out Fletcher's habit of obscuring some of his stylistic habits for collaborative plays in '*Henry VIII* and Fletcher', *Shakespeare Quarterly*, 12 (1961), 239–60 (pp. 239–40).

18 For a thorough account of the play's 'disunities' see Vickers, *Shakespeare, Co-author*, pp. 480–91.

19 For further discussion see *The Two Noble Kinsmen*, edited by Eugene M. Waith (Clarendon Press, 1989), p. 22.

20 Michael M. Wagoner, 'The Dramaturgical Space of Solo Scenes in Fletcher and Shakespeare, Or a Study of the Jailer's Daughter', *Shakespeare Bulletin*, 35.1 (2017), 97–118 (p. 97).

21 For a fascinating account see Gary Taylor's 'A History of *The History of Cardenio*', in *The Quest for Cardenio: Shakespeare, Fletcher, Cervantes, and the Lost Play*, edited by David Carnegie and Gary Taylor (Oxford University Press, 2012), pp. 11–61.

22 Brean Hammond discusses whether Theobald was aware of the documentary evidence concerning *Cardenio* in his edition of *Double Falsehood* (Methuen Drama, 2010), pp. 80–4.

23 The play's styles are subjected to detailed analysis by MacDonald P. Jackson in 'Looking for Shakespeare in *Double Falsehood*: Stylistic Evidence', in *The Quest for Cardenio: Shakespeare, Fletcher, Cervantes, and the Lost Play*, edited by David Carnegie and Gary Taylor (Oxford University Press, 2012), pp. 133–61, and Richard Proudfoot in 'Can *Double Falsehood* Be Merely a Forgery by Lewis Theobald?', in *The Quest for Cardenio: Shakespeare, Fletcher, Cervantes, and the Lost Play*, pp. 162–79.

Conclusion: Our other Shake-scenes

1 Ann Thompson, '*The Taming of the Shrew* and *The Spanish Tragedy*', *Notes and Queries*, 31 (1984), 182–4 (p. 182).

2 J. M. Robertson, *An Introduction to the Study of the Shakespeare Canon: Proceeding on the Problem of Titus Andronicus* (London: Routledge, 1924), p. 392.

3 William Wells, 'Thomas Kyd and the Chronicle-History', *Notes and Queries*, 30 (1940), 218–24, 238–43 (p. 243).

4 MacDonald P. Jackson, *Determining the Shakespeare Canon: Arden of Faversham and A Lover's Complaint* (Oxford University Press, 2014), p. 23.

5 Alfred Hart, *Stolne and Surreptitious Copies: A Comparative Study of Shakespeare's Bad Quartos* (Melbourne University Press, 1942), p. 468.

6 Peter Bull proposes Alleyn as the 'upstart crow' in 'Tired with a Peacock's Tail: All Eyes on the Upstart Crow', *English Studies*, 101.3 (2020), 284–311.

7 The play doesn't fit Greene's style at all. Robert Wilson is a far likelier candidate. See Darren Freebury-Jones, *Reading Robert Greene: Recovering Shakespeare's Rival* (Routledge, 2022), pp. 152–68, pp. 175–8.

8 Emma Smith, 'Shakespeare: the apex predator', *Times Literary Supplement*, 4 May 2017, https://www.the-tls.co.uk/articles/we-over-privilege-shakespeare-is-that-a-bad-thing-essay-emma-smith/ (accessed 3 April 2024).

9 This figure is provided by David McInnis in *Shakespeare and Lost Plays: Reimagining Drama in Early Modern England* (Cambridge University Press, 2021), p. 1.

10 These figures are taken from Lukas Erne's *Shakespeare and the Book Trade* (Cambridge University Press, 2013), p. 95.

11 Stanley Wells suggests the payment was an informal contract in *Shakespeare for All Time* (Macmillan, 2002), p. 99.

12 John Jowett, *Shakespeare and Text*, rev. edn (Oxford University Press, 2019), pp. 19–20.

13 Chris Laoutaris proposes that the First Folio's history play sequence could be regarded as a 'grand compliment' to Shakespeare's patron, King James, 'ratifying the divinely preordained inevitability of the king's reign', in *Shakespeare's Book: The Intertwined Lives behind the First Folio* (William Collins, 2023), p. 240.

14 These figures are given in Brian Vickers's *Shakespeare, Co-author: A Historical Study of Five Collaborative Plays* (Oxford University Press, 2002), pp. 16–17.

15 For further discussion, see *The Oxford Shakespeare: Timon of Athens*, edited by John Jowett (Oxford University Press, 2004), p. 132, and Emma Smith, *The Making of Shakespeare's First Folio* (Oxford University Press, 2015), pp. 13–15.

Bibliography

Adger Law, Robert, '*Richard the Third*, Act I Scene 4', *Publications of the Modern Language Association of America*, 27.2 (1912), 117–41.

Alberge, Dalya, 'Poetic justice as Shakespeare rival Robert Greene takes play credit', *The Telegraph*, 28 November 2020, p. 3.

Alexander, Peter, *Shakespeare's Henry VI and Richard III* (Cambridge University Press, 1929).

Andrews, Meghan C., 'Shakespeare the Formalist: Reading and Rewriting John Marston in the Poets' War', *Texas Studies in Literature and Language*, 63.1 (2021), 1–27.

Artese, Charlotte, *Shakespeare's Folktale Sources* (University of Delaware Press, 2015).

Aubrey, John, *Brief Lives: Volume II*, edited by Andrew Clark, 2 vols (Clarendon Press, 1898).

Auden, W. H., *The Dyer's Hand and Other Essays* (Faber and Faber, 1948).

Auerbach, David, '"A cannon's burst discharged against a ruinated wall": A Critique of Quantitative Methods in Shakespearean Authorial Attribution', *Authorship*, 7.2 (2018), 1–16.

Auerbach, David, 'Review of *The New Oxford Shakespeare: Authorship Companion*', *American Notes and Queries*, 33.2 (2020), 236–41.

Auerbach, David, 'Statistical Infelicities in *The New Oxford Shakespeare Authorship Companion*', *American Notes and Queries*, 33.1 (2020), 28–31.

Austin, Warren B., 'A Computer-Aided Technique for Stylistic Discrimination: The Authorship of *Greene's Groatsworth of Wit*', Final Report, Project No. 7-G-036, US Department of Health, Education, and Welfare (Washington, DC), April 1969.

Baird, Caroline, 'From Court to Playhouse and Back: Middleton's Appropriation of the Masque', *Early Theatre*, 18.2 (2015), 57–85.

Baldwin, T. W., *William Shakspere's Small Latine and Lesse Greeke: Volume I*, 2 vols (University of Illinois Press, 1944).

Baldwin, T. W., *On the Literary Genetics of Shakespeare's Plays* (University of Illinois Press, 1959).

Bancroft, Thomas, *Time's Out of Tune* (W. Godbid, 1658).

Barber, Charles, '"You" and "Thou" in Shakespeare's *Richard III*', *Leeds Studies in English*, 12 (1981), 273–89.

Barber, Rosalind, 'Function Word Adjacency Networks and Early Modern Plays', *American Notes and Queries*, 33.2 (2020), 204–13.

Barber, Rosalind, 'Big Data or Not Enough? Zeta Test Reliability and the Attribution of *Henry VI*', *Digital Scholarship in the Humanities*, 36.3 (2021), 542–64.

Barbour, Reid, 'Peele, George', in *Oxford Dictionary of National Biography*, edited by Henry Colin Grey Matthew and Brian Harrison (Oxford University Press, 2004).

Barish, Jonas, *Ben Jonson and the Language of Prose Comedy* (Harvard University Press, 1960).

Barton, Anne, *Ben Jonson, Dramatist* (Cambridge University Press, 1984).

Bate, Jonathan (ed.), *Titus Andronicus* (Routledge, 1995).

Bate, Jonathan, *The Genius of Shakespeare* (Oxford University Press, 1998).

Bate, Jonathan (ed.), *Titus Andronicus: Revised Edition* (Bloomsbury, 2018).

Bate, Jonathan, and Eric Rasmussen (eds), *The RSC Complete Works of Shakespeare* (Macmillan, 2007).

Bate, Jonathan, and Eric Rasmussen (eds), *William Shakespeare & Others: Collaborative Plays* (Macmillan, 2013).

Beard, Thomas, *The Theatre of God's Judgements: Collection of histories out of sacred, ecclesiastical, and profane authors, concerning the admirable judgements of God upon the transgressors of his commandments* (Adam Islip and Spark, 1597).

Bednarz, James, *Shakespeare and the Poets' War* (Columbia University Press, 2001).

Bentley, G. E., *The Jacobean and Caroline Stage* (Clarendon Press, 1971).

Bevington, David (ed.), *Henry IV Part 1* (Oxford University Press, 1987).

Bevington, David (ed.), *Endymion* (Manchester University Press, 1996).

Bevington, David, 'Jonson and Shakespeare: A Spirited Friendship', *Ben Jonson Journal*, 23.1 (2016), 1–23.

Bevington, David, and Eric Rasmussen (eds), *Christopher Marlowe: Doctor Faustus, A- and B-Texts (1604, 1616)* (Manchester University Press, 1993).

Bevington, David, Martin Butler, and Ian Donaldson (eds), *The Cambridge Edition of the Works of Ben Jonson*, 7 vols (Cambridge University Press, 2012).

Boas, Frederick S. (ed.), *The Works of Thomas Kyd* (Clarendon Press, 1901).

Bond, R. Warwick (ed.), *The Complete Works of John Lyly*, 3 vols (Clarendon Press, 1902).

Boswell, James (ed.), *The Plays and Poems of William Shakespeare*, 21 vols (F. C. and J. Rivington, 1821).

Bourus, Terri, and Farah Karim-Cooper, '*All's Well that Ends Well* 4.3: Dramaturgy', in *The New Oxford Shakespeare: Authorship Companion*, edited by Gary Taylor and Gabriel Egan (Oxford University Press, 2017), pp. 303–6.

Bowers, Fredson, 'Ben Jonson the Actor', *Studies in Philology*, 34.3 (1937), 392–406.

Bowers, Fredson (ed.), *The Dramatic Works of Thomas Dekker*, 4 vols (Cambridge University Press, 1953–61).

Bowers, Fredson (ed.), *The Dramatic Works in the Beaumont and Fletcher Canon*, 10 vols (Cambridge University Press, 1966–97).

Bradbrook, M. C., 'Shakespeare's Recollections of Marlowe', in *Shakespeare's Styles: Essays in Honour of Kenneth Muir*, edited by Philip Edwards, Inga-Stina Ewbank, and G. K. Hunter (Cambridge University Press, 1980), pp. 191–204.

Braden, Gordon, *Renaissance Tragedy and the Senecan Tradition: Anger's Privilege* (Yale University Press, 1985).

Brooke, C. F. Tucker (ed.), *The Shakespeare Apocrypha* (Clarendon Press, 1908).

Brooks, Harold F., '*Richard III*, Unhistorical Amplifications: The Women's Scenes and Seneca', *Modern Language Review*, 75.4 (1980), 721–37.

Brown, Ford K., 'Marlowe and Kyd', *Times Literary Supplement*, 2 June 1921, p. 355.

Bruster, Douglas, *Seeing Shakespeare's Style* (Routledge, 2022).

Bruster, Douglas, and Nell McKeown, 'Wordplay in Earliest Shakespeare', *Philological Quarterly*, 96.3 (2017), 293–322.

Bull, Peter, 'Tired with a Peacock's Tail: All Eyes on the Upstart Crow', *English Studies*, 101.3 (2020), 284–311.

Bullough, Geoffrey (ed.), *Narrative and Dramatic Sources of Shakespeare*, 8 vols (Routledge, 1957–75).

Burnett, Mark Thornton (ed.), *Christopher Marlowe: The Complete Plays* (Everyman, 1999).

Burns, Edward (ed.), *King Henry VI Part 1* (Thomson Learning, 2000).

Burrow, Colin, 'Shakespeare and Humanistic Culture', in *Shakespeare and the Classics*, edited by Charles Martindale and A. B. Taylor (Cambridge University Press, 2004), pp. 9–32.

Burrow, Colin, 'Ben Jonson', in *The Cambridge Companion to English Poets*, edited by Claude Rawson (Cambridge University Press, 2011), pp. 122–38.

Butler, Martin, 'Jonson's London and Its Theatres', in *The Cambridge Companion to Ben Jonson*, edited by Richard Harp and Stanley Stewart (Cambridge University Press, 2000), pp. 15–29.

Butler, Martin, '*The Tempest* and the Jonsonian Masque', in *Performances at Court in the Age of Shakespeare*, edited by S. Chiari and J. Mucciolo (Cambridge University Press, 2019), pp. 150–61.

Cairncross, A. S., 'Pembroke's Men and Some Shakespearean Piracies', *Shakespeare Quarterly*, 2 (1960), 335–49.

Capell, Edward, *Prolusions; or select pieces of antient Poetry* (J. and R. Tonson, 1760).

Carrère, Félix (ed.), *Arden de Faversham. Etude Critique, Traduction et Notes* (Montaigne, 1950).

Cathcart, Charles, '*Hamlet*: Date and Early Afterlife', *Review of English Studies*, 52.207 (2001), 341–59.

Cathcart, Charles, *Marston, Rivalry, Rapprochement, and Jonson* (Ashgate, 2008).

Chambers, E. K., *The Elizabethan Stage*, 4 vols (Clarendon Press, 1923).

Chambers, E. K., *William Shakespeare a Study of Facts and Problems*, 2 vols (Oxford University Press, 1930).

Chaney, Maurice, 'Marlowe's *Edward II* as a Model for Shakespeare's *Richard II*', *Research Opportunities in Renaissance Drama*, 33 (1994), 31–41.

Cheney, Patrick, and Brian J. Striar (eds), *The Collected Poems of Christopher Marlowe* (Oxford University Press, 2006).

Chernaik, Warren, 'The Dyer's Hand: Shakespeare and Jonson', in *The Cambridge Companion to Shakespeare and Contemporary Playwrights*, edited by Ton Hoenselaars (Cambridge University Press, 2012), pp. 54–69.

Chernaik, Warren, 'Theatrical Companies and Their Plays', *Medieval and Renaissance Drama in England*, 33 (2020), 167–87.

Chernaik, Warren, 'Review of *Early Shakespeare, 1588–1594*', *Modern Philology*, 118.3 (2021), 209–14.

Chettle, Henry, *Kind-Hartes Dream 1592*, edited by G. B. Harrison (London, 1923).

Clare, Janet, *Shakespeare's Stage Traffic: Imitation, Borrowing and Competition in Renaissance Theatre* (Cambridge University Press, 2014).

Clark, W. G., and William Aldis Wright (eds), *Macbeth* (Clarendon Press, 1869).

Clemen, Wolfgang, *English Tragedy before Shakespeare: The Development of Dramatic Speech* (Methuen, 1961).

Cockayne, Aston, *Small Poems of Divers Sorts* (William Godbid, 1658).

Coleridge, Samuel Taylor, *The Collected Works of Samuel Taylor Coleridge: Volume XIV*, edited by Carl Woodring, 14 vols (Princeton University Press, 1990).

Collins, John Churton (ed.), *The Plays & Poems of Robert Greene*, 2 vols (Oxford University Press, 1905).

Coral, Jordi, 'Seneca, what Seneca? The Chorus in *The Spanish Tragedy*', *The Spanish and Portuguese Society for English Renaissance Studies*, 17 (2007), 5–26.

Corballis, R. P., 'The "second Pen" in the Stage Version of "Sejanus"', *Modern Philology*, 76 (1979), 273–7.

Correll, Barbara, 'Schooling *Coriolanus*: Shakespeare, Translation and Latinity', in *Shakespeare and the Translation of Identity in Early Modern England*, edited by Liz Oakley-Brown (Bloomsbury, 2011), pp. 22–45.

Craig, Hugh, 'The Three Parts of *Henry VI*', in *Shakespeare, Computers, and the Mystery of Authorship*, edited by Hugh Craig and Arthur F. Kinney (Cambridge University Press, 2009), pp. 40–77.

Craig, Hugh, and Arthur F. Kinney, 'Methods', in *Shakespeare, Computers, and the Mystery of Authorship*, edited by Hugh Craig and Arthur F. Kinney (Cambridge University Press, 2009), pp. 15–39.

Crawford, Charles, *Collectanea: First Series* (Shakespeare Head Press, 1906).

Dahl, Marcus, 'Authors of the Mind', *Journal of Early Modern Studies*, 5 (2016), 157–73.

Dawson, Anthony B., and Gretchen E. Minton (eds), *Timon of Athens* (Arden Shakespeare, 2008).

Dekker, Thomas, *A Knight's Conjuring Done in Earnest: Discovered in Jest* (William Barley, 1607).

Dessen, Alan, *Elizabethan Stage Conventions and Modern Interpreters* (Cambridge University Press, 1984).

Deutermann, Allison K., *Listening for Theatrical Form in Early Modern England* (Edinburgh University Press, 2016).

Dickinson, Thomas H. (ed.), *Robert Greene* (T. Fisher Unwin, 1909).

Dickson, Vernon Guy, *Emulation on the Shakespearean Stage* (Ashgate, 2013).

Dimmock, Matthew, 'Tamburlaine's Curse: An Answer to a Great Marlowe Mystery', *Times Literary Supplement*, 19 November 2010, pp. 16–17.

Donaldson, Ian, 'Jonson, Benjamin [Ben]', in *Oxford Dictionary of National Biography*, edited by Henry Colin Grey Matthew and Brian Harrison (Oxford University Press, 2004).

Donaldson, Ian, 'Looking Sideways: Jonson, Shakespeare and the Myths of Envy', in *Shakespeare, Jonson, Marlowe: New Directions in Biography*, edited by Takashi Kozuka and J. R. Mulryne (Ashgate, 2006), pp. 241–58.

Donaldson, Ian, *Ben Jonson: A Life* (Oxford University Press, 2012).

Doran, Madeleine, *Henry VI, Parts II and III: Their Relation to the Contention and the True Tragedy* (University of Iowa Humanistic Studies, 1928).

Drakakis, John (ed.), *The Merchant of Venice* (Bloomsbury, 2011).

Drakakis, John, *Shakespeare's Resources* (Manchester University Press, 2021).

Drawdy, Miles, '"See here my show": Providence and The Theatrum Mundi in Thomas Kyd's *The Spanish Tragedy*' (Honors thesis: College of William and Mary, Virginia, 2014).

Eliot, T. S., *The Sacred Wood: Essays on Poetry and Criticism* (Methuen, 1920).

Eliot, T. S., 'Introduction', in *Seneca, His Tenne Tragedies* (Constable, 1927).

Elliott, Ward, 'Notes from the Claremont Shakespeare Clinic', *The Shakespeare Newsletter* (2011), pp. 105–12.

Empson, William, *Some Versions of Pastoral* (Chatto and Windus, 1935).

Enterline, Lynn, *Shakespeare's Schoolroom: Rhetoric, Discipline, Emotion* (University of Pennsylvania Press, 2012).

Erne, Lukas, *Beyond The Spanish Tragedy: A Study of the Works of Thomas Kyd* (Manchester University Press, 2001).

Erne, Lukas, *Shakespeare as Literary Dramatist* (Cambridge University Press, 2003).

Erne, Lukas, *Shakespeare and the Book Trade* (Cambridge University Press, 2013).

Erne, Lukas (ed.), *Soliman and Perseda [1592/93]* (Malone Society Reprints, 2014).

Erne, Lukas, 'Disintegrating Marlowe', *Studies in Philology*, 119.2 (2021), 272–97.

Es, Bart van, '"Johannes fac Totum"?: Shakespeare's First Contact with the Acting Companies', *Shakespeare Quarterly*, 61.4 (2010), 551–77.

Es, Bart van, *Shakespeare in Company* (Oxford University Press, 2013).

Es, Bart van, 'Reviving the Legacy of Indoor Performance', in *Moving Shakespeare Indoors: Performance and Repertoire in the Jacobean Playhouse*, edited by Andrew Gurr and Farah Karim-Cooper (Cambridge University Press, 2014), pp. 237–50.

Farley-Hills, David, *Shakespeare and the Rival Playwrights, 1600–1606* (Routledge, 1990).

Farnham, Willard, 'Colloquial Contractions in Beaumont, Fletcher, Massinger, and Shakespeare as a Test of Authorship', *Publications of the Modern Language Association of America*, 31.2 (1916), 326–58.

Fernández, José María Pérez, 'Stoicism and Plain Style in Ben Jonson: An Analysis of Some of His Verse Epistles', *Atlantis*, 18.1 (1996), 337–47.

Fleay, F. G., 'On Metrical Tests as Applied to Dramatic Poetry. Part II. Fletcher, Beaumont, Massinger', *Transactions of the New Shakspere Society*, 1 (1874), 51–72.

Fleay, F. G., 'On the Authorship of *Timon of Athens*', *Transactions of the New Shakspere Society*, 1 (1874), 130–51.

Fleay, F. G., *Shakespeare Manual* (Macmillan, 1876), p. 306.

Fleay, F. G., *A Biographical Chronicle of the English Drama*, 2 vols (Reeves and Turner, 1891).

Foakes, R. A. (ed.), *Henslowe's Diary*, 2nd edn (Cambridge University Press, 2002).

Ford, Howard Lee, 'A Comparison of Christopher Marlowe's *Edward II* and William Shakespeare's *Richard II*' (MA thesis: North Texas State College, 1960).

Forker, Charles R., '*The Troublesome Reign, Richard II*, and the Date of *King John*: A Study in Intertextuality', *Shakespeare Survey*, 63 (2010), 127–48.

Forker, Charles R. (ed.), *The Troublesome Reign of John, King of England* (Manchester University Press, 2011).

Forman, Simon, *The Bocke of Plaies and Notes therof per forman for Common Pollicie* (1611), Bodleian Library, Oxford University, MS Ashmole 208, fols 200–207v, transcribed by *Shakespeare Documented* (2020). https://shakespearedocumented.folger.edu/resource/document/formans-account-seeing-plays-globe-macbeth-cymbeline-winters-tale (accessed 12 February 2023).

Freebury-Jones, Darren, 'Exploring Co-authorship in *2 Henry VI*', *Journal of Early Modern Studies*, 5 (2016), 201–16.

Freebury-Jones, Darren, 'Possible Light on the Authorship of *Fair Em*', *Notes and Queries*, 64.2 (2017), 252–4.

Freebury-Jones, Darren, 'Exploring Verbal Relations between *Arden of Faversham* and John Lyly's *Endymion*', *Renaissance and Reformation*, 41.4 (2018), 93–108.

Freebury-Jones, Darren, 'Unique Phrases and the Canon of Thomas Kyd', *Notes and Queries*, 67.2 (2020), 220–3.

Freebury-Jones, Darren, 'Unsound Deductions in Early Modern Attribution: The Case of Thomas Watson', *American Notes and Queries*, 33.2 (2020), 164–71.

Freebury-Jones, Darren, 'Determining Robert Greene's Dramatic Canon', *Style*, 54.4 (2020), 377–98.

Freebury-Jones, Darren, 'John Fletcher's Collaborator on *The Noble Gentleman*', *Studia Metrica et Poetica*, 7.2 (2020), 43–60.

Freebury-Jones, Darren, 'Collocations and N-grams', *Early Modern Digital Review*, 4.4 (2021), 210–16.

Freebury-Jones, Darren, 'Elevating Thomas Watson: An Investigation into New Authorship Claims', *Early Modern Literary Studies*, 22.1 (2021), 1–19.

Freebury-Jones, Darren, 'New Perspectives on Thomas Kyd's Restored Canon', *Notes and Queries*, 69.1 (2022), 15–17.

Freebury-Jones, Darren, *Reading Robert Greene: Recovering Shakespeare's Rival* (Routledge, 2022).

Freebury-Jones, Darren, *Shakespeare's Tutor: The Influence of Thomas Kyd* (Manchester University Press, 2022).

Freebury-Jones, Darren, 'Kyd, Shakespeare, and *Arden of Faversham*: Rerunning a Two-Horse Race', *American Notes and Queries*, 36.3 (2023), 347–50.

Freebury-Jones, Darren (ed.), *The Collected Plays of Robert Greene* (Edinburgh University Press, 2028).

Freebury-Jones, Darren, and Marcus Dahl, 'The Limitations of Microattribution', *Texas Studies in Literature and Language*, 60.4 (2018), 467–95.

Freebury-Jones, Darren, and Marcus Dahl, 'Searching for Thomas Nashe in *Dido, Queen of Carthage*', *Digital Scholarship in the Humanities*, 35.2 (2020), 296–306.

Freebury-Jones, Darren, Marina Tarlinskaja, and Marcus Dahl, 'Attributing John Marston's Marginal Plays', *Studia Metrica et Poetica*, 5.1 (2018), 28–51.

Freebury-Jones, Darren, Marina Tarlinskaja, and Marcus Dahl, 'The Boundaries of John Marston's Dramatic Canon', *Medieval and Renaissance Drama in England*, 31 (2018), 43–77.

Freeman, Arthur, *Thomas Kyd: A Study of Facts and Problems* (Clarendon Press, 1967).

Fretz, Claude, *Dreams, Sleep, and Shakespeare's Genres* (Palgrave, 2020).

Frost, David L., *The School of Shakespeare: The Influence of Shakespeare on English Drama 1600–42* (Cambridge University Press, 1968).

Fuller, Thomas, *History of the Worthies of England* (Thomas Williams, 1662).

Fusillo, Robert J., 'The Staging of Battle Scenes on the Shakespearean Stage' (Doctoral thesis: University of Birmingham, 1966).

Garber, Marjorie, *Dream in Shakespeare: From Metaphor to Metamorphosis* (Yale University Press, 1974).

Gibbons, Brian, *Jacobean City Comedy* (Methuen, 1980).

Gildon, Charles, *The Post-Man Robb'd of his Mail* (A. Bettesworth and C. Rivington, 1719).

Gillespie, Stuart (ed.), *King John*, in *The Complete Works of William Shakespeare: The Alexander Text* (HarperCollins, 2006).

Godman, Maureen, '"Plucking a Crow" in *The Comedy of Errors*', *Early Theatre*, 8.1 (2005), 53–68.

Gossett, Suzanne (ed.), *Philaster* (Arden Shakespeare, 2009).

Grantley, Darryll, 'Thomas Dekker and the Emergence of City Comedy', in *The Cambridge Companion to Shakespeare and Contemporary Playwrights*, edited by Ton Hoenselaars (Cambridge University Press, 2012), pp. 83–96.

Greatley-Hirsch, Brett, and Jack Elliott, '*Arden of Faversham*, Shakespearian Authorship, and "The Print of Many"', in *The New Oxford Shakespeare: Authorship Companion*, edited by Gary Taylor and Gabriel Egan (Oxford University Press, 2017), pp. 139–81.

Green, William, 'Thomas Middleton and the Adaptation of Shakespeare: Late Jacobean Politics in Print and Performance, 1616–1623' (Doctoral thesis: University of Birmingham, 2021).

Greenblatt, Stephen, *Will in the World: How Shakespeare Became Shakespeare* (The Bodley Head, 2004).

Greer, C. A., 'Revision and Adaptation in *1 Henry VI*', *Studies in English*, 22 (1942), 110–20.

Greer, C. A., 'Shakespeare's Use of *The Famous Victories of Henry V*', *Notes and Queries*, 1 (1954), 238–41.

Greg, W. W. (ed.), *The Elder Brother*, in *The Works of Francis Beaumont and John Fletcher: Volume II*, edited by A. H. Bullen, 4 vols (G. Bell and Sons, 1905).

Greg, W. W., 'Review of *The Plays & Poems of Robert Greene*; J. Churton Collins', *Modern Language Review*, 1.3 (1906), 238–51.

Greg, W. W. (ed.), *Henslowe's Diary, Part II*, 2 vols (A. H. Bullen, 1908).

Greg, W. W., *A Bibliography of the English Printed Drama to the Restoration*, 4 vols (Bibliographical Society, 1939–59).

Greg, W. W., 'Shakespeare and *King Leir*', *Times Literary Supplement*, 9 March 1940, p. 124.

Greg, W. W., 'The Date of *King Lear* and Shakespeare's Use of Earlier Versions of the Story', *The Library*, 20 (1940), 377–400.

Greg, W. W., *The Shakespeare First Folio: Its Bibliographical and Textual History* (Clarendon Press, 1955).

Grosart, A. B. (ed.), *The Complete Works of John Davies of Hereford*, 2 vols (printed privately, 1878).

Grosart, A. B. (ed.), *The Life and Complete Prose Works of Robert Greene*, 15 vols (printed privately, 1881–86).

Grosart, A. B. (ed.), *The Works of Gabriel Harvey*, 3 vols (printed privately, 1884–85).

Grosart, A. B. (ed.), *The Tragical Reign of Selimus, Sometime Emperor of the Turks* (J.M. Dent and Co., 1898).

Gurr, Andrew, 'Another Jonson Critic', *Ben Jonson Journal*, 18.1 (2011), 27–44.

Hackett, Helen, '"As the Diall Hand tells Ore": The Case for Dekker, Not Shakespeare, as Author', *Review of English Studies*, 63 (2011), 34–57.

Hadfield, Andrew, 'Marlowe and Nashe', *English Literary Renaissance*, 51.2 (2021), 190–216.

Hadfield, Andrew, 'A More Brilliant Bird: Compiling the Canon of Shakespeare's First Critic and Rival', *Times Literary Supplement*, 7 October 2022, pp. 20–1.

Halliwell-Phillipps, J. O., *Outlines of the Life of Shakespeare* (Longmans, Green, and Company, 1883).

Hammond, Brean (ed.), *Double Falsehood* (Methuen Drama, 2010).

Harbage, Alfred, *Shakespeare and the Rival Traditions* (Macmillan, 1952).

Harbage, Alfred, 'Intrigue in Elizabethan Tragedy', in *Essays on Shakespeare and Elizabethan Drama in Honor of Hardin Craig*, edited by Richard Hosley (University of Missouri Press, 1962), pp. 37–44.

Harbage, Alfred, '*Love's Labour's Lost* and the Early Shakespeare', *Philological Quarterly*, 41 (1962), 18–36.

Hart, Alfred, *Shakespeare and the Homilies* (Melbourne University Press, 1934).

Hart, Alfred, *Stolne and Surreptitious Copies: A Comparative Study of Shakespeare's Bad Quartos* (Melbourne University Press, 1942).

Hattaway, Michael, 'Dating *As You Like It*, Epilogues and Prayers, and the Problems of "As the Dial Hand Tells O'er"', *Shakespeare Quarterly*, 60 (2009), 154–67.

Henze, Catherine, 'Francis Beaumont and John Fletcher's Tragicomedy as Musical Melodrama', in *The Cambridge Companion to Shakespeare and Contemporary Playwrights*, edited by Ton Hoenselaars (Cambridge University Press, 2012), pp. 149–64.

Hieatt, Charles W., 'Multiple Plotting in *Friar Bacon and Friar Bungay*', *Renaissance Drama*, 16 (1985), 17–34.

Higgins, Martin, '"Flowers of this purple dye, / Hit with Cupid's archery": Lyly, Shakespeare, and Early Modern Cupid', in *Critical Insights: A Midsummer Night's Dream*, edited by Nicolas Tredell (Grey House Publishing, 2020), pp. 118–34.

Hoenselaars, Ton, 'Shakespeare: Colleagues, Collaborators, Co-authors', in *The Cambridge Companion to Shakespeare and Contemporary Playwrights*, edited by Ton Hoenselaars (Cambridge University Press, 2012), pp. 97–119.

Holden, Anthony, *William Shakespeare: His Life and Work* (Little, Brown, and Company, 1999).

Holdsworth, Roger, 'Shakespeare and Middleton: A Chronology for 1605–6', in *The New Oxford Shakespeare: Authorship Companion*, edited by Gary Taylor and Gabriel Egan (Oxford University Press, 2017), pp. 366–84.

Honan, Park, *Christopher Marlowe: Poet and Spy* (Oxford University Press, 2005).

Honigmann, E. A. J., *Shakespeare's Impact on His Contemporaries* (Macmillan, 1982).

Horne, David, *The Life and Minor Works of George Peele* (Yale University Press, 1952).

Hotson, Leslie, *The Death of Christopher Marlowe* (Nonesuch Press, 1925).

Howard, Jean E., *Theater of a City: The Places of London Comedy, 1598–1642* (University of Pennsylvania Press, 2011).

Hoy, Cyrus, 'The Shares of Fletcher and His Collaborators in the Beaumont and Fletcher Canon', *Studies in Bibliography*, 8–15 (1956–62).

Hulse, Mark, 'The Case for Peele's Authorship of *Titus Andronicus* 4.1: Cross-Examining Attribution Methods in a Disputed Scene', *Review of English Studies*, 72 (2021), 860–81.

Hulse, Mark, 'Review of "Determining Authorship: A New Technique"', *Renaissance and Reformation*, 4.4 (2021), 204–10.

Hunter, G. K., *John Lyly: The Humanist as Courtier* (Routledge, 1962).

Hunter, G. K. (ed.), *Antonio and Mellida* (University of Nebraska Press, 1965).

Hunter, G. K., *English Drama 1586–1642: The Age of Shakespeare* (Clarendon Press, 1997).

Hunter, G. K., 'Lyly, John', in *Oxford Dictionary of National Biography*, edited by Henry Colin Grey Matthew and Brian Harrison (Oxford University Press, 2004).

Hutchings, Mark, 'The "Turk Phenomenon" and the Repertory of the Late Elizabethan Playhouse', *Early Modern Literary Studies*, 13.2 (2007).

Ioannidis, John P. A., 'Why Most Published Research Findings Are False', *PLoS Medicine*, 2.8 (2005). https://doi.org/10.1371/journal.pmed.0020124 (accessed 29 October 2022).

Ioppolo, Grace, 'The Transmission of an English Renaissance Play-Text', in *A Companion to Renaissance Drama*, edited by Arthur F. Kinney (Blackwell, 2002), pp. 163–79.

Jackson, MacDonald P., 'Material for an Edition of *Arden of Faversham*' (B.Litt. thesis: Oxford University, 1963).

Jackson, MacDonald P., 'Determining Authorship: A New Technique', *Research Opportunities in Renaissance Drama*, 41 (2002), 1–14.

Jackson, MacDonald P., *Defining Shakespeare: Pericles as Test Case* (Oxford University Press, 2003).

Jackson, MacDonald P., 'The Date and Authorship of Hand D's Contribution to *Sir Thomas More*: Evidence from "Literature Online"', *Shakespeare Survey*, 59 (2006), 69–78.

Jackson, MacDonald P., 'Parallels and Poetry: Shakespeare, Kyd, and *Arden of Faversham*', *Medieval and Renaissance Drama in England*, 23 (2010), 17–33.

Jackson, MacDonald P., 'Looking for Shakespeare in *Double Falsehood*: Stylistic Evidence', in *The Quest for Cardenio: Shakespeare, Fletcher, Cervantes, and the Lost Play*, edited by David Carnegie and Gary Taylor (Oxford University Press, 2012), pp. 133–61.

Jackson, MacDonald P., *Determining the Shakespeare Canon: Arden of Faversham and A Lover's Complaint* (Oxford University Press, 2014).

Jackson, MacDonald P., 'Shakespeare, *Arden of Faversham*, and *A Lover's Complaint*: A Review of Reviews', in *The New Oxford Shakespeare: Authorship Companion*, edited by Gary Taylor and Gabriel Egan (Oxford University Press, 2017), pp. 123–38.

Jackson, MacDonald P., '*Locrine* and Robert Greene's Dramatic Canon', *Notes and Queries*, 70.3 (2023), 154–9.

Jackson, MacDonald P., and Michael Neill (eds), *The Selected Plays of John Marston* (Cambridge University Press, 1986).

Jackson, MacDonald P., and Gary Taylor, 'Works Excluded from this Edition', in *Thomas Middleton and Early Modern Textual Culture: A Companion to the Collected Works*, edited by Gary Taylor and John Lavagnino (Oxford University Press, 2007), pp. 444–8.

Jansohn, Christa, '*Arden of Faversham*', in *Studying English Literature in Context: Critical Readings*, edited by Paul Poplawski (Cambridge University Press, 2022), pp. 101–16.

Jones, John, *Shakespeare at Work* (Oxford University Press, 1995).

Jong, Ian H. De, and Eric Rasmussen, 'Non-English Words in *The Spanish Tragedy*', *American Notes and Queries*, 33.2 (2020), 133–42.

Jowett, John, 'Johannes Factotum: Henry Chettle and *Greene's Groatsworth of Wit*', *Papers of the Bibliographical Society of America*, 87.4 (1993), 453–86.

Jowett, John (ed.), *The Oxford Shakespeare: Timon of Athens* (Oxford University Press, 2004).

Jowett, John, '*Measure for Measure*: A Genetic Text', in *Thomas Middleton: The Collected Works*, edited by Gary Taylor and John Lavagnino (Oxford University Press, 2007), pp. 1542–6.

Jowett, John (ed.), *Sir Thomas More* (Arden Shakespeare, 2011).

Jowett, John, *Shakespeare and Text*, rev. edn (Oxford University Press, 2019).

Jowett, John, William Montgomery, Gary Taylor, and Stanley Wells (eds), *The Oxford Shakespeare: The Complete Works* (Oxford University Press, 2005).

Kane, Eilidh, 'Shakespeare and Middleton's Co-Authorship of *Timon of Athens*', *Journal of Early Modern Studies*, 5 (2016), 217–35.

Kapitaniak, Pierre, 'Bending One's Eye on Vacancy? Stage Ghosts, Shakespeare and the Question of Visibility in English Drama', *Arrêt sur scène / Scene Focus*, 11 (2022), 1–26.

Keller, Stefan D., 'Shakespeare's Rhetorical Fingerprint: New Evidence on the Authorship of *Titus Andronicus*', *English Studies*, 84.2 (2003), 105–18.

Kesson, Andy, *John Lyly and Early Modern Authorship* (Manchester University Press, 2011).

Kesson, Andy, 'His Fellow Dramatists and Early Collaborators', in *The Shakespeare Circle: An Alternate Biography*, edited by Paul Edmondson and Stanley Wells (Cambridge University Press, 2015), pp. 235–47.

Kesson, Andy, 'John Lyly and Shakespeare's Early Career', in *Early Shakespeare, 1588–1594*, edited by Rory Loughnane and Andrew J. Power (Cambridge University Press, 2020), pp. 167–79.

Kesson, Andy, Lucy Munro, and Callan Davies, 'London Theatrical Culture, 1560–1590', *Oxford Research Encyclopedia of Literature* (2021). doi. org/10.1093/acrefore/9780190201098.013.1194 (accessed 16 October 2022).

Kidnie, M. J., 'Shakespeare's Audiences', in *Shakespeare: An Oxford Guide*, edited by Stanley Wells and Lena Cowen Orlin (Oxford University Press, 2003), pp. 32–43.

Kimbrough, Robert (ed.), *Sir Philip Sidney: Selected Prose and Poetry* (Holt, Rinehart and Winston, 1969).

King, Walter N., 'John Lyly and Elizabethan Rhetoric', *Studies in Philology*, 52 (1955), 149–61.

Kinney, Arthur F., 'Shakespeare's Falstaff as Parody', *Connotations*, 12.2–3 (2002), 105–25.

Kinney, Arthur F., 'Authoring *Arden of Faversham*', in *Shakespeare, Computers, and the Mystery of Authorship*, edited by Hugh Craig and Arthur F. Kinney (Cambridge University Press, 2009), pp. 78–99.

Kinney, Arthur F., and David A. Katz (eds), *Renaissance Drama: An Anthology of Plays and Entertainments*, 3rd edn (Wiley, 2022).

Kirwan, Peter, *Shakespeare and the Idea of the Apocrypha: Negotiating the Boundaries of the Dramatic Canon* (Cambridge University Press, 2015).

Kirwan, Peter, 'The Shakespeare Canon from the Sixteenth to the Twenty-first Century', in *The Arden Research Handbook of Shakespeare and Textual Studies*, edited by Lukas Erne (Bloomsbury, 2021), pp. 150–67.

Knowles, James, 'Marston, John', in *Oxford Dictionary of National Biography*, edited by Henry Colin Grey Matthew and Brian Harrison (Oxford University Press, 2004).

Knutson, Roslyn, *The Repertory of Shakespeare's Company 1594–1613* (University of Arkansas Press, 1991).

Knutson, Roslyn, 'Falconer to the Little Eyases: A New Date and Commercial Agenda for the "Little Eyases" Passage in *Hamlet*', *Shakespeare Quarterly*, 46.1 (1995), 1–31.

Knutson, Roslyn, 'The Start of Something Big', in *Locating the Queen's Men, 1583–1603: Material Practices and Conditions of Playing*, edited by Helen Ostovich, Holger Schott Syme, and Andrew Griffin (Routledge, 2009), pp. 99–108.

Knutson, Roslyn, 'Ur-Plays and Other Exercises in Making Stuff Up', in *Lost Plays in Shakespeare's England*, edited by David McInnis and Matthew Steggle (Palgrave, 2014), pp. 31–54.

Koskenniemi, Inna, *Studies in the Vocabulary of English Drama 1550–1600* (Turun Yliopisto, 1962).

Lake, David, *The Canon of Thomas Middleton's Plays* (Cambridge University Press, 1975).

Lake, David, 'Three Seventeenth-Century Revisions: *Thomas of Woodstock*, *The Jew of Malta*, and *Faustus* B', *Notes and Queries*, 228 (1983), 133–43.

Laoutaris, Chris, *Shakespeare's Book: The Intertwined Lives behind the First Folio* (William Collins, 2023).

Leggatt, Alexander, *Citizen Comedy in the Age of Shakespeare* (University of Toronto Press, 1974).

Leishman, J. B. (ed.), *The Three Parnassus Plays* (Nicholson and Watson, 1949).

Lodge, Thomas, *Wit's Misery* (A. Islip, 1596).

Logan, Robert, *Shakespeare's Marlowe: The Influence of Christopher Marlowe on Shakespeare's Artistry* (Ashgate, 2007).

Logan, Terence P., and Denzell S. Smith (eds), *The Predecessors of Shakespeare: A Survey and Bibliography of Recent Studies in English Renaissance Drama* (University of Nebraska Press, 1973).

Loughnane, Rory, 'Re-editing Non-Shakespeare for the Modern Reader: The Murder of Mutius in *Titus Andronicus*', *Review of English Studies*, 68.284 (2017), 268–95.

Loughnane, Rory, 'Thomas Middleton in *All's Well that Ends Well*? Part One', in *The New Oxford Shakespeare: Authorship Companion*, edited by Gary Taylor and Gabriel Egan (Oxford University Press, 2017), pp. 278–302.

Loughnane, Rory, 'Thomas Middleton in *All's Well that Ends Well*? Part Two', in *The New Oxford Shakespeare: Authorship Companion*, edited by Gary Taylor and Gabriel Egan (Oxford University Press, 2017), pp. 307–20.

Lunney, Ruth, and Hugh Craig, 'Who Wrote *Dido, Queen of Carthage*?', *Journal of Marlowe Studies*, 1 (2020), 1–31.

Maguire, Laurie, *Shakespearean Suspect Texts: The 'Bad' Quartos and Their Contexts* (Cambridge University Press, 1996).

Maguire, Laurie, 'Marlovian Texts and Authorship', in *The Cambridge Companion to Christopher Marlowe*, edited by Patrick Cheney (Cambridge University Press, 2006), pp. 41–54.

Maguire, Laurie, and Emma Smith, 'Many Hands: A New Shakespeare Collaboration?', *Times Literary Supplement*, 20 April 2012, pp. 13–15.

Maguire, Laurie, and Emma Smith, 'What Is a Source? Or, How Shakespeare Read His Marlowe', *Shakespeare Survey*, 68 (2015), 15–31.

Malone, Edmond, 'A Dissertation on the *Three Parts of King Henry VI*. Tending to show that those plays were not written originally by Shakespeare' (1787), reprinted in *The Plays and Poems of William Shakespeare: Volume XVIII*, edited by James Boswell, 21 vols (F. C. and J. Rivington, 1821), pp. 562–97.

Manley, Lawrence, and Sally-Beth MacLean, *Lord Strange's Men and Their Plays* (Yale University Press, 2014).

Mardock, James, and Eric Rasmussen, 'What Does Textual Evidence Reveal about the Author?', in *Shakespeare Beyond Doubt: Evidence, Argument, Controversy*, edited by Paul Edmondson and Stanley Wells (Cambridge University Press, 2013), pp. 111–20.

Maxwell, Baldwin, *Studies in the Shakespearean Apocrypha* (King's Crown Press, 1956).

McCarthy, Jeanne, *The Children's Troupes and the Transformation of English Theater 1509–1608: Pedagogue, Playwrights, Playbooks, and Play-boys* (Routledge, 2016).

McDonald, Russ, 'Othello, Thorello, and the Problem of the Foolish Hero', *Shakespeare Quarterly*, 30 (1979), 51–67.

McDonald, Russ, 'Jonson and Shakespeare and the Rhythm of Verse', in *The Cambridge Companion to Ben Jonson*, edited by Richard Harp and Stanley Stewart (Cambridge University Press, 2000), pp. 103–18.

McDonald, Russ, *Shakespeare's Late Style* (Cambridge University Press, 2009).

McInnis, David, *Shakespeare and Lost Plays: Reimagining Drama in Early Modern England* (Cambridge University Press, 2021).

McKerrow, R. B. (ed.), *The Spanish Curate*, in *The Works of Francis Beaumont and John Fletcher: Volume II*, edited by A. H. Bullen, 4 vols (G. Bell and Sons, 1905).

McKerrow, R. B. (ed.), *The Works of Thomas Nashe*, 5 vols (Basil Blackwell, 1958).

McMillin, Scott, *The Elizabethan Theatre and The Book of Sir Thomas More* (Cornell University Press, 1987).

McMillin, Scott, and Sally-Beth MacLean, *The Queen's Men and Their Plays* (Cambridge University Press, 1998).

McMullan, Gordon, 'Fletcher, John', in *Oxford Dictionary of National Biography*, edited by Henry Colin Grey Matthew and Brian Harrison (Oxford University Press, 2004).

McNeal, Thomas H., 'Margaret of Anjou: Romantic Princess and Troubled Queen', *Shakespeare Quarterly*, 9 (1958), 1–10.

Melchiori, Giorgio (ed.), *Edward III: The New Cambridge Shakespeare* (Cambridge University Press, 1998).

Melnikoff, Kirk, and Edward Gieskes (eds), *Writing Robert Greene: Essays on England's First Notorious Professional Writer* (Ashgate, 2008).

Merriam, Thomas, 'New Light on a Possible Kyd Canon', *Notes and Queries*, 240 (1995), 340–1.

Meyer, Edward, *Machiavelli and the Elizabethan Drama* (Felber, 1897).

Miksch, Walter, *Die Verfasserschaft des Arden of Feversham* (Breslau, 1907).

Mincoff, Marco, 'Shakespeare and Lyly', *Shakespeare Survey*, 14 (1961), 15–24.

Mincoff, Marco, '*Henry VIII* and Fletcher', *Shakespeare Quarterly*, 12 (1961), 239–60.

Mincoff, Marco, *Shakespeare: The First Steps* (Bulgarian Academy of Sciences, 1976).

MOLA, 'The Curtain Theatre: The citizen's playhouse for high-octane drama' (2018). https://www.mola.org.uk/discoveries/news/curtain-theatre-citizens-playhouse-high-octane-drama (accessed 2 April 2023).

Mueller, Martin, 'From *Leir* to *Lear*', *Philological Quarterly*, 73 (1994), 195–218.

Mueller, Martin, 'Vickers is right about Kyd' (2009). https://darrenfj.files.word press.com/2017/11/N-grams-and-the-Kyd-Canon-and-Vickers-is-right-about-Kyd.pdf (accessed 16 October 2022).

Mueller, Martin, 'Authors are trumps' (2011). https://literaryinformatics.word press.com/2011/03/31/authors-are-trumps/ (accessed 1 October 2022).

Muir, Kenneth, *The Sources of Shakespeare's Plays* (Routledge, 1977).

Mulryne, J. R., 'Kyd, Thomas', in *Oxford Dictionary of National Biography*, edited by Henry Colin Grey Matthew and Brian Harrison (Oxford University Press, 2004).

Nance, John V., 'From Shakespeare "To ye Q."', *Shakespeare Quarterly*, 67 (2016), 204–31.

Nance, John V., '"We, John Cade": Shakespeare, Marlowe, and the Authorship of 4.2.33–189 2 Henry VI', *Shakespeare*, 13.1 (2017), 30–51.

Nance, John V., 'Middleton and the King's Speech in *All's Well that Ends Well*', in *The New Oxford Shakespeare: Authorship Companion*, edited by Gary Taylor and Gabriel Egan (Oxford University Press, 2017), pp. 321–36.

Nance, John V., 'Early Shakespeare and the Authorship of *The Taming of the Shrew*', in *Early Shakespeare, 1588–1594*, edited by Rory Loughnane and Andrew J. Power (Cambridge University Press, 2020), pp. 261–83.

Nason, Arthur Huntington, 'Shakespeare's Use of Comedy in Tragedy', *Sewanee Review*, 14 (1906), 28–37.

Nelson, Alan H., and Paul H. Altrocchi, 'William Shakespeare, "Our Roscius"', *Shakespeare Quarterly*, 60.4 (2009), 460–9.

Ness, F. W., *The Use of Rhyme in Shakespeare's Plays* (Yale University Press, 1941).

Newcomb, Lori Humphrey, 'Greene, Robert', in *Oxford Dictionary of National Biography*, edited by Henry Colin Grey Matthew and Brian Harrison (Oxford University Press, 2004).

Nicholl, Charles, *The Reckoning: The Murder of Christopher Marlowe* (Vintage Books, 2002).

Nicholl, Charles, 'Marlowe [Marley], Christopher', in *Oxford Dictionary of National Biography*, edited by Henry Colin Grey Matthew and Brian Harrison (Oxford University Press, 2004).

Nicol, David, *Middleton and Rowley: Forms of Collaboration in the Jacobean Playhouse* (University of Toronto Press, 2012).

Norland, Howard R., *Neoclassical Tragedy in Elizabethan England* (Associated University Presses, 2009).

Nosworthy, J. M., *Shakespeare's Occasional Plays: Their Origin and Transmission* (Edward Arnold, 1965).

O'Callaghan, Michelle, 'Thomas Middleton and the Early Modern Theatre', in *The Cambridge Companion to Shakespeare and Contemporary Playwrights*, edited by Ton Hoenselaars (Cambridge University Press, 2012), pp. 165–80.

Öğütcü, Murat, 'Old Wives' Humour: George Peele's *The Old Wives Tale*', in *Humour in Western Literature*, edited by Şeyda Sivrioğlu, Meryem Ayan, Nejdet Keleş, and Gamze Yalçın (Kriter, 2016), pp. 307–29.

Oliphant, E. H. C., *The Plays of Beaumont and Fletcher: An Attempt to Determine Their Respective Shares and the Shares of Others* (Yale University Press, 1927).

Oras, Ants, '"Extra Monosyllables" in *Henry VIII* and the Problem of Authorship', *Journal of English and Germanic Philology*, 52 (1953), 198–213.

Østerberg, Valdemar, 'Nashe's "Kid in Aesop": A Danish Interpretation', *Review of English Studies*, 18 (1942), 385–94.

Ota, Kazuaki, 'Was Marlowe Shakespeare's Collaborator?: Computational Stylometry and the Authorship of the Three Parts of *Henry VI*', *Studies in Languages and Cultures*, 50 (2023), 1–17.

Owens, Rebekah, 'The Reception History of Frederick Samuel Boas' *Works of Thomas Kyd*' (Doctoral thesis: Anglia Ruskin University, 2020).

Paleit, Edward, 'Shakespeare's Faulty Learning? Classical Reference in *2 Henry VI* and the Authorship Question', *Notes and Queries*, 48.4 (2018), 506–11.

Partridge, A. C., *The Problem of Henry VIII Reopened* (Cambridge University Press, 1949).

Pask, Kevin, 'Caliban's Masque', *English Literary History*, 70.3 (2003), 739–56.

Patterson, R. F. (ed.), *Ben Jonson's Conversations with William Drummond of Hawthornden* (Blackie and Son, 1924).

Pearlman, Elihu, 'Shakespeare at Work: The Two Talbots', *Philological Quarterly*, 75.1 (1996), 1–22.

Perrett, Wilfrid, *The Story of King Lear from Geoffrey of Monmouth to Shakespeare* (Mayer and Muller, 1904).

Perry, Curtis, *Shakespeare and Senecan Tragedy* (Cambridge University Press, 2020).

Petersen, Lene B., *Shakespeare's Errant Texts: Textual Form and Linguistic Style in Shakespearean 'Bad' Quartos and Co-authored Plays* (Cambridge University Press, 2010).

Philo, John-Mark, 'Ben Jonson's *Sejanus* and Shakespeare's *Othello*: Two Plays Performed by the King's Men in 1603', *Shakespeare Survey*, 75 (2022), 122–36.

Pikli, Natália, '"As for that light hobby-horse, my sister": Shakespearean Influences and Popular Discourses in *Blurt Master Constable*', *Shakespeare Survey*, 70 (2017), 259–71.

Pope, Maurice, 'My Kingdom for a Horse', *Notes and Queries*, 41 (1994), 472–7.

Price, Eoin, 'Marlowe in Miniature: *Dido, Queen of Carthage* and the Children of the Chapel Repertory', in *Christopher Marlowe, Theatrical Commerce, and the Book Trade*, edited by Kirk Melnikoff and Roslyn L. Knutson (Cambridge University Press, 2018), pp. 41–55.

Price, Eoin, 'The Dearth of the Author: Philip Massinger and the Beaumont and Fletcher Folio', *Review of English Studies*, 74.313 (2023), 78–94.

Price, Hereward T., 'Mirror-scenes in Shakespeare', in *Joseph Quincy Adams Memorial Studies*, edited by James G. McManaway, Giles E. Dawson, and Edwin E. Willoughby (Folger Shakespeare Library, 1948), pp. 101–13.

Proudfoot, Richard, '*The Reign of King Edward the Third* (1596) and Shakespeare', *Proceedings of the British Academy*, 71 (1985), 159–85.

Proudfoot, Richard, 'Can *Double Falsehood* Be Merely a Forgery by Lewis Theobald?', in *The Quest for Cardenio: Shakespeare, Fletcher, Cervantes, and the Lost Play*, edited by David Carnegie and Gary Taylor (Oxford University Press, 2012), pp. 162–79.

Proudfoot, Richard, and Nicola Bennett (eds), *King Edward III* (Bloomsbury, 2017).

Prouty, C. T. (ed.), *The Life and Works of George Peele*, 3 vols (Yale University Press, 1952–70).

Pruitt, Anna, 'Refining the *LION* Collocation Test: A Comparative Study of Authorship Test Results for *Titus Andronicus* Scene 6 (= 4.1)', in *The New Oxford Shakespeare: Authorship Companion*, edited by Gary Taylor and Gabriel Egan (Oxford University Press, 2017), pp. 92–106.

Ravenscroft, Edward, *Titus Andronicus, or the Rape of Lavinia* (J. Hindmarsh, 1687).

Ribner, Irving, *The English History Play in the Age of Shakespeare* (Princeton University Press, 1957).

Richardson, Brenda, 'Robert Greene's Yorkshire Connexions: A New Hypothesis', *Yearbook of English Studies*, 10 (1980), 160–80.

Riggs, David, *The World of Christopher Marlowe* (Faber and Faber, 2004).

Ritchie, Brian B., *The Plays of Christopher Marlowe and George Peele: Rhetoric and Renaissance Sensibility* (Universal Publishers, 1999).

Rizvi, Pervez, 'The Use of Spellings for Compositor Attribution in the First Folio', *Papers of the Bibliographical Society of America*, 110 (2016), 1–53.

Rizvi, Pervez, *Collocations and N-grams* (2017). www.shakespearestext.com/can/index.htm (accessed 1 October 2022).

Rizvi, Pervez, '*Arden of Faversham* and the Extended Kyd Canon' (2018). https://www.shakespearestext.com/can/experiments/ (accessed 5 December 2022).

Rizvi, Pervez, 'The Interpretation of Zeta Test Results', *Digital Scholarship in the Humanities*, 34.2 (2018), 401–18.

Rizvi, Pervez, 'The Problem of Microattribution', *Digital Scholarship in the Humanities*, 34.3 (2019), 606–15.

Rizvi, Pervez, 'Authorship Attribution for Early Modern Plays Using Function Word Adjacency Networks: A Critical View', *American Notes and Queries*, 33.4 (2020), 328–31.

Rizvi, Pervez, 'Shakespeare and Principal Component Analysis', *Digital Scholarship in the Humanities*, 36.4 (2021), 1030–41.

Rizvi, Pervez, 'The Interpretation of Zeta Test Results: A Supplement', *Digital Scholarship in the Humanities*, 37.4 (2022), 1172–8.

Rizvi, Pervez, 'The Unsoundness of the Stylometric Case for Thomas Watson's Authorship of *Arden of Faversham*', *American Notes and Queries*, 35.3 (2022), 261–70.

Rizvi, Pervez, 'An Analysis of the Word Adjacency Network Method – Part 1 – The Evidence of Its Unsoundness', *Digital Scholarship in the Humanities*, 38.1 (2023), 347–60.

Roberts, Josephine A., and James F. Gaines, 'Kyd and Garnier: The Art of Amendment', *Comparative Literature*, 31 (1979), 124–33.

Roberts, P. B., '"Sheep-skin-weaver": Ben Jonson in Thomas Dekker's *Satiromastix*', *Early Modern Literary Studies*, 19.2 (2017), 1–21.

Robertson, J. M., *An Introduction to the Study of the Shakespeare Canon: Proceeding on the Problem of Titus Andronicus* (Routledge, 1924).

Rollins, H. E. (ed.), *The Letters of John Keats*, 2 vols (Cambridge University Press, 1958).

Routh Jr, James E., 'Thomas Kyd's Rime Schemes and the Authorship of *Soliman and Perseda* and of *The First Part of Jeronimo*', *Modern Language Notes*, 20.2 (1905), 49–51.

Rowe, Nicholas (ed.), *The Works of Mr William Shakespeare*, 6 vols (Jacob Tonson, 1709).

Rubow, Paul V., *Shakespeare og hans samtidige* (Gyldendubidal, 1948).

Rutter, Tom, *Shakespeare and the Admiral's Men: Reading across Repertoires on the London Stage, 1594–1600* (Cambridge University Press, 2017).

Sanderson, John Russell, *The Elizabethan and Jacobean Two-part Play: A Study of the Composition and Structure of Dramatic Sequels* (Doctoral thesis: University of Birmingham, 1975).

Sarrazin, Gregor, *Thomas Kyd und sein Kreis. Eine Litterarhistorische Untersuchung* (E. Felber, 1892).

Schoenbaum, Samuel, *William Shakespeare: A Compact Documentary Life* (Oxford University Press, 1987).

Schoone-Jongen, Terence, *Shakespeare's Companies: William Shakespeare's Early Career and the Acting Companies, 1577–1594* (Ashgate, 2008).

Scott, Michael, 'Marston's Early Contribution to *The Insatiate Countess*', *Notes and Queries*, 222 (1977), 116–17.

Scragg, Leah, *The Metamorphosis of Galatea: A Study in Creative Adaptation* (University Press of America, 1982).

Segarra, Santiago, Mark Eisen, Gabriel Egan, and Alejandro Ribeiro, 'Attributing the Authorship of the *Henry VI* Plays by Word Adjacency', *Shakespeare Quarterly*, 67 (2016), 232–56.

Shapiro, James, *Rival Playwrights: Marlowe, Jonson, Shakespeare* (Columbia University Press, 1991).

Shapiro, Michael, *Gender in Play on the Shakespearean Stage: Boy Heroines and Female Pages* (Ann Arbor, 1996).

Sharpe, Will, 'Authorship and Attribution', in *William Shakespeare & Others: Collaborative Plays*, edited by Jonathan Bate and Eric Rasmussen (Macmillan, 2013), pp. 641–730.

Shepherd, R. H. (ed.), *The Dramatic Works of Thomas Heywood*, 6 vols (John Pearson, 1874).

Shrank, Cathy L., and Paul Werstine, 'The Shakespeare Manuscripts', in *The Arden Research Handbook of Shakespeare and Textual Studies*, edited by Lukas Erne (Bloomsbury, 2021), pp. 53–70.

Simpson, Percy, 'The Additions to the *Spanish Tragedy*', in *Ben Jonson: Volume II*, edited by Charles Harold Herford, Percy Simpson, and Evelyn Simpson, 11 vols (Clarendon Press, 1925).

Simpson, Richard, 'Are There Any Extant MSS. in Shakespere's Handwriting?', *Notes and Queries*, 183 (1871), 1–3.

Sisson, Charles Jasper, *Lost Plays of Shakespeare's Age* (Cambridge University Press, 1936).

Skura, Meredith, *Shakespeare the Actor and the Purposes of Playing* (University of Chicago Press, 1993).

Skura, Meredith, 'What Shakespeare Did with the Queen's Men's *King Leir* and When', *Shakespeare Survey*, 63 (2010), 316–25.

Slaney, Helen, *The Senecan Aesthetic: A Performance History* (Oxford University Press, 2016).

Smart, John Semple, *Shakespeare: Truth and Tradition* (E. Arnold, 1928).

Smith, Emma, *The Making of Shakespeare's First Folio* (Oxford University Press, 2015).

Smith, Emma, 'Shakespeare: the apex predator', *Times Literary Supplement*, 4 May 2017. https://www.the-tls.co.uk/articles/we-over-privilege-shakespea re-is-that-a-bad-thing-essay-emma-smith/ (accessed 3 April 2024).

Smith, R. M., '*Edward III* A Study of the Authorship of the Drama in the Light of a New Source', *Journal of English and German Philology*, 10 (1911), 90–104.

Southworth, John, *Shakespeare the Player: A Life in the Theatre* (Sutton, 2000).

Spedding, James, 'Who Wrote *Henry VIII*?', *Gentleman's Magazine*, 34, August 1850, pp. 115–23.

Stagg, Robert, 'Rhyme's Voices: Hearing Gender in *The Taming of the Shrew*', *Studies in Philology*, 119.2 (2021), 323–46.

Stagg, Robert, 'Shakespeare's Bombastic Blanks', *Review of English Studies*, 72.307 (2021), 882–99.

Stanivukovic, Goran, 'The Language and Style of Early Shakespeare', in *Early Shakespeare, 1588–1594*, edited by Rory Loughnane and Andrew J. Power (Cambridge University Press, 2020), pp. 76–101.

Steggle, Matthew, 'Urbane John Marston: Obscenity, Playfulness, Co-operation', in *The Cambridge Companion to Shakespeare and Contemporary Playwrights*, edited by Ton Hoenselaars (Cambridge University Press, 2012), pp. 70–82.

Stephenson, Henry Thew, '*The Spanish Tragedy* and *Hamlet*', *Sewanee Review*, 14.3 (1906), 294–8.

Stephenson, Joseph F., 'Review of *The New Oxford Shakespeare: Authorship Companion*', *Sixteenth Century Journal*, 49.4 (2018), 1314–17.

Stern, Tiffany, *Rehearsal from Shakespeare to Sheridan* (Oxford University Press, 2000).

Stern, Tiffany, *Documents of Performance in Early Modern England* (Cambridge University Press, 2009).

Stevenson, Stanley Warren, 'Shakespeare's Hand in *The Spanish Tragedy* 1602' (Doctoral thesis: McGill University, 1954).

Stoll, E. E., *John Webster: The Periods of His Work as Determined by His Relations to the Drama of His Day* (Alfred Mudge, 1905).

Sutton, C. W., rev. Alan G. Crosby, 'Heywood, Thomas', in *Oxford Dictionary of National Biography*, edited by Henry Colin Grey Matthew and Brian Harrison (Oxford University Press, 2004).

Swinburne, Algernon Charles, *The Age of Shakespeare* (Chatto and Windus, 1908).

Sykes, H. Dugdale, *Sidelights on Shakespeare* (Shakespeare Head Press, 1919).

Syme, Holger, *Theatre History, Attribution Studies, and the Question of Evidence* (Cambridge University Press, 2023).

Tarlinskaja, Marina, *Shakespeare and the Versification of Elizabethan Drama 1561–1642* (Ashgate, 2014).

Taylor, Gary, 'Rare Vocabulary in the Two Texts of *King Lear*', in *The Division of the Kingdoms: Shakespeare's Two Versions of King Lear*, edited by Gary Taylor and Michael Warren (Clarendon Press, 1983), pp. 462–4.

Taylor, Gary, 'Shakespeare and Others: The Authorship of *Henry the Sixth Part One*', *Medieval and Renaissance Drama*, 7 (1995), 145–205.

Taylor, Gary, 'Middleton, Thomas', in *Oxford Dictionary of National Biography*, edited by Henry Colin Grey Matthew and Brian Harrison (Oxford University Press, 2004).

Taylor, Gary, 'Works Included in this Edition', in *Thomas Middleton and Early Modern Textual Culture: A Companion to the Collected Works*, edited by Gary Taylor and John Lavagnino (Oxford University Press, 2007), pp. 335–444.

Taylor, Gary, 'A History of *The History of Cardenio*', in *The Quest for Cardenio: Shakespeare, Fletcher, Cervantes, and the Lost Play*, edited by David Carnegie and Gary Taylor (Oxford University Press, 2012), pp. 11–61.

Taylor, Gary, 'Empirical Middleton: *Macbeth*, Adaptation, and Microauthorship', *Shakespeare Quarterly*, 65 (2014), 239–72.

Taylor, Gary, 'Did Shakespeare Write *The Spanish Tragedy* Additions?', in *The New Oxford Shakespeare: Authorship Companion*, edited by Gary Taylor and Gabriel Egan (Oxford University Press, 2017), pp. 246–60.

Taylor, Gary, '*All's Well that Ends Well*: Text, Date, and Adaptation', in *The New Oxford Shakespeare: Authorship Companion*, edited by Gary Taylor and Gabriel Egan (Oxford University Press, 2017), pp. 337–65.

Taylor, Gary, 'Shakespeare's Early Gothic *Hamlet*', in *Shakespeare & the First Hamlet*, edited by Terri Bourus (Berghahn Books, 2022), pp. 7–34.

Taylor, Gary, and John Jowett, *Shakespeare Reshaped, 1606–1623* (Clarendon Press, 1993).

Taylor, Gary, and John Lavagnino (eds), *Thomas Middleton and Early Modern Textual Culture: A Companion to the Collected Works* (Oxford University Press, 2007).

Taylor, Gary, and John Lavagnino (eds), *Thomas Middleton: The Collected Works* (Oxford University Press, 2007).

Taylor, Gary, John Jowett, Terri Bourus, and Gabriel Egan (eds), *The New Oxford Shakespeare: Modern Critical Edition* (Oxford University Press, 2016).

Taylor, Gary, and Doug Duhaime, 'Who Wrote the Fly Scene (3.2) in *Titus Andronicus*?: Automated Searches and Deep Reading', in *The New Oxford Shakespeare: Authorship Companion*, edited by Gary Taylor and Gabriel Egan (Oxford University Press, 2017), pp. 67–91.

Taylor, Gary, and Doug Duhaime, 'Dataset 1.2', in *The New Oxford Shakespeare: Authorship Companion*, edited by Gary Taylor and Gabriel Egan (Oxford University Press, 2017), pp. 605–7.

Taylor, Gary, and Rory Loughnane, 'The Canon and Chronology of Shakespeare's Works', in *The New Oxford Shakespeare: Authorship Companion*, edited by Gary Taylor and Gabriel Egan (Oxford University Press, 2017), pp. 417–603.

Thomas, Sidney, '"Enter a Sheriff": Shakespeare's *King John* and *The Troublesome Raigne*', *Shakespeare Quarterly*, 37 (1986), 98–100.

Thompson, Ann, '*The Taming of the Shrew* and *The Spanish Tragedy*', *Notes and Queries*, 31 (1984), 182–4.

Thompson, Craig R. (ed.), *Collected Works of Erasmus: De Copia* (University of Toronto Press, 1978).

Thomson, Peter, 'Rogues and Rhetoricians: Acting Styles in Early Modern Drama', in *A New History of Early English Drama*, edited by John D. Cox and David Scott Kastan (Columbia University Press, 1997), pp. 320–35.

Thorndike, A. H., *The Influence of Beaumont and Fletcher on Shakespeare* (O. B. Wood, 1901).

Thorndike, A. H., 'The Relations of *Hamlet* to Contemporary Revenge Plays', *Modern Language Association*, 17.2 (1902), 125–220.

Timberlake, Philip, *The Feminine Ending in English Blank Verse: A Study of Its Use by Early Writers in the Measure and Its Development in the Drama up to the Year 1595* (Banta, 1931).

Tobin, John, 'Elizabethan Theater', in *Hamlet: Evans Shakespeare Editions*, edited by John Tobin (Wadsworth, 2012), pp. 15–26.

Trimpi, Wesley, *Ben Jonson's Poems: A Study in the Plain Style* (Stanford University Press, 1962).

Twyning, John, 'Dekker, Thomas', in *Oxford Dictionary of National Biography*, edited by Henry Colin Grey Matthew and Brian Harrison (Oxford University Press, 2004).

Vaughan, Virginia Mason, and Alden T. Vaughan (eds), *The Tempest* (Bloomsbury, 1999).

Verplanck, G. C. (ed.), *Shakespeare's Plays; with His Life: Volume II*, 3 vols (Harper and Brothers, 1847).

Vickers, Brian, *Shakespeare, Co-author: A Historical Study of Five Collaborative Plays* (Oxford University Press, 2002).

Vickers, Brian, 'The Troublesome Reign, George Peele, and the Date of *King John*', in *Words that Count: Essays on Early Modern Authorship in Honor of*

MacDonald P. Jackson, edited by Brian Boyd (Associated University Presses, 2004), pp. 76–118.

Vickers, Brian, 'Incomplete Shakespeare: Or, Denying Coauthorship in *1 Henry VI*', *Shakespeare Quarterly*, 58.3 (2007), 311–52.

Vickers, Brian, 'Thomas Kyd, Secret Sharer', *Times Literary Supplement*, 18 April 2008, pp. 13–15.

Vickers, Brian, 'Disintegrated: Did Thomas Middleton Really Adapt *Macbeth*?', *Times Literary Supplement*, 28 May 2010, pp. 14–15.

Vickers, Brian, 'Shakespeare and Authorship Studies in the Twenty-First Century', *Shakespeare Quarterly*, 62.1 (2011), 106–42.

Vickers, Brian, 'Identifying Shakespeare's Additions to *The Spanish Tragedy* (1602): A New(er) Approach', *Shakespeare*, 8 (2012), 13–43.

Vickers, Brian, 'The Two Authors of *Edward III*', *Shakespeare Survey*, 67 (2014), 102–18.

Vickers, Brian, 'Marlowe in *Edward II*: Lender or Borrower?', in *The Text, the Play, and the Globe: Essays on Literary Influence in Shakespeare's World and His Work in Honor of Charles R. Forker*, edited by Joseph Candido (Fairleigh Dickinson University Press, 2016), pp. 43–74.

Vickers, Brian, '"Upstart Crow"? The Myth of Shakespeare's Plagiarism', *Review of English Studies*, 68.284 (2017), 244–67.

Vickers, Brian (ed.), *The Collected Works of John Ford: Volume II*, 5 vols (Oxford University Press, 2017).

Vickers, Brian, '"The Dial Hand" Epilogue: by Shakespeare, or Dekker?', *Authorship*, 7.2 (2018), 1–18.

Vickers, Brian, 'Kyd's Authorship of *King Leir*', *Studies in Philology*, 115.3 (2018), 433–71.

Vickers, Brian, 'Is EEBO-TCP / LION Suitable for Attribution Studies?', *Early Modern Literary Studies*, 22.1 (2019), 1–34.

Vickers, Brian, 'Kyd, *Edward III*, and "The Shock of the New"', *American Notes and Queries*, 33.2 (2020), 172–88.

Vickers, Brian, 'Compositors' Spelling Preferences and the Integrity of *2 Henry VI*', *The Library*, 24.2 (2023), 141–53.

Vickers, Brian (ed.), *The Collected Works of Thomas Kyd*, Associate Editor Darren Freebury-Jones (Boydell and Brewer, 2024).

Vickers, Brian, and Marcus Dahl, '"What is infirm ..." *All's Well That Ends Well*: An Attribution Rejected', *Times Literary Supplement*, 11 May 2012, pp. 14–15.

Vincent, Paul, 'Unsolved Mysteries in *Henry the Sixth, Part Two*', *Notes and Queries*, 246 (2001), 270–4.

Vincent, Paul, 'When *harey* Met Shakespeare: The Genesis of *The First Part of Henry the Sixth*' (Doctoral thesis: University of Auckland, 2005).

Vitkus, Daniel, *Turning Turk: English Theater and the Multicultural Mediterranean, 1570–1630* (Macmillan, 2003).

Wagoner, Michael M., 'The Dramaturgical Space of Solo Scenes in Fletcher and Shakespeare, Or a Study of the Jailer's Daughter', *Shakespeare Bulletin*, 35.1 (2017), 97–118.

Waith, Eugene M. (ed.), *The Two Noble Kinsmen* (Clarendon Press, 1989).

Warren, Michael, *The Verse Style of Ben Jonson's Roman Plays* (Doctoral thesis: University of California, 1968).

Wayne, Valerie (ed.), *Cymbeline* (Bloomsbury, 2017).

Weber, William W., 'Shakespeare After All? The Authorship of *Titus Andronicus* 4.1 Reconsidered', *Shakespeare Survey*, 67 (2014), 69–84.

Wells, Stanley, *Shakespeare for All Time* (Macmillan, 2002).

Wells, Stanley, *Shakespeare & Co.* (Penguin, 2006).

Wells, Stanley, and Gary Taylor, *William Shakespeare: A Textual Companion* (Clarendon Press, 1987).

Wells, William, '*Timon of Athens*', *Notes and Queries*, 12.6 (1920), 266–9.

Wells, William, 'The Authorship of *King Leir*', *Notes and Queries*, 25 (1939), 434–8.

Wells, William, 'Thomas Kyd and the Chronicle-History', *Notes and Queries*, 30 (1940), 218–24, 238–43.

Wentersdorf, Karl, 'The Authenticity of *The Taming of the Shrew*', *Shakespeare Quarterly*, 5 (1954), 11–32.

Wernham, E. B., 'Christopher Marlowe at Flushing in 1592', *English Historical Review*, 91 (1976), 344–5.

Westley, Richard, 'Computing Error: Reassessing Austin's Study of *Groatsworth of Wit*', *Literary and Linguistic Computing*, 21.3 (2006), 363–78.

Whitworth, Charles (ed.), *The Old Wife's Tale*, 2nd edn (A. & C. Black, 1996).

Wiggins, Martin, *British Drama 1533–1642: A Catalogue* (Oxford University Press, 2012–).

Wilson, F. P., 'The English History Play', in *Shakespearian and Other Studies*, edited by Helen Gardner (Clarendon Press, 1969), pp. 1–53.

Wilson, John Dover (ed.), *All's Well that Ends Well* (Cambridge University Press, 1929).

Wilson, John Dover (ed.), *Titus Andronicus* (Cambridge University Press, 1948).

Wilson, John Dover (ed.), *The First Part of King Henry VI* (Cambridge University Press, 1952).

Wilson, Richard, '"The words of Mercury": Shakespeare and Marlowe', in *The Cambridge Companion to Shakespeare and Contemporary Playwrights*, edited by Ton Hoenselaars (Cambridge University Press, 2012), pp. 34–53.

Witherspoon, Alexander Maclaren, *The Influence of Robert Garnier on Elizabethan Drama* (Yale University Press, 1924).

Withington, Phil, 'Putting the City into Shakespeare's City Comedy', in *Shakespeare and Early Modern Political Thought*, edited by David Armitage, Conal Condren, and Andrew Fitzmaurice (Cambridge University Press, 2009), pp. 197–216.

Yang, Albert, 'Validating the Enlarged Kyd Canon: A New Approach', *American Notes and Queries*, 33.2 (2020), 189–97.

Yang, Albert, Chung-Kang Peng, and Ary L. Goldberger, 'The Marlowe-Shakespeare Authorship Debate: Approaching an Old Problem with New Methods', *The Calvin & Rose G Hoffman Marlowe Memorial Trust Prize* (2003).

Index